Dedication

In loving memory of my father
Joshua Sunday Adenigba Arowosegbe
and my grandfather
Matthew Olaseinde Arowosegbe

About the Series

The African Humanities Series is a partnership between the African Humanities Program (AHP) of the American Council of Learned Societies and academic publishers NISC (Pty) Ltd*. The Series covers topics in African histories, languages, literatures, philosophies, politics and cultures. Submissions are solicited from Fellows of the AHP, which is administered by the American Council of Learned Societies and financially supported by the Carnegie Corporation of New York.

The purpose of the AHP is to encourage and enable the production of new knowledge by Africans in the five countries designated by the Carnegie Corporation: Ghana, Nigeria, South Africa, Tanzania, and Uganda. AHP fellowships support one year's work free from teaching and other responsibilities to allow the Fellow to complete the project proposed. Eligibility for the fellowship in the five countries is by domicile, not nationality.

Book proposals are submitted to the AHP editorial board which manages the peer review process and selects manuscripts for publication by NISC. In some cases, the AHP board will commission a manuscript mentor to undertake substantive editing and to work with the author on refining the final manuscript.

The African Humanities Series aims to publish works of the highest quality that will foreground the best research being done by emerging scholars in the five Carnegie designated countries. The rigorous selection process before the fellowship award, as well as AHP editorial vetting of manuscripts, assures attention to quality. Books in the series are intended to speak to scholars in Africa as well as in other areas of the world.

The AHP is also committed to providing a copy of each publication in the series to university libraries in Africa.

*early titles in the series was published by Unisa Press, but the publishing rights to the entire series are now vested in NISC

Published in this series

Claude E. Ake

The making of an organic intellectual

JEREMIAH O. AROWOSEGBE

AHP
Publications

NISC

Originally published in 2018 by Unisa Press, South Africa
under ISBN: 978-1-86888-808-5

This edition published in South Africa on behalf of the African Humanities
Program by NISC (Pty) Ltd, PO Box 377, Grahamstown, 6140, South Africa
www.nisc.co.za

NISC first edition, first impression 2019

ISBN: 978-1-920033-53-8 (print)
ISBN: 978-1-920033-54-5 (PDF)
ISBN: 978-1-920033-55-2 (ePub)

Copy Editor: Shakira Hoosain
Series designer: Thea Bester-Swanepoel
Typesetting: Maria Kirstein
Cover design: Nozipho Noble
Indexer: Elsabé Nell

Contents

Abbreviations and acronyms

AAPS	African Association of Political Science
AG	Action Group
AISA	Africa Institute of South Africa
ANC	African National Congress
AAI	African-American Institute
AHP	African Humanities Programme
ACLS	American Council of Learned Societies
ASA	African Studies Association
ASC	African Studies Centre
CAS	Centre for African Studies
CASS	Centre for Advanced Social Science
CHR	Centre for Humanities Research
CODESRIA	Council for the Development of Social Science Research in Africa
CODICE	CODESRIA Documentation and Information Centre
CSSSC	Centre for Studies in Social Sciences, Calcutta
DAAD	German Academic Exchange Service

HIV/AIDS	Human Immune-deficiency Virus/Acquired Immune Deficiency Syndrome
HSRC	Human Sciences Research Council
ICSSR	Indian Council of Social Science Research
IDIs	In-depth Interviews
IISH	International Institute of Social History
IISS	International Institute of Social Studies
IMF	International Monetary Fund
IPSA	International Political Science Association
IPSR	International Political Science Review
NCNC	National Council for Nigeria and Cameroons
NDES	Niger Delta Environmental Survey
NGOs	Non-Governmental Organizations
NPSA	Nigerian Political Science Association
NUC	National Universities Commission
OAU	Organization of African Unity
OPEC	Organization of Petroleum Exporting Countries
PhD	Doctor of Philosophy
SSHC	Senior Staff Housing Committee
SSNSA	Social Sciences Network of South Africa
UNECA	United Nations Economic Commission for Africa
USA	United States of America
UCT	University of Cape Town
UNU-WIDER	United Nations University World Institute for Development Economics Research
UWC	University of the Western Cape
WARA	West African Research Association
WARC	West African Research Centre

Preface and acknowledgements

The contributions and profiles of intellectuals and nationalist figures in Africa and the diaspora are still a largely underdeveloped genre. Such contributions are however, very crucial for understanding politics in Africa, a region where the roles of individuals have been central in making history. Although Claude Ake is one of the most instructive voices in African political thought, most works on him have been limited to a celebration of his intellectual pedigree and stature. Barring a few exceptions, most scholarly commentaries on political and social theorists in Africa have been treated either as part of the biographical accounts of various African intellectuals or as part of the colonial liberation struggles, with the veiled objective of denying the existence and reality of African political thought. In particular, in spite of his contributions and insights, Ake's works are yet to be fully explored in terms of their prospects, not just for understanding the problematic underpinnings of Africa's contradictory trajectory, but also for transcending its historic intellectual lag in the area of history writing and knowledge production. The consequence of this oversight is that whereas, within the humanities, accomplished scholars have been extensively studied, within the social sciences, very few works have been carried out on political and social theorists in Africa and on Ake in particular. This book is a start towards filling this gap and rectifying this omission. It offers a critical examination of Claude Ake's works and an intellectual biography that demonstrates the relevance of such works for understanding the constitutive elements, precepts and prospects for knowledge production on Africa. It argues out and discusses the connections between Claude Ake's works and the subject field of postcolonial studies. In doing this, the aim is to establish the relevance of Ake's works for mapping the genealogies of the colonial and postcolonial in African history.

My debts on completing this book are numerous. It is therefore only by relying on a longstanding convention that I can effectively claim its authorship. The large body of literature cited in the book also testifies to my indebtedness to several authors, too numerous to be mentioned individually. These have, however, been acknowledged in the work. They have also been given the pride of place in the bibliography.

Adigun Agbaje supervised the doctoral dissertation from which the production and revision of this book emanated. Other colleagues across the continent helped in discussing and reading the drafts of the manuscript. Archie Mafeje, Bernard Magubane, Dani Nabudere, Fantu Cheru, Mahmood Mamdani, Olujimi Adesina, Samir Amin and Thandika Mkandawire inspired me greatly, through their responses to my oral interviews and the interactions I had with them. They also provided me an affectionate and constantly available conversational community within the permissible limits of the cyberspace. I hope that they find their continuing interest in my work justified by my efforts in this book.

I am happy to acknowledge the guidance I received at the Centre for Studies in Social Sciences. Calcutta. India, while developing the doctoral dissertation, from which this book emanated. Anjan Ghosh, Dwaipayan Bhattacharyya, Manabi Majumdar, Partha Chatterjee, Rosinka Chaudhuri and Uday Kumar deserve my appreciation for their mentoring and support for my work. For permission to reprint from my published articles, my thanks go to the editors of the journals *Africa Spectrum*, which published 'The Social Sciences and Knowledge Production in Africa: The Contribution of Claude Ake' (2008, 43 (3):333–351); and *International Affairs*, which published 'State Reconstruction in Africa: The Relevance of Claude Ake's Political Thought' (2011, 87 (3):651–670).

Finally, I pay a glowing tribute to my immediate family. My wife, Cynthia, and our children – Emmanuel, Daniel, Samuel, Abraham and Victoria – gave me the encouragement I needed and took my absence from home with understanding. My parents, Joshua S. A. Arowosegbe and Victoria O. Arowosegbe, provided me immeasurable support during the period of producing this book. I am very grateful to them. Lastly, I thank the Almighty God for the gift of life as well as the grace to commence and complete this assignment with appreciable success. I thank the Spirit controlling the star of my destiny for always leading me in the path of life (Isaiah 30: 21).

Jeremiah O. Arowosegbe
Ibadan. October 2017

Introduction

Capitalism, Marx said, was the first universal social form, at least the first form capable of a possible universality. It imposed, on most people with whom it came in touch, certain peculiar forms of suffering. These several sufferings at the various frontiers of capitalism gave rise to critiques in which those who suffered at its hands tried to make sense of their history. In a sense, each critique analysed and held up for criticism aspects of sufferings related to capitalism which were opaque, unperceived and unreported to the others. But as critiques they are potentially connectable; they, as it were, waited to meet each other. It is only now, in the writing of history, that such a meeting is possible. In this, the critique of an aggressive, uncritical, all-conquering rationalist colonialism by the early nationalists is a necessary part. And it is only when these critiques are stitched together that a true map of the unhappy consciousness of humanity, when capitalism reigned, can be put together.

— Sudipta Kaviraj, 1992, 34

Claude E. Ake (1939–1996) is one of Africa's foremost political philosophers who worked extensively in the area of political theory and made original and unique contributions to the political economy of democracy and development in the continent. As a major praxiological figure from whose works the real world in the continent can best be understood, his writings constitute a significant entry point not just for understanding contemporary Africa, but also for rethinking globalisation, modernity and the larger theoretical concerns shared by postcolonial theorists throughout the world. The enduring significance and topicality of his contribution to African political thought assuredly place him alongside great African political thinkers, such as Cheikh Anta Diop and

Samir Amin. Ake's works are particularly instructive given his successful application of the radical critical theory to illuminate the African condition and provide a guide to political action (Martins 1996; Harris 2005).

However, in spite of his contributions, Ake's works are yet to be fully explored in terms of their prospects, not only for understanding the problematic underpinnings of Africa's contradictory trajectory, but also for transcending its intellectual lag in the area of knowledge production. This book takes on this task. To illustrate, while the academies in Asia and Latin America shifted to postcolonial studies in the 1980s, Africa remained – trapped – within the dependency, political economy and under development paradigm as the dominant mode of analysis. Consequently, history writing and more broadly knowledge production on the continent has neither benefitted much from, nor engaged substantially with, the expansive debate and rich literature on postcolonial studies especially as we see it in the subaltern studies intellectual project in Asia and Latin America.

This lag is not just individual and institutional, but is also epistemological, paradigmatic and philosophical. As Frederick Cooper explains, while subaltern studies emerged in the 1980s (about forty years or so after India's independence) as a critique of an established nationalist interpretation of history, and of progressive arguments generally (both liberal and Marxist), Africa's independence movements are rather more recent, their histories only beginning to be written.[1] Africans' and Africanists' responses to the disillusionment with the failings of independence in the 1970s took the form of an emphasis on the external determinants of economic and social problems. Hence their resort to Latin America for the theories of development and underdevelopment. The catastrophic economic situation faced by the continent, especially since the 1980s, together with the harsh material conditions in which its cultural and educational institutions and its intellectuals function, have undermined the density of debate made possible in India and South Asia (Cooper 1994, 1519).

Known exceptions to this gap on the continent include Paulin Hountondji (1977, 1983, 1997); Valentin Y. Mudimbe (1988, 1994); Mamadou Diouf (1994, 1996, 2003); Achille Mbembe (2001, 2002) and Premesh J. Lalu (2009). To rectify this limitation, this book critically assesses Claude Ake's intellectual works and draws attention to vital aspects of those works that are relevant not just for accounting for, but also for transcending, Africa's intellectual lag in the areas of history writing and knowledge production.

From all available sources, few works on Ake have been critical and engaging enough for rethinking the conclusions reached in his philosophical corpus. Hardly does one find any rigorous engagement with his published works and theoretical positions. Yet, his analyses have far reaching implications for (i) African studies as a field of enquiry, (ii) theoretical questions of autochthoneity and endogeneity in knowledge production on Africa, and (iii) theoretical reflections on the state in Africa as well as the geopolitics of knowledge production on the continent. In addition, academics across the humanities and social sciences working on Africa have a lot to learn from critiquing aspects of such works. This objective is central to the conception of this book. It offers an intellectual history of Africa rooted in an understanding of colonialism which no imperial account on the continent wants us to see. It articulates the relevance of endogenous African knowledges as subjugated knowledges and presents Ake's works as one of the foremost attempts at combating Africa's domination by Western knowledge systems. It seeks to further an understanding of Africa as discursively constituted as a problem. To achieve this task, it engages with those sources and texts that discursively construct the continent as a problem. Following Jacques Derrida's (1967) famous assertion that, 'there is nothing outside the text',[2] it contextualises and problematises the global representations of interests as well as the structures of power that undermine the capacity of subordinated subjects from expressing their freedom within historically delineated systems of power. The aim is to intervene substantially in ongoing debates on the need to reconstitute the humanities and social sciences in Africa.

Aspects of the intellectual traditions into which Ake's works are inserted are not only rooted in Marxist thought, but also feed into the more contemporary debates on postcolonial studies and subaltern studies – the connections of which are yet to be explicitly established and foregrounded in the literature. While Ake's publications are marked by an original brand of Marxism, some of his contributions and insights can be linked to the discussions on postcolonial studies and subaltern studies scholarship. This book attempts to make this linkage explicit.

At the moment, the interventions made to Ake's works can be grouped into three. First are those which directly focus on the celebration of his intellectual pedigree and stature through the biographical accounts and tributes that they provided. These include J. 'Bayo Adekanye (1996), L. Adele Jinadu (1996), Guy Martins (1996), the Yale Bulletin and Calendar (1996), CASS (1997, 1998) and James H. Mittleman (1997a, 1997b). The second comprises his interlocutors, who engaged with some of the issues raised in his corpus. Julius O. Ihonvbere (1989), Okechukwu O. Ibeanu (1993), Archie Mafeje (1997), Andrew O. Efemini (2000) and Kelly Harris (2005) are known examples in this respect. Although indirectly, the third draws on the works of leading authorities within the subject field of postcolonial studies and subaltern studies, which help to deepen historical and theoretical understandings of the questions bearing on autochthoneity and endogeneity in knowledge production; the state and other postcolonial concerns examined in Ake's works. Of particular relevance are those texts which help to animate the debate on the relationship between the colonial and postcolonial in African history. In speaking to this issue, the book draws heavily on the works of Frantz Fanon, Fanonist scholars like Aimé Césaire and Albert Memmi as well as the writings of members of the subaltern studies intellectual project in India and South Asia.

How does Ake aid our understanding of the relations of power in the very conception of knowledge production on Africa? To what extent does his corpus help in questioning the colonial foundations of the dominant knowledge systems and their links with the constellation of power vis-à-vis the operations of the state in Africa? How relevant are those texts for recreating the imagination of the African subject using a knowledge-driven liberatory project? What prospects do they offer for rethinking Africa's future beyond the early colonial vision of westernising the continent? These questions are central to the discussions in the chapters that follow. However, before sketching the outlines of my argument, I consider it necessary to clarify my theoretical point of departure.

Development and endogenous knowledge

An apt analogy for speaking to Africa's experience with development is offered by the twinning of colonialism and modernisation. While colonialism left behind some forms of hybridity and mimicry, the urge to decolonise – to be free from the coloniser's control in every possible way – was integral to all anti-colonial criticism after the Second World War.[3] The politics of decolonisation followed by the 'new state' in the mid-20th century, however displayed an uncritical emphasis on modernisation, in which development, pursued – with technology and tools of scientific progress – was a catching-up exercise with the West. As an epistemological export from the West, taking the form of science as hegemony and ideology within the colonial discourse, this has not delivered material progress for Africa. Not surprisingly, the concern about the intractability and magnitude of the problems facing the continent has made development a popular theme within the literature on African studies. The disappointment across various academic circles and the popular press over its dwindling prospects – illustrated in its food insecurity, low life expectancy and the familiar litany of its ills – has made the debates about the continent both compelling and timely. Much has consequently been written on what development is or should be about in Africa. It is thus increasingly important to reflect on how knowledge about Africa is produced; by whom and to what ends it is put. It is also worthwhile to relate such questions to Africa's position in global economic and political structures.

To illustrate, while empirical research has widely shown that economic development has a significant, positive effect on political democracy (Frank 1969; Bollen 1983), the relationship between and in particular, the relevance of endogenous knowledge for autonomous – capitalist or socialist – development has not been adequately explored. A substantial amount of the literature on African development is unquestionably qualitatively oriented, investigating important cultural, economic, political and social factors that influence society. Such studies have also assumed many different forms, including the examination of (i) contemporary case studies, (ii) contemporary comparative studies, (iii) historical case studies, (iv) comparative historical studies and (v) ethnographic studies (Bradshaw et al 1995:46). These studies emphasise complex qualitative analysis and widely deploy descriptive explanations. This literature also occasionally combines descriptive data with the utilisation of inferential statistical techniques that formally test the existence of possible causal relationships. Such works have however not paid attention to the connection between the role of endogenous knowledge and the development question in Africa. This section addresses this gap.

As a hegemonically produced discourse, development occupies a central position within historically dominant explanations and schools of thought on the reasons why Africa and postcolonial societies generally are not developing. While most recent usages link it up with globalisation and modernity, development has manifested under different guises and has been used as the most powerful influence for structuring economic transformation and social progress in this century, especially in developing societies (Harvey 1989). It is clearly one of the most politicised discourses as well as a performed practice and a formation to be explained. The development discourse is therefore best understood as an ideological apparatus with which the core capitalist societies assert their dominance on backward regions of the world – an assertion that generates numerous counterreactions for economic and political independence from the South.

The high point in its emergence as a power-driven mode of thought was perhaps the declaration in 1951 by a group of experts convened by the United Nations with the objective of designing concrete policy measures for the economic development of underdeveloped countries based on the ideas of hard choices, necessary trade-offs and unavoidable sacrifices. Much of the ideological warfare – Cold War – which reached its climax in the 1960s was fought over development, that is, to determine whether the so-called free world model – capitalism – or the communist model – communism – would be adopted by the developing nations.[4] The critical view point reveals that, although it has a relatively recent history, it has featured prominently within past attempts at dominating non-Western societies. It is thus, in the discontinuities, shifts and slides as well as in the unintended moves – what is asserted as much as what is suppressed in the histories of these societies – that one can get a clear sense of its actual operations. Just like nationalism, development has been the cause of the most destructive wars ever seen. It has been used as justification for the brutality of Fascism and Nazism. It informed the ideology of racial hatred in the colonies and has given birth to some of the most irrational revivalist movements as well as the most oppressive political regimes in the contemporary world.[5]

Not surprisingly, 'everywhere and at all times,' Jacques René Hébert wrote in 1794 in *Le Père Duchesne*, 'men of commerce have had neither heart nor soul; their cash box is their God ... They traffic in all things, even human flesh'.[6] For the sake of the cash box, they have also penetrated the discourse of development and systems of education with the intent to confuse and fetishise them (Arowosegbe 2016). 'In business', Joseph B. Mathews and R. E. Smalleross (1976) have contended, 'plunder is the essence'. The springs of thought together with the sources of physical life for the working people are poisoned in so far as such a poisoning act is deemed profitable; adulterated when adulteration is profitable; and otherwise exploited in ways that blight and despoil. In the colonies, imperial conquest was put in place, supposedly in defence of the human, and in the name of development. Development was presented as the complementary veneer to civilisation, for legitimising colonisation.

During the early years of colonial rule, the ideology of development was advanced as justification for colonial domination. This was later corroborated with the notion of the plural society. The concept of the plural society grew out of the study of colonial societies by European anthropologists. It was particularly popularised by John S. Furnivall, a British colonial administrator who spent his lifetime as a civil servant in Burma. In his studies of the Dutch East Indies, he defines the plural society as comprising two or more elements of social orders living side by side, yet without mingling, in one political unit (Furnivall 1939). In such a setting, communities were separated on the basis of language, race and religion, with each having a distinct set of cultural values incompatible with those of the other communities. Since there was consequently, a total lack of consensus in such polities, only an externally imposed authority could hold such a society together. The self-appointed candidates for such a task were the colonial powers (Chatterjee 1974).

Subsequently, developmentalism, which first appeared in African colonies as official state policy in the 1920s, 'became central to the legitimation imperative of the terminal colonial state, now subject to an increasingly hostile international environment and a rising torrent of nationalist criticism' (Young 2004:27). Developmentalism thus became the defining discourse of the late colonial state from the 1940s onwards. This much was the case in Asia and other centres of imperial control.

It was not limited to the terminal colonial state-craft. It continued into the postindependence period. Unfortunately, its postcolonial projection was born into the limitations of the old colonial situation. While the decade of African independence coincided with the zenith of confidence in state-led development, formal decolonisation was accompanied by two developments, namely, the politics of modern imperialism and two, the emergence of the United States as the unquestioned leader of the capitalist powers. These two developments must be borne in mind when assessing the post-Second World War literature in the social sciences, for as Partha Chatterjee (1974:26) has shown, the upsurge of interest by American scholars in the postcolonial world is not unconnected to the emergence of the United States of America as a global power of the highest rank. Throughout the 1950s and 1960s, American social scientists immersed themselves in studying the cultures and institutions of underdeveloped societies. The product of that curious academic activity was the theory of political development (Rostow 1960). Its fundamental conclusion was that the political development of underdeveloped countries could only be the result of economic development – a rapid industrialisation of their productive systems and a thorough modernisation of their cultural superstructures. However, its actual aim was the preservation of vital interests of the United States and other Western powers. And since the moment of African independence also coincided with the apogee of the

Cold War, the new states became a diplomatic battlefield for the capitalist and communist blocs (Cooper 2006:159–61).

As this idea of development travels to other parts of the world, it seeks to produce societies along the Western model. In such instances where deviations are established from the Western standard, its disposition is to describe them as backward, pre-modern or traditional. Using a set of predetermined Eurocentric assumptions and understandings of the modern and the universal, this idea of development replicates Western social forms in non-Western parts of the world. Yet, the history of development does not constitute an entirely homogenous narration. Besides, these societies may not wish to emulate the West since the experience of Western modernity itself, is diverse and not uniformly attractive. My point here is that, the trajectory of state and power in Africa and the postcolonial world does not always conform to the known experience of the state in the West. The task of critical political theory – in this respect – is not to characterise or dismiss these societies in terms of any lack, but to study them – on their own terms – as an interesting contrast and establish the implications of such differences on the manner in which societies are constituted across the East (Kaviraj 2000).

It is my contention that development for Africa cannot be a catching-up strategy within the globalised system of international capitalism. A critical examination of the leading issues in African development – conflict resolution, debt management, democratisation, economic reform, environmental protection and poverty reduction – underlines the need for critical thinking and a departure from the manner in which public policies have been made in the past. There is, in particular, the need to address the problematic character of the state in Africa (Deng 1998:1–9, 11–64, 65–140).

The basic lacuna for Africa, in this regard, is the absence of a recognisable body of ideology guiding and informing the ordering of priorities in tackling its development-related problems. To illustrate, while colonialism achieved remarkable success in Africa and Asia – not necessarily by relying on the deployment of force but through the operation of a system of knowledge that enabled the imperial powers reconcile might to right and transform domination into hegemony[7] – there is no recognisable ideology guiding the development agenda by the state in postcolonial Africa. Fanon (1967, 1968) decries this absence of a working ideology as one of the greatest dangers threatening Africa. Yet, we cannot fully emancipate ourselves unless we strive for the endogenous articulation and development of our practices and thoughts.

Relatedly, throughout the heritage of human civilisation, no society has achieved autonomous and sustainable development – whether along the capitalist or socialist models – through relying entirely and exclusively on the particularities of an alien culture. Unfortunately, for the most parts, Africa is not a knowledge-driven society; while the historically created gulf between its knowledge bearers and state actors has remained entrenched and unbreached. It is therefore not surprising that potentially self-reliant and other self-sustainable internally-generated development initiatives have been supplanted by colonial and neo-colonial theories of development.[8] Bade Onimode, Claude Ake, Samir Amin and Walter Rodney have written extensively about the extent to which the West impoverished and underdeveloped Africa. More recently, Adebayo Adedeji, Thandika Mkandawire and Yusuf Bangura have illustrated how the West and its major financial institutions – the Bretton Woods family and the Washington Consensus – have slowed down socioeconomic progress in sub-Saharan Africa. There is therefore no point, restating their positions.

As John Stuart Mill (Mill 2003) has surmised, 'No great improvements in the lot of mankind are possible, until a great change takes place in the fundamental constitution of their modes of thought'. To think of development in Africa therefore, is to ask the compelling and critical questions consistent with its historical and continuing experiences namely: What are the actual development needs of the continent as defined by its history, intelligentsia and people? What aspects of the Western and other external experiences does the continent actually need to borrow from? What must be the beneficial limits of such borrowing? What system of knowledge ought to guide the continent's development agenda? Put differently, on what knowledge system, are Africa's development models and priorities anchored or hinged? And how relevant are African knowledge systems for rethinking development on the continent? These questions are central for African development. Clearly, the failure to properly mark the limits of external borrowing and interventionism has made the continent a dumping ground of all sorts of foreign recipes and solutions since its independence. As Abdulkarim H. Somjee (1984:1) observes, the absence of such endogenous knowledge systems, in driving development on the continent, is a major basis of difference between the state in peripheral societies and its counterparts in the advanced capitalist societies.

I argue that development in Africa must be explored as a retrieval project. One needs to pursue it as an invention of another kind, fundamentally different from what colonial-peripheral capitalism offers. While

autarchy is neither advocated nor feasible,[9] the idea of development –
based on a critical and selective borrowing from other epistemic contexts
– readily becomes suggestive (Amin 1990a; Dieng 2007). It must entail
a process of inventing a new kind of civilisation. Its exploration must
transcend the mechanical replacement of the old by the new. It must
entail a radical process of socio-economic engineering as well as the
reconstruction of inherited institutions of the past.[10] To do this is to
undertake a critique of the continent's past as a basis for contributing
towards a productive transformation of its future. To do this is also to
appreciate that there are a great many contributions and legacies to be
mined from various African cultures and pasts as well as other texts on
the continent that radically critique hierarchy. To explore development as
a retrieval project – in Africa – would be to work hard towards bringing
back such distant traditions that appear increasingly lost to us – in all
their richness – and which we have so far neither reconnected with nor
revived except in the most perfunctory of manners. Hitherto, much of
what is written about African heritages, pasts and traditions are a bundle
of unexamined assertions and assumptions based on the knowledge of
these traditions, which in a serious textual sense, are rather scanty.

As is widely known, Europe achieved modernity by capturing the
classic past of the ancient Greece and Rome, which led to renaissance, a
strategy which allowed renaissance Europe to make the secularisation of
social life a basis for modernity and decide that individuals could make
their own destiny and history and therefore should have the right to innovate
and transcend tradition. Likewise, Africa must explore development as a
retrieval project. To do this requires that all developmental aspirations
are rooted in endogenous African cultures. There is also the need to draw
lessons from the experiences of other postcolonial societies across the
global South. How is China, India and Japan constructing new conceptions
of nationalism and the state on the heels of their colonial experiences?
How relevant are Africa's pasts for imagining development? What lessons
can it learn from the intellectual, nationalist and other experiences in
China, India and Japan? What might we draw from the legacies of the
ancient Egyptian and other civilisations in the continent? These questions
underline the centrality of endogenous African knowledge systems as the
material precondition for development. To decolonise Africa in this sense,
is to decolonise knowledge production – as well as the very strategies of
knowledge production – on the continent.

Placed in the context of its encounters with the outside world, 'the
problem of development in Africa' is here formulated in terms of how

to undertake social change on a large scale while also minimising the disruptive impact of such change. As the epitaph at the beginning of this chapter illustrates, while the idea of 'world history' has not always existed, the rise of capitalism in Europe and the imperialist adventures that followed it, marked the beginning of modern history, especially as capital accumulation acquired a pronounced globalised character. Consequently, how can Africans borrow and learn from the experiences of other societies without necessarily compromising and losing their Africanity; tradition and other aspects of their humanity. Answering this question is compelling because, while development must be contemplated and explored as a retrieval project – drawing from the heritages of their pasts – Africans cannot develop entirely in isolation without learning from the already consummated experiences of other postcolonial societies and the West in particular. Our reference to the West in this regard is not a contradiction. While postcolonial societies must connect to their pasts as a basis for autocentric development, such societies cannot, however, afford to entirely ignore the West while aspiring to be modern. This is mainly because, while Europe has historically – and continues to dominate the global access to human and natural resources, it is also within the Western epistemic modes of thought that modern understandings of development and progress are constructed. The task for Africans in this regard is therefore, how to concatenate its local cultures with the beneficial and productive heritages of the Western experience in a manner that is autochthonous, endogenous and idiographic to its existence.

The major question for Africa here is that of how to develop significant scientific skills as well as technological techniques without compromising 'the Africanness of its identity' by accepting the full force of Western influences. The critical issue here is therefore, the question of how knowledge appropriated and developed by Africans on the basis of their historical experiences can be valorised for empowering the state in the pursuit of democracy and development.

To engender development in Africa, efforts must be made not only to retrieve the continent's illustrious heritages and traditions of the pasts, but also to revive relevant aspects of its imaginary golden pasts as a basis for making sense of modernity. Viewed from the perspective of knowledge production, there is the need to build a system of knowledge based on an appreciation of the different histories which produce the different knowledge bases and systems across the world. This is a criterion for transcending the restrictive contexts of knowledge production in the modern world. Furthermore, there is the need to develop a system of knowledge which, in actual epistemic terms, is rooted in its culture and locale to create canons in its own right, especially one that (i) borrows carefully and selectively from other epistemic contexts, (ii) derives the source codes of its epistemologies from the life forms, lived experiences and practices of its people, and (iii) takes the African policymaking nexus seriously. This is a requirement for pursuing development beyond its constraining conception as a catching-up exercise. Put together, these considerations are central for imagining development and history writing on the continent. After all, history is never more compelling than when it gives us insights into oneself and the ways in which one's experiences are constituted. As a critical component to the development agenda, history writing in Africa must therefore, create those conditions that would enable us redeem ourselves by ourselves. While good history writing on the continent may well involve acknowledging the efforts of non-African collaborators and contributors in the development agenda, it must centrally involve making our own choices and judgments – as Africans. The modernising impulse must never be premised on a renouncement of the national culture by Africans, for it is the national culture that enables one account for the past and productively imagine the future. According to Marcus Garvey cited in E. U. Essien-Udom (1962:17), 'The reliance of our race upon the progress and achievements of others for a consideration in sympathy, justice and rights is like a dependence upon a broken stick, resting upon which will eventually consign you to the ground'.

Postcoloniality and the African condition

What is postcoloniality? How relevant is it for understanding Ake's works? And what relationship exists between this concept and Ake's characterisation of the African condition? This work answers these questions and draws attention to some of Ake's contribution and insights which speak to the debate on postcoloniality.[11] Postcolonial studies is the intellectual engagement developed over the past three decades on a set of issues, debates and articulations of points of intervention, performed as a tricontinental project within the institutional sites of research centres and universities across the world, particularly outside the metropolitan intellectual centres (Young 1990) and across a range of disciplinary fields. Characterised by its geographical capaciousness and multiple sites of production, its lineage embraces Albert Memmi's analysis in the 1950s of the drama of North African decolonisation; Frantz Fanon's theorisation of anti-colonialism and the complex psychology of racism articulated in the 1950s; Edward Said's elaboration of Fanon's (1968:102) thesis, that Europe is literally the creation of the Third World, in his *Orientalism* (1978), which sparked off decades of scholarship on occidental representations of the East; the wide ranging scholarship of Caribbeanists like C. L. R. James, Walter Rodney and Wilson Harris, whose early lives in Trinidad and Guyana respectively, shaped their very different approaches to the history of colonialism after their migration to England; the works of theorists of the Hispanophone Americas, from Gloria Anzaldua to Jose David Saldivar; and the contribution of the subaltern studies group in India initiated by Ranajit Guha, with Dipesh Chakrabarty, Gayatri C. Spivak, Partha Chatterjee and Sumit Sarkar as its founding members. Hinged on deconstruction historiography, the subaltern studies intellectual project, for example, radically emphasises the question of representing and writing history from below, as an alternative form of historiography. According to Frederick Cooper (1994:1516), by putting the process of making history at the centre of history writing as an enterprise, the subaltern studies intellectual project has had an empowering effect on the scholarship of the once-colonised societies.

Postcolonial theory insists that the centre has no meaning apart from the periphery; the West apart from the East; the Occidental apart from the Oriental; the coloniser apart from the colonised. The dominant party within the binaries and parings thus gets its character shaped by the identity or shape it gives to the other. This is a major contribution made by postcolonial theory to the understanding of colonial practice. Although it was developed between the 1980s and 1990s, the terms 'postcolonial' and 'postcoloniality' have become common currency in intellectual and political debates across the world in recent times, especially following the unrest that hit the French suburbs in 2005. Notwithstanding their popularity across global academic and scholarly circles, these words are yet to be fully explained. In fact, as Jean-François Bayart (2010) illustrates, the seemingly straightforward question of their spelling remains as yet unclear.

Its emergence was inspired by the realisation by these scholars that (i) post-Enlightenment traditions of European historiography had led to a longstanding neglect of history writing from the South, (ii) disciplinary practices had failed to address the full complexity of historical change in the era that they studied (Ashcroft et al 1995) and (iii) that there are lots more to be learnt from opening up the spaces of enquiry and examining historically shared experiences across the postcolonial world. Hence the determination to make the perspectives of other contexts as well as disciplines integral to the historical enterprise. Although the histories of the capitalist penetration and underdevelopment of the postcolonial world do not constitute an entirely homogenous narration, nevertheless, such histories have potentially connectible strands. Unless an intellectual history of anticolonialism is written in a manner reflective of 'shared historical experiences', the history of colonialism will permanently remain unfinished (Holsinger 2002, 1195).

It is also an intellectual-political discourse inspired inter alia by Marxist, structuralist, post-modernist and post-structuralist writings and deals with the legacies of the Enlightenment for postcolonial societies generally and Africa, Asia and Latin America in particular. These societies are engaged – in different ways – with closely related debates and experiences. Their historiographies also wrestle with – but do not entirely escape – the dichotomous visions characteristic of colonial ideologies, originating in the oppositional identities of civilised coloniser and primitive colonised. Postcolonial studies therefore, brings their historiographies into dialogue as well as their particular blind spots, insights and scholarly traditions into relationship with each other, avoiding the assumption that interaction strictly means borrowing from more developed historiographies. Postcoloniality is therefore an intellectual field in which no single historical perspective can have a monopoly over the elaboration of the postcolony or the postcolonial condition. This is mainly because, history is continually in the making and there is always a lot in the telling and retelling of the past. History writing therefore, cannot stake claims to any finality, fixity or even an oracular form. There is also no single way of producing or representing the past.[12] By attempting to give an epistemological agency to the hitherto unheard subalternised voices from the South, postcolonial studies is therefore a politically charged intellectual project hinged mainly on the epistemological critique of Eurocentrism through seeking to invert the agency of domination in favour of the South.

Can the deconstruction of the West's misrepresentation of 'the Other' open the door for a true representation of the Orient? While this is a critical question for postcolonial studies, there is however, no common position on it among its experts. Following Jacques Derrida, most postcolonial theorists, especially those within the purist mode, argue that any effort to retrieve the attitudes and experiences of the colonised is doomed to failure because such efforts are inescapably enmeshed in the positivist premises of Western knowledge. Homi K. Bhabha (1994) for example, argues that the best that can be done is to follow the traces of the colonised inscribed in the margins and narratives of the coloniser's discourse.

Gayatri C. Spivak (1988:271–313) says the voice of the colonised subject, particularly the colonised female subject, can never be recovered – it has been permanently drowned out by the oppressive collusion of colonial and patriarchal discourses. For Gyan Prakash (1994:1482, 1483), 'the shift to the analysis of discourses' implies the abandonment of a 'positivist retrieval' of the experience of the colonised and search instead for the random discursive threads from that experience that have become 'woven into the fabric of dominant structures'.

Arguing that the coupling of imperial expansion with wanton violence 'shapes' South Africa's past – thus forming residues of anger, guilt, nostalgia and resentment, thereby surfacing to the top of contemporary historical writing and politics – Premesh J. Lalu (2009:62) states that postcolonial critiques of apartheid and the task of rewriting South African history remain unviable having been trapped in the colonial archive and its mode of evidence, best distinguished by their ability to fabricate subjectivity. He questions the possibility of inaugurating an indigenous tradition of historical writing by South African historians and concludes that the attempt at reversing colonial representations end up confirming the same ambiguities of dependence. Evidently, one way of marking these voices is to understand them as saying that the colonial encounter led colonial and postcolonial societies into irretrievable pasts and paths. Yet, in the midst of these positions, overcoming its tendency to abstract the colonised other as an undifferentiated and unknowable category is compelling for postcolonial theory in its efforts at delivering a historicised and nuanced understanding of the colonial experience. As Dane Kennedy (2003:16–17) surmises, 'Critics complain that the Derridean turn in postcolonial theory denies agency and autonomy to the colonised, whose struggles against colonial rule and strategies to turn it in their favour are too abundantly recorded to be dismissed as mere echoes in the chambers of Western discourse.

One of the strongest merits of postcolonial studies is that it has opened up the spaces of enquiry not just for people to appreciate experiences, but also historically shared experiences across different postcolonial societies. While postcolonial studies – just like the other intellectual practices within the provenance of critical theory – has an understandably multidisciplinary character, literary studies has been outstanding in articulating the colonial and postcolonial experience. It has also been most audacious in its application of poststructuralist theories as well as the most uncompromising in its relationship to historiographical traditions. With Edward W. Said, Gayatri C. Spivak and Homi K. Bhabha as the leading path-finding torchbearers of the academic firmament, teaching positions in colonial and postcolonial literatures have become booming fields in the English departments of several universities across the world. These scholars recognise the distinction existing between history as a text and history as a tool; between its presence as a discursive product and its use as an analytic practice. They have also enriched our understanding of the imperial experience by placing their arguments in their appropriate historical contexts, reading them against the grains of the historical evidence.

One of the major characteristics of postcolonial studies is its theoretical promiscuity. However, one of its most obvious limitations is the complex and sometimes impenetrable writing styles in which postcoloniality is articulated by most of its exponents – a practice that alienates a massive chunk of the global subalterns (the original target of its analytic articulation and theoretical engagement) from such path-finding revolutionary works (Kennedy 2003:13). The major source of this is its infiltration by several theoretical influences. Drawing on the heritages of the 20th century, which saw the development of a wide range of analytical theories, individual theorists now mix and pick from the catalogue of theories to put together various synthetic models for whatever their task may happen to be. Feminism can thus be crossed with deconstruction or Marxism; Marxism with postmodernism, post-structuralism or even post-colonialism, and so on, continuously in a variety of analytical and theoretical permutations. Except for the most committed enthusiasts of particular movements, most critics and theorists tend to operate in magpie fashion these days; selecting a bit of this theory and a bit of that, for their own personalised approach. The sheer profusion of the theories with which experts are confronted today promotes this kind of experimental possibility. Consequently, postcolonial studies, subaltern studies, together with the full range of theories within critical theory, have all been adapted by various movements to help further particular political programmes, as in the case of black criticism and queer theory (Stuart and Van Loon 2009, 6–7).

Some postcolonial theorists were influenced by the cultural and political critiques developed over time by structuralist and poststructuralist theorists like Ferdinand de Saussure (1857–1913), Martin Heidegger (1889–1976), Antonio Gramsci (1891–1937), Walter B. S. Benjamin (1892–1940), Mikhail M. Bakhtin (1895–1975), Jacques M. E. Lacan (1901–1981), Roland G. Barthes (1915–1980), Louis P. Althusser (1918–1990), Paul de Man (1919–1983), Frantz Fanon (1925–1961), Giles Deleuze (1925–

Introduction

1995), Michel Foucault (1926–1984), Pierre-Felix Guattari (1930–1992) and Jacques Derrida (1930–2004).

Ake was influenced mainly by the intellectual legacies of Marxist scholarship, especially the writings of Karl Marx (1818–1883), Frederick Engels (1820–1895), Vladimir I. Lenin (1870–1924), Rosa Luxemburg (1871–1919), Rudolf Hilferding (1877–1941) and Nikolai Ivanovich Bukharin (1888–1938), particularly as articulated in the Latin American contributions to the theories of dependency, political economy and underdevelopment.[13] A number of other approaches and epistemologies also claim to be, and in fact, describe themselves as 'postcolonial' in many remarkable respects. For example, Achille Mbembe (2001) focuses on 'imagining' and 'reimagining' the city, the nation-state as well as locations and places generally in colonial and postcolonial Africa. Armed with the latest interventions in critical theory in his engagement with colonial discourse analysis[14] and postcolonial theory,[15] Edward W. Said (1978) works from the poststructuralist premise that knowledge is a discursive field derived from language and draws from Antonio Gramsci, Erich Auerbach and Michel Foucault the insight that its significance lies embedded within various systems of power. From this, he exposes the epistemological system underlining imperial power, thus transcending its conventional understanding as a merely material phenomenon. According to Said, the West is able to survive the full weight of political decolonisation fundamentally because its power, which is linked to the cultural and ideological representations it constructs and imposes on the rest of the world remains intact, a reality characterising, albeit subtly – even the supposedly objective scholarship of the Western academia. Any assessment of centre-periphery relations that ignores the cultural dimension – underlined by the mutual representations of the self and the Other – misses one of the most persistent and profound legacies of the colonial experience.

The implication of this analysis is that the deconstruction of Western structures as well as systems of knowledge on non-Western societies is a *sine qua non* for dismantling Western modes of domination.[16] For Said, it is this compelling task that underlines the *post*, in 'postcolonial' and 'postcolonial theory'. Ngugi Wa Thiong'o (1986) describes language, especially the indigenous language, as the key to emancipation from colonial modes of thought. Drawing on Senegal, Mamadou Diouf harps on the transformations taking place in youth identities and subjectivities under changing cultural, economic and socio-political conditions across Africa. Hinged on deconstruction historiography in their works on India and South Asia, Ashis Nandy (1983; 1995b:65),[17] Dipesh Chakrabarty, Gayatri C. Spivak (1985:332),[18] Homi K. Bhabha, Partha Chatterjee and Ranajit Guha interpret the world beyond the boundaries of rationality and disciplinary reason.[19] Paulin Hountondji (1977; 1983; 1997) takes on the theme of endogeneity in knowledge production on Africa, while Valentin Y. Mudimbe (1988; 1994) advances a deconstruction of the concept of 'Africa'. Mahmood Mamdani (1996) examines the question of identities as historically produced in colonial and postcolonial Africa.

Postcolonial theory's insight into the pervasive nature of Western constructions of the Other has made it clear that much of what we thought we knew about the once-colonised-societies was deliberately distorted by the discursive designs of the colonisers. This realisation has informed a re-examination of the circumstances under which particular peoples became identified as members of various castes, faiths, nations, races, tribes and other culturally-defined collectivities. Mahmood Mamdani's engagement in this regard represents an important and lively examination of the construction of various identities under colonial and postcolonial conditions. Through such works, what had been thought to be primordial affiliations of castes and tribes are now better understood as having assumed their modern shapes from the contestatory processes arising from the efforts of colonial authorities to impose order over subject populations who sought to resist those demands. Following the intellectual tradition of Edward Said's *Orientalism*, Premesh J. Lalu engages with theoretical questions of disciplinary knowledge and reason; nationalism and the nation-state in Africa.[20]

As Ake's works reveal, barring the historicist reading noted in his epistemological and methodological formulations, Marx remains relevant not just as a critic of capitalism and liberalism but also to any postcolonial and postmodernist project of history writing. And, as Kelly Harris (2005:78) explains, 'Underdevelopment theorists clearly embrace much of the philosophy of Marx and Engels and Ake was no different'. 'The Marxist vision of development seems closer to Ake's notion of development'.

While postcoloniality makes clear the legacies of inherited power relations and their continuing effects on modern global culture and politics, its exponents seek to replace the hermeneutic approach to the construction of history by competing constructions of the past.[21] Its spirit is found in the writings of Hichem Djait, the Tunisian historian who accused imperial Europe of denying Africa its own vision of humanity. It is also found in Fanon's (1968) articulation of 'the African liberation struggle', which held on to the Enlightenment idea of the equality of the human person. The engagement with European thought is thus marked by the fact that the European intellectual tradition is the most dominant in the social sciences departments of most, if not all modern universities today. And as Samir Amin (1989) observes, although the idea of the European intellectual tradition stretching back to ancient Greece and Rome, is merely a fabrication of a relatively recent European history, it is nevertheless, the genealogy of the thought in which historians and social scientists across the world find themselves inserted. While the idea of Europe existing as a source of signification and subtle referent to historical knowledge is a major epistemological problem underlining the struggle by postcolonial scholars to reconstruct history from a non-Eurocentric perspective, there are, however, important variations in the positions of these scholars. For example, while some of them like Dipesh Chakrabarty (1992) are content mainly at decentring Europe as the sole source of all legitimate signification, others like Ashis Nandy (1983) aim at entirely replacing the prevailing historical mode of understanding the world altogether. Given the opposing claims to history around which the genealogy of the social sciences is constructed, the critique of historicism is therefore an integral part of the unended story of postcolonial studies.

Ake did not use the very notion of postcoloniality, which is central in this chapter.[22] He was also never directly identified with the debate on postcoloniality, which only became common currency and took the centre stage in major intellectual circles and political debates across the world, about a decade before his sudden and tragic death in a plane crash in November 1996. While his publications are marked by an original brand of Marxism, nevertheless, some of his contribution and insights can be linked to the discussions on postcoloniality. In other words, in Ake's works, one certainly sees the beginning of an engagement with postcoloniality – an intonation rather cut short by his sudden death in November 1996. The idea of narrowly boxing or fixing his works into political economy, therefore, does not seem fair enough. As this book suggests, beyond the domain of political economy, such works are extendable into critical theory and especially postcolonial studies. This work attempts to make such a linkage explicit. It explores the relevance of Ake's works for mapping the genealogies of the colonial and the postcolonial in African history.

Although recent efforts at extending the postcolonial inquiry to non-Western authorities is a remarkably welcome achievement, attention has been limited to those Westernised experts who have received – at least – some provisional admission into the Western academic canon.

Such scholars are yet to be carefully situated within the class structures of their home societies as well as the cultural context of a transnational intelligentsia so as to avoid simplistic generalisations that their work necessarily embodies some nationalist or 'Third World' essence. Such work also needs to be freed from its Eurocentric character. Lastly, there is the challenge for postcolonial theory to open up the scope of its enquiries to a wider range of disciplines, other than literature and welcome other voices, especially those across various colonial and postcolonial territories of the world. Drawing on Claude Ake's intellectual works, this study attempts an intervention in that regard.

A note on methods and sources

This book relied on data generated from primary and secondary sources. Primary data took the form of extensive unstructured in-depth interviews conducted to a selected group of twenty strategic informants purposively sampled, five each from the colleagues, contemporaries, old friends and past students of the late Claude Ake. Secondary data were drawn from Ake's original texts; the published commentaries, critiques and tributes written in his honour before and after his death by his colleagues, friends and other institutional bodies; the information available in Ake's curriculum vitae and the texts which focused not only on the debates and issues on which Ake worked and wrote, but also the general context of scholarship in Africa during his lifetime and beyond. Equally relevant were those texts which explain the context of scholarship among the 'progressive opinion'at the University of Dar es Salaam, in Tanzania, in the 1970s-1980s as well as other developments, which characterised the period of his paradigm shifts. Particular attention was paid to the Cold War era, during which critical scholarship and radical Marxist perspectives were quite popular and indeed influenced many scholars across Africa and the Third World. Other developments also examined are the impact of the collegiate spirit and peer influences, especially Ake's interactions with Abdulrahman M. Babu, Dani W. Nabudere, Samir Amin, Walter Rodney, his access to the works of Frantz Fanon and the impact of the great debate at the University of Dar es Salaam, in Tanzania, in the 1970s.

While the entire work is grounded in relevant published literature on the subject matter, with respect to the period marking the end of Ake's life – the 1990s – much written evidence has been lost, some deliberately destroyed or carefully not recorded, out of fear of reprisal in a fearful age underwritten by the excesses of autocratic military rule. Ake's account on this period, therefore, draws substantially from interviews. Most of these were done with his colleagues, contemporaries and past students. Interviews, however, are not without their weaknesses as historical sources. They are subjective and also rely on memory – often blurred and distorted by perspective and time. Furthermore, describing another's life is sometimes unconsciously appropriated as a projection of one's own.

On the whole, the book placed Ake in conversation with other authorities from the early classical to the modern periods and examined their works on political and social theory generally as well as on Africa, Asia and Latin America. The objectives were one, to establish the influences and inspirations of some of these authorities and scholars on Ake. The book interrogated aspects of the issues raised in Ake's works and placed them in conversation with those noted in the works of these scholars. Doing this enabled us not only to see the extent of Ake's indebtness to these sources, but also in establishing an informed sense of change and continuity in terms of the development of those ideas and views. Two, it helped us in establishing the extent of consistence and relevance of Ake's writings on the issues under consideration in relation to the works of other authorities. Three, it helped in foregrounding the noted differences, and where applicable reservations, which some of these scholars have demonstrated directly and indirectly to aspects of Ake's works. Finally we sought to explore the prospects for deepening an understanding of African intellectual history drawing on Ake's works.

By drawing on China, India and other postcolonial societies, the aim is to answer two compelling questions. One, what does Africa stand to learn from the intellectual, nationalist and other experiences in these societies? Two, how do the experiences in these societies enable the African continent in fulfilling and making sense of the African revolution? This effort should be understood against the backdrop of Ake's (1967a; 1967b) repeated reference to Burma, Ceylon, India and Pakistan among other South-Asian states, especially in his earlier works. This is added to the fact that the draft chapters of the doctoral dissertation from which this book is produced, were written in India. Consequently, in addition to the rich collection on Africa from the social sciences community in Africa, the study examined the works of authorities in other parts of the global South, particularly India and Latin America. This is meant to produce the critique of Ake's works in a manner that fundamentally differs from the conventional idea of uncritically eulogising him while also hoping to explore the possibilities of a South–South intellectual exchange, as is the original intention of the South–South Exchange Programme for Research on the History of Development, one of the institutions which funded the production of this work. The idea of raising issues on India, South-Asia and Latin America is therefore not meant to drift its focus from Africa to these societies, but to draw useful illustrations and insights from the writings of scholars in these and other postcolonial societies which focused on related issues for their analyses. The aim is to enrich our examination of the issues posed for assessment in Ake's works by drawing from aspects of the critical and rich arguments and illustrations that have engaged the attention of scholars in those regions of the South. After all, these societies share similar predicaments – although in varying measures and are also products of similar historical experiences – with Africa.

Lastly, it should be recalled that Ake (1978; 1979) conceives of scholarship as a collective enterprise and describes social reality as complex, dialectical and dynamic, so much so that we will hardly understand it unless we learn to think dialectically. One way of interpreting Ake's position here is to understand him as implying that the issues which engage the attention of scholars in Africa and Asia are also parts of the collective experiences shared in other regions of the postcolonial world. Hence, in addition to an eclectic method, the idea of a dialectical approach towards understanding such issues produces a comparative and detailed research orientation. The reference to India and other societies within the South should hopefully enrich the analysis of Ake's writings on Africa.

The book therefore presents the postcolonial world as a text in which the peculiar African and Asian experiences are chapters and sections within the larger system of textualised narration. The immediately foreseeable advantage of this approach is that it helps to establish a transcontinental account of the intellectual and nationalist histories of these societies as provided in the works of the major scholars across these regions, while also emphasising the Africa-specific issues captured from the perspectives of Ake's analyses. The approach therefore privileges the use of arguments and ideas in a highly intellectualised sense through engaging the works of such scholars with reference to the trajectories of the debates and lived experiences which such ideas have generated. It is hoped that this approach will help not only in enriching vital aspects of Ake's works but also in retrieving the contributions of other thinkers and writers on Africa and other postcolonial societies who share similar intellectual exceptionalities and pedigrees with Ake.

Organisation of the work

The book is divided into five chapters. The first introduces Claude Ake's corpus as a major entry point for South-driven intellectual discourses within the humanities and social sciences. Arguing that South–South initiatives on endogenous knowledge production owe a great debt to Claude Ake, it positions his works as an illustration of the contributions of critical thinkers to knowledge production on Africa and highlights their relevance for understanding the African condition from uniquely African perspectives. In particular, it introduces the themes of development and endogenous knowledge as well as the subject field of postcolonial studies in relation to Africa and explores their connections with Ake's works. While there are several other approaches and epistemologies which describe themselves as linked with postcoloniality, this chapter highlights a major sense in which Ake's works fit into postcolonial studies. It underlines the book's orientation as a project on African intellectual history and engages the theme of knowledge production from the perspective of Ake's intellectual works. It ends with a discussion of the contents of the other chapters in the book. The second provides a genealogical account of the career and scholarship of the late Claude Ake. It examines the historical experiences and factors which shaped his worldview and writings. The aim is to explain the contexts and implications of his paradigm shifts as well as other contentious issues noted in his writings. Among the developments and experiences that influenced his career and life, the chapter emphasises the impact of the neo-Marxist debate at the University of Dar es Salaam in Tanzania on his theoretical paradigm shifts, thoughts and writings. Following Jacques Derrida's (1967) assertion that, 'there is nothing outside the text', the chapter pays attention to those texts which explain the context of scholarship among 'the progressive opinion' at the University of Dar es Salaam, in Tanzania, and other developments which characterised the period of his paradigm shifts. Particular attention is also paid to the Cold War era during which critical radical perspectives – especially Marxist scholarship – were quite popular and indeed influenced many scholars across Africa and the Third World.

Chapter three engages Africa as a question for critical thought. Evidently, the question of how one thinks about Africa is certainly an object of intense debate. It demands answering difficult, irritating and sometimes almost teleological questions about the human. It also entails having to live with the indetermination of seeking to keep open what others struggle to keep closed. To explore Africa as a question for critical thought, it revisits the debate on the legacy of colonialism for African history as well as the implications of that understanding for imagining and thinking about Africa's future. The critical question to engage in this respect is formulated thus, 'Is colonialism merely an episode or is it a unique experience in the modern regime of power in Africa?' While the argument on colonialism as an episode emphasises the ending of the colonial impact based on the termination of formal colonial rule and the acquisition of self-rule, its description as an epoch hinges on three major positions. One, is the argument that 'the colonial' created fundamental historical and continuing conditions, which in producing the colonised populations, reproduces them within a particular mode of thinking about the self – in relation to the 'other' and the world – strictly in terms of reinscribing the self into the same conditions created by the colonial system. The contradiction of critiquing imperial hierarchies of power while also reinscribing oneself into it is a major illustration of this continuity of the logic of the colonial condition. Two, there is the argument that colonialism not only left behind 'indelible' or 'permanent marks', but also that it led the colonised into 'irretrievable pasts' and paths. Three, that given the manner in which the 'colonial' continues to energise and shape the 'postcolonial', development in the postcolony – defined either as change, policy or process – is already destined to failure.[23]

To instantiate our position on the place of the colonial legacy in the determination of postcolonial anxieties, the chapter examines the theme of African studies and the bias of Eurocentricism, and closes with the author's position on this debate. As is widely known, the relationship between the colonial and the postcolonial in African history is a compelling issue and a critical question of continuing importance for postcolonial theorists throughout the world. While understanding colonialism as Africa's counter experience or counterpoint, one major way by which one can make historical analysis increasingly sensitive to some of the changes that have taken place as a result of European colonisation, is to think of colonialism and decolonisation as dialogical processes. This is especially the case, as Partha Chatterjee (1986:18–22) shows, given that nationalism, that is, the national question in Africa – as elsewhere in the postcolonial world – is historically and continues to be tied to the colonial question. Within that discursive space, the question of Africa's place in world history has been a huge basis of a genealogy of discourse. How can one acquire the intellectual sovereignty – as an African – over one's imagination of the self in relation to 'the Other' and 'the world'? How does one possibly explore the relationship between 'agency' and 'passivity' within the knowledge economy in Africa? How does the colonial reinscribe itself into the postcolonial in Africa, and what is the extent of its penetration in that regard? In what ways is it productive to think of colonialism as Africa's counter experience or counterpoint?[24] What is the 'human' and what is the 'social', and how are these constituted in Africa? Why have Africans not been able to effectively recover and retrieve their pasts, especially within the discipline of history?[25] Why have Africans not been capable of preserving their pasts? In answering these questions, the book suggests the need to historicise, problematise and further make colonialism a question to be examined, re-examined and answered, rather than making it appear as a self evident answer already produced, and a source, from which one only needs to draw.

Chapter four examines the connections between Claude Ake's contribution to the social sciences in Africa and the subject field of postcolonial studies. It discusses the relevance of his works for understanding 'the postcolonial condition' in contemporary Africa. It also highlights the shortcomings noted in his epistemological orientation to expatriate knowledge generally and the Western social sciences in particular. Given his advocacy of the need to reconstruct existing disciplinary fields following uniquely African critiques and interpretations, the chapter presents Ake's works as a corrective intervention to Eurocentrism and advocates the practices of 'cross-regional non-hierarchical dialogue' in which neither the East nor the West is taken as the paradigm against which the 'other' is measured and pronounced inadequate. Chapter five recapitulates and sums up the discussions in the book. It seeks to inspire and provoke further research on some of the issues at the centre of its enquiry. It does this, not necessarily by answering all of the questions the book poses, but primarily by raising issues and drawing attention to areas in need of further intellectual enquiry on Africa.

Notes

1. On the newness of efforts in providing written accounts on African history, see Steven Feierman (1993) and Albert M. Craig et al (2008, 156–7).

2. By this statement, Jacques Derrida (1967) means that 'there is nothing outside context'. With this, he suggests that one pays attention to the contexts within which experiences are acquired and lived. He is complemented here by Harold J. Laski's (1948, i) famous quotation that, 'No theory of the state is ever intelligible save in the context of

its time. What men think about the state is the outcome always of the experiences in which they are immersed'.

3. While the classic statement on hybridity is Homi K. Bhabha (1994), the connection between the definition of development as a 'catching-up' alternative and the failure of such a strategy to deliver developmental expectations for Africa and other postcolonial societies, receives careful attention in Dipesh Chakrabarty (2005) and Samir Amin (1990a).

4. This point has been pursued rigorously elsewhere by Daniel A. Offiong (1980).

5. Partha Chatterjee (1986:1–35) provides a compelling account with telling evidence on some of the epistemological violence that the modern world has witnessed with nationalism.

6. Quoted in *The Current*, 17 January 1976, Bombay.

7. Bernard Cohn (1996) and Christopher Bayly (1996) illustrate this point in relation to India.

8. For a critique of inherited theories of development and an advocacy for indigenous development strategies in Africa, see Olatunde Ojo (1985b:141–72) and S. K. B. Asante (1991:36–57).

9. The option of autarchy, which was vigorously advocated by Walter Rodney (1972) in Africa, has been the subject of numerous criticisms, especially within the literature on development in African and Latin American studies.

10. For a recapitulation of this position, see Samir Amin (2004).

11. Unless we first establish from the beginning what postcoloniality is, it may not be convincing to see how Ake's works are linked to the debate on it.

12. For probing analyses of postcoloniality, especially in the context of colonialism, imperialism and neocolonialism, see Aijaz Ahmed (1992) and Rajagopalan Radhakrishnan (1993).

13. In Marxist analysis, the materiality of knowledge production is very central for understanding its epistemological and ontological implications for power relations.

14. Colonial discourse analysis broadly refers to the examination and interpretation of particular colonial texts.

15. Postcolonial theory on the other hand, refers to the ideological and political position of the critic engaged in colonial discourse analysis. While postcolonial theory has rapidly become one of the great growth areas in academic life and cultural analysis over the past few decades, a great deal of its value stems from its ability to be politically charged and engaged. In this sense, being critical is being political. It thus represents an intervention into a much wider debate than the aesthetic alone.

16. This is an important connection between Edward Said (1978) and Claude Ake's (1990:7–21) thesis on the need for endogeneity in knowledge production on Africa.

17. Ashis Nandy (1983:XV; 1995b:65) denounces historical consciousness as a cultural and political liability for non-Western societies. He describes history as a mythography concocted by the West to further its hegemonic hold on the rest of the world and advances an alternative mythography that defies and denies the values of history.

18. Gayatri C. Spivak (1985:332) advocates the need to engage in a project based on the deconstruction of hegemonic historiographies.

19. Suffice it to say that theoretical thinking on civilisation, colonialism and nationalism has remained central to Indian and South-Asian scholars working within the subject field of postcolonial studies.

20. Given its coupling with power, the suspicion of history as a central accomplice to the West's discursive drive to dominate Southern African historiography is a disturbing motif, to which Premesh Lalu (2009) critically draws attention. He questions the discipline of history, especially its relevance for recovering the colonised and subjugated African voice. Although Lalu draws from Edward Said (1978), however, unlike Lalu, Said's position in this regard, is ambiguous. On the one hand, he highlights the importance of a historicised understanding of *Orientalism*, on the other; he suggests that the discipline of history is itself deeply implicated in the orientalist enterprise.

21. Friedrich Nietzsche's (1957) text is a seminal treatment of the selective privileging of issues and peoples in world history by the West. For an in-depth critique of historicism and the idea of the political or political modernity, see Dipesh Chakrabarty (2000).

22. This is an important caution for our purpose in this work.

23. On the argument that colonialism left behind 'indelible' or 'permanent marks' for colonial and postcolonial societies, see Edward Thompson and Garret T. Garratt (1934).

24. One way of doing this, is to problematise and think of colonialism, decolonisation and nationalism as dialogical processes, in which metropolitan and satellite voices carry equal weight.

25. While not seeking to make a fetishism of history, its cohabitation with power makes it difficult to be ignored.

Biographical and theoretical orientations

Men make their own history, but they do not make it just as they please;
they do not make it under circumstances chosen by themselves, but under
circumstances directly encountered, given and transmitted from the past. The
tradition of all the dead generations weighs like a nightmare on the minds of
the living

— Karl Marx, 1852/1869[1]

Although the ideas of political leaders in Africa provide a popular entrée
to African politics, the exploration of their contributions and profiles still
remains a largely underdeveloped genre. This is especially the case with
intellectuals and scholar-activists on the continent. Yet by challenging
existing hierarchies and oppressive institutions as well as truth regimes and
the structures of power that produce and support them, engaged scholars
occupy a critical position in society as vanguards of various popular
struggles. The world therefore has a lot to learn from their contributions
and failings as progressive social forces. This chapter examines Claude
Ake's corpus as a basis for filing this gap. Being a political scientist with an
unusually broad intellectual formation and horizon, the chapter highlights
the developments and shifts which shaped his worldview and writings. It
pays attention to his production – over a period of four decades – of a wide
ranging body of works which have been quite instructive not only for their
analytic acuity, methodological rigour and theoretical sophistication, but
also for being remarkable works of magisterial erudition, the products of

an exceptionally great mind, written with a deftly profound authority and also constituting a significant attempt to adapt the intellectual legacies of Marxist scholarship towards understanding the political economy and social history of contemporary Africa from a broadly critical perspective. The chapter provides a genealogical account of the career and scholarship of the late Claude Ake. It examines the historical experiences and factors that shaped his worldview and writings. The aim is to explain the contexts and implications of his paradigm shifts and other contentious issues noted in his writings.[2]

Covering a complex range of issues, the scope of Ake's corpus is broad. Such issues have also attracted numerous attentions within the African and Africanist communities. For example, his account of traditional African cultures (Ake 1985a, 1985b), his theses on pan-Africanism (Ake 1965) and elite construction of the state in the continent (Ake 1996), civil society and social movements as well as the connections between his thoughts and those of other scholars are examples of subjects where Ake's works have been examined extensively within the literature on African studies (Mamdani et al 1988; Mamdani 1992; Mamdani and Wamba-dia-Wamba 1995). These issues are however not at the centre of attention in this chapter. This is a very important clarification. Ake's engagement with African cultures; his positions on their contradictions within the framework of the modern state system in the continent; his thesis on their contributions and relevance to the state in postcolonial Africa as well as the connections and parallels between his works and those of Amilcar L. Cabral, Cheikh A. Diop, Frantz Fanon, Samir Amin and other leading African political thinkers are entirely separate themes. These are not the focus of this chapter. They have also been treated in other works. Following the note on his biography, the connections between, as well as the relevance of his works for understanding Africa's intellectual and political history – drawing on insights from the sociology of knowledge production on Africa – are the focus of attention in this chapter.

The chapter relied on data generated from both primary and secondary sources. Primary data took the form of extensive, unstructured in-depth interviews (IDIs) conducted to a selected group of twenty strategic informants purposively sampled, five each from the (i) colleagues, (ii) contemporaries, (iii) old friends and (iv) past students of the late Claude Ake.[3] Secondary data were drawn from (i) Ake's original texts, (ii) the published commentaries, critiques and tributes written in his honour before and after his death by his colleagues, friends and other institutional bodies, (iii) the information available in his curriculum vitae and (iv) the texts which focused not only on the debates and issues on which Ake worked and wrote, but also the general context of scholarship in Africa during his lifetime and beyond. Of particular relevance are those texts which explain the context of scholarship among the progressive opinion at the University of Dar es Salaam, in Tanzania, in the 1970s–1980s and other developments which characterised the period of his paradigm shifts. According to Dani W. Nabudere (1978, VI):

> These developments…remain a testimony to the vibrant intellectual atmosphere that has characterised the University of Dar es Salaam over the last few years, despite various reactionary efforts to stifle it, and to the democratic sentiments of the people of Tanzania and in particular the very enlightened leadership of Mwalimu Nyerere, despite the imperialist domination of the country which tends to negate democracy in general.

Particular attention was also paid to the Cold War era, during which critical scholarship and radical Marxist perspectives were quite popular and indeed influenced many scholars across Africa and the Third World. Other developments also examined are the impact of the collegiate spirit and peer influences, especially Ake's interactions with Abdulrahman M. Babu, Dani W. Nabudere, Samir Amin, Walter Rodney, his access to the works of Frantz Fanon and the impact of the neo-Marxist debate at the University of Dar es Salaam, in Tanzania, in the 1970s, in his transformation.

In historicising Africa, the chapter avoids particularist or reductionist approaches which limit analyses to one moment or trajectory, but focuses on the entire historical span of the continent and the periods both antedating and predating the development and emergence of nation-states across the regions. It theorizes the whole of Ake's life and scholarship as a lived essentialism. As Abubakar Momoh (2002, 25–6) puts it, this is necessary mainly because aspects and moments of one's life may throw up developments and features that could make primary determinants of one's consciousness assume the form of secondary determinants of the individual's scholarship and vice versa. It is therefore, methodologically erroneous and theoretically incorrect for anyone to use specific aspects and manifestations of Ake's life to generalise about the entire character of his career and scholarship. Rather, the contents, contexts and forms of those manifestations should be critically analysed, examined and interrogated by focusing on the details of his lifetime sojourn and trajectory. As will be shown shortly, it is necessary to examine Ake's biographical and intellectual accounts, and historicise him in relation to Africa's social history for a number of reasons. One, Ake's shift from *homo erectus* to *homo sapiens* is not properly accounted for, unless we critically analyse and interrogate his career and scholarship in relation to the material conditions and social processes which facilitated the developments and transformations noted therein.

Two, establishing such connections helps one to show that, far from being abstract, Ake's experiences and theoretical positions are products of the material world in which he lived and concerning which he wrote. In other words, just like those of other scholars, Ake's theoretical positions were historically constituted and socially developed in Africa. This suggests that the consciousness of men can neither be entirely abstracted nor independently understood from the specific social contexts and experiences within which they were developed. Consciousness therefore includes fundamental aspects of criticality, which is indomitable and is also not mechanically determinable. Hence, the twin concepts of engagement and relevance, which help in appreciating the concept of socialisation in relation to Ake, and by which reference is made to the material conditions within which his actions and thoughts were conceived and given expression. This also suggests the need to critically interrogate and problematise Ake's works in relation to his specific context and social milieu. Doing these will reveal that Ake's works did not and were not developed in a vacuum. Neither did they arise independently of the complex social realities which informed his thoughts and concerning which he wrote. In fact, those ideas make sense only when juxtaposed with, rather than isolated or separated from the complex interactions of social forces and the mode of production of his time. The idea of narrating Ake's biographical accounts and other crucial details, is therefore, meant not only to capture the specific material conditions and the distinctive social history within which his actions, experiences and thought were constituted and given expression, but also to explain the details of how he came into existence as an intellectual, and how he concretised and made sense of that existence.

Three, through such an approach, one is able to appreciate his praxis of knowledge production in Africa and thus overcome the temptation of vainly condemning or glorifying either his paradigm shift or contribution to different areas and aspects of the social sciences in Africa, without properly understanding the context of such contributions, especially the specific social history that gave rise and meaning to them (see Momoh 1999, 142–4). These considerations make the examination of Ake's life and works in the context of the African condition and experience *sui generis*.

From yet another perspective, Ake's ideas on African politics and the summation of his experiences and scholarship are expressions of the struggles of the African people as a collectivised social force. To deny the historical significance of such struggles is to abstract Ake, not only from his historical context, but also to undermine the struggles themselves, which informed his entire development. The chapter therefore theorises Ake's life and scholarship as a lived essentialism. This is necessary because moments of his life may throw up developments and features that could make primary determinants of his consciousness[4] assume the forms of secondary determinants of his scholarship and vice versa. It is thus methodologically erroneous and theoretically incorrect to use specific aspects and manifestations of his life to generalise about the character of his scholarship. Rather, the contexts and forms of those manifestations should be critically analysed, explained and interrogated, focusing on the details of his lifetime sojourn and trajectory. It is important to examine Ake's biographical and intellectual accounts and historicise him in relation to the complex social history of Africa for a number of reasons. One, Ake's intellectual shifts are not properly accounted for, unless we critically interrogate and analyse his career and scholarship vis-à-vis the material conditions and the complex social history which facilitated such a transformation. Two, establishing such vital connections helps one to show that, far from being independent, Ake's theoretical positions were historically developed and socially constituted in the material world in which he lived and concerning which he wrote. This suggests that human consciousness can neither be independently understood nor entirely abstracted from the specific social contexts and experiences within which they were developed. Consciousness therefore includes fundamental elements of criticality which are not mechanically determinable. Hence the concepts of engagement and relevance which help us in appreciating the concept of socialisation in relation to Ake, and by which reference is made to the material conditions within which his thought was conceived and given expression (Swingewood 2000; Booth et al 2003; Burke 2005; Moore and Parker 2007).

This approach enables one understand that Ake's ideas about African politics are expressions of the struggles of the African people as a collectivised social force. It also helps one appreciate his praxis of knowledge production on Africa and thus avoid the temptation of wrongly condemning or glorifying either his contributions or paradigm shifts without properly understanding their contexts and the specific social history that gave rise and meaning to them. To deny the significance of such struggles is therefore, to abstract Ake not only from his historical context, but also to undermine the struggles themselves which informed the development of his career. Two positions emerge from this exercise which underscores the central argument of the article. One, theories as a peculiar genre of writings in the social sciences are special forms of discourses based largely on established relations, imagined categories and objectified realities grounded in the experiences and mindsets of the theorists themselves and the environments on which they are based. Theories are therefore products of the literary imaginations of men and thus must be critically engaged and painstakingly scrutinised in terms of their boundaries, which are constrained by the institutional parameters that inform and limit them. This is because, theory, by any definition of it, has always been born out of social reality. Its content and forms have always been to some extent derived from attempts to codify experience. Its internal structures recreate and simulate epistemic paradigms from a realm of possibilities already defined by its specialised community of practitioners – communicative producers and consumers. What the social sciences generally recognise as classical social theory – Durkheim, Marx and Weber among others – began in fact as systematic attempts to critically assess the nature of the social experiences that dominated the world in which they lived, namely capitalism, modernity and rationality. In that regard, modern theories are not theories of modernity per se but rather social theories that mimicked to some extent the underlying axioms and structure of modern experiences in their codification of the world. Two, the successful revision of theories is contingent upon a sufficient understanding of the theorists' experiences and mindsets not only as historically constituted in specific contexts, but also as such theories condition the subjectivities of the theorists themselves both as agents and proponents of historical change. There is therefore, a fundamental difference in the way social thought in the classical era – such as that of Durkheim, Marx and Weber – was articulated in reference to their own intellectual and socio-political context as well as the way their work has been appropriated in the context of contemporary disciplines as theory.

This chapter explains Ake's intellectual biography not as an independent episteme but locates it within the complex interplay of different social forces, and the entire social structure in Africa as an organic whole. Following the note on Ake as an organic intellectual, this chapter comprises five sections. The first provides the account of Ake's biographical factors and other early influences. The second discusses his paradigm shift, from liberalism to radical scholarship. The third examines the impact of the neo-Marxist debate at the University of Dar es Salaam, in Tanzania, in the 1970s, in the making of his paradigm shift. The fourth offers a note on his death in November 1996. This is followed by the conclusion.

Claude E. Ake as an organic intellectual

Conceptually, intellectuals are members of the petit-bourgeois class within the modern bourgeois society. As a collectivity, the intelligentsia represents that social class which occupies the intermediate position between the bourgeoisie and proletariat under capitalism. It comprises the category of artisans, intellectuals, shopkeepers, small manufacturers, subalterns as well as those in the distributive sector. Its existence is not exclusive to the capitalist mode of production. Intellectuals exist under feudalism as well as other non-capitalist modes of production. We have focused on the context of capitalism to highlight and underline its particularities and uniqueness under that stage of history. According to Antonio Gramsci (1891–1937),[5] all men[6] are potentially intellectuals, at least, in the sense of having an intellect and using it, but not all have the social functions of an intellectual.[7] Functionally, he identifies the organic and the traditional as two distinct categories or groups of the intellectual historically existing. While every social group[8] coming into existence on the original terrain of an essential function in the world of economic production, creates and possesses along with itself – organically – one or more strata of intellectuals that give it homogeneity and an awareness of its existence and functions within the economic, political and social spheres (Gramsci 2001, 1135–43), every mode of production or stage of history is identified with an intellectual class that articulates the interests of the dominant class within that social order. Thus for example, under capitalism, the capitalist entrepreneur creates alongside himself a group of economists, industrial technicians and lawyers, in short, an elite among its rank of entrepreneurs possessing the capacity to organise the dominant class and society in general, including all its complex organism of classes as well as services right up to the level of the state organism. Furthermore, he points out that 'every class that emerges into history out of the preceding economic structure and as an expression of the development of this structure has found … categories of intellectuals already in existence.' By this, he underlines an 'historical continuity uninterrupted even by the most complicated and radical changes in political and social forms' (Gramsci 2001, 1139). To expand Gramsci's shorthand here is to understand him as suggesting that the existence of the intelligentsia is not exclusive to the capitalist mode of production. Feudal lords as well as several other social classes within various pre-capitalist modes of production all possessed particular military and technical capacities. It is precisely from the moment at which the aristocracy loses its monopoly of techno-military capacity that the crisis of feudalism begins. This is also true of the other modes of production. The formation of intellectuals in the feudal world and the preceding classical world is therefore a question to be examined separately and thoroughly. For while the mass of the peasantry performs an essential function in the world of production, it does not elaborate its own organic intellectuals, nor does it assimilate any stratum of traditional – even though it is from the peasantry that other social groups draw many of their intellectuals – and a high proportion of traditional intellectuals are of peasant origin.

Gramsci's characterisation of and distinction between the organic and traditional intellectuals need not detain us. The more compelling task for us is to underline the essential elements of his thought on the role of the intellectual. Comprising the categories of literary writers, philosophers, priests and professors, among others, traditional intellectuals are members of those elite groups who see themselves as autonomous and independent of their social contexts, and perceive their work as both changeless and timeless in relation to the leading problems of their societies. Arguing that these constitute a rather conservative and reactionary force, Gramsci describes them as the leading agents of various passive revolutions. He notes that far from their seemingly autonomous and independent positions, their work has sinister implications which, more often than not, support the status quo and stultify the prospects for progressive and radical change towards an egalitarian or humane society. Organic intellectuals, on the other hand, spring from their own social classes and contexts and act functionally as the organisational and thinking force for their specific social classes and contexts. While the examples of members of this group include cultural organisers, economic and political analysts, industrial technicians and others who may or may not belong to the dominant classes, they are distinguished less by their profession, which may be any job characteristic of their class, than by their function in directing the aspirations and ideas of the classes to which they organically belong.

Gramsci points out that there is basically no human activity or sphere of life from which intellectual articulation can be entirely excluded.

Central to his thought in this regard, is the argument that intellectuals are not independent but are rather products of their societies and in particular the specific classes into which they are born and for which they speak. He describes intellectuals as members of various social groups who are (i) deeply rooted in their historical and social contexts, (ii) meaningfully and sufficiently aware of the oppressive forces undermining the economic freedom and material comfort of the class/es that they represent, (iii) bold enough to openly and publicly denounce unjust representations of power, (iv) unconditionally committed to mobilising and organising their social groups towards an intended progressive, revolutionary change, and (v) whose knowledge and political action are fused together. His understanding of the intellectual is neither fixed nor limited to the ivory tower professors who have, or are still publishing academic articles and books at the highest levels in the world. The critical consideration for Gramsci is the question of an attachment to as well as the functional representation of members of the social classes to which their affiliation and commitment are pledged. It is thus in reference to this attachment, bond and intimacy between the intellectuals and the classes that they represent, that Gramsci talks of organic intellectuals (Gramsci 1971, 3–23). In Gramsci therefore, the question of identifying with the material conditions of members of a social class as well as representing their interests and speaking for them is the most important demand of the organic intellectual. It is also in doing this, that intellectuals become integral in relation to their social contexts and thus acquire their organicity vis-à-vis the social classes that they represent.

Contrary to Gramsci's postulation, not all intellectuals represent and speak for the social classes into which they are born. Marx for example – although was born into an upper class family in Trier – spoke for the industrial working class in Europe. To clarify, intellectuals and philosophers generally are usually the products of their material conditions and socio-political milieux. This is a major thesis that Gramsci underlines. As David Caute (1970, 2) illustrates:

> In an overturned, humane world, a global society harmonized by abiding principles of equity and mutual respect among men, the mystique of the prophet would no longer be relevant ... Marx was 'created' by capitalism ... Lenin by Russian autocracy; Gandhi by British imperialism; Fanon was created by the white man ... Throughout his life Fanon was plagued and embittered by his encounters with racism.

Environmental factors and material conditions alone do not make any intellectual. Fanon, for example, 'had everything ... to become assimilated into the middle class black elite which the French colonial system carefully nurtured,' but did not (Caute 1970, 2). What marked him out, however, was 'some distinctive personal quality, some force of temperament.' As L. Adele Jinadu (1972, 433–6) observes, Fanon gives us a clue to this 'distinctive personal quality' when in the closing sentence of *Black Skin, White Masks*, he exclaims, 'My final prayer: O my body make me always a man who questions.'

Gramsci accepted Marx's analysis of capitalism put forward in the previous century and conceded that the struggle between the ruling class and the subordinate working class was the actual driving force that moved society forward. His reading of Marx's works had to be entirely from memory since communist books were not allowed in prison. He however, rejected the traditional Marxist view of how the ruling class ruled. Following this rejection and an insistence on an alternative mode of analysis, he made a major contribution to modern thought through his imaginative articulation of the role played by ideology in the construction of consciousness. While Marxism had premised its conception of power entirely on the role of coercion and force as the domination exerted by the ruling class, Gramsci felt that an understanding of the pervasive albeit subtle forms of ideological control and manipulation by the dominant class, that served to perpetuate all repressive structures of every class based society, was missing. He identified domination – that is, the direct physical coercion by the armed forces and the police and hegemony, which referred to both ideological control and consent – as two distinct forms of political control. He argued that no regime, however authoritarian, could sustain its control and dominance exclusively through the deployment of coercion and force. Ultimately, it had to rely on some measure of legitimacy derived from popular support in order to stabilise its hold onto power.

By hegemony, he meant the permeation throughout society of a body of values, or a set of attitudes, beliefs and morality capable of legitimising and supporting the status quo in power relations. Conceived in this light, hegemony thus becomes an organising principle diffused through socialisation into every area of the daily life of all men in society. To the extent that this consciousness becomes accepted and internalised by the governed or ruled, it also becomes part of the prevailing common sense such that the entire system of culture, morality and philosophy of the ruling elite appears as the natural order of things (Boggs 1976, 39). This way, the ruling class maintained its dominance mainly by eliciting the consent of the people and only using its coercive apparatuses as a last resort. This way also, beyond the known orientation of traditional Marxism, Gramsci's analysis provides an explanation of why the working class in Europe had on the whole failed to develop a revolutionary consciousness after the First World War and had moved instead towards reformism – manipulating and tinkering with the system rather than working towards entirely overthrowing it. His thesis on hegemony was thus foregrounded into a subtle theory of power – than whatever was developed by any of his contemporaries – that most profoundly explains how the ruling class ruled.

Using the concept of hegemony, Gramsci explained that the reason the much anticipated revolution of the proletariat had not yet occurred was because within the realm of civil society[9] the working class had come to identify their own best interests as being in tandem with the best interests of the bourgeoisie.[10] To transcend this situation, Gramsci says, the proletariat must possess its own intelligentsia – a standing army of organic intellectuals – representing the working masses that, in contrast to the ivory tower intellectuals, do not see themselves as separate from society. In other words, to bring about historical change or transition from an existing system, Gramsci argues that, the proponents of that intended change must advance a break in the prevailing ideological bond, through the articulation and development of a counter hegemony to that of the existing ruling class. According to Gramsci, the mass of the people must be mobilised to see ideological and structural change as part of the same struggle.[11] In other words, although the labour process is at the centre of the class struggle, it is the ideological struggle that will have to be addressed if the mass of the people were to come to a consciousness that allowed them effectively question the economic and political rights of their masters to rule. Thus, as the organising and thinking element of the classes that they represent, the role of the intellectual in relation to the creation of a counter hegemony as a basis for mass participation is very crucial. Considering the particular context of capitalism, for example, there was no question that historical change towards socialism could be brought about mainly by an organised elite of dedicated and well informed radical thinkers – organic revolutionary intellectuals – acting for the working class (Entwistle 1979).

Neither Gramsci nor Marx addressed attention to the revolutionary role of the intellectual as a theoretical problem in the world outside Europe. I will also not delve into what either of them had to say about these societies in any of their many works.[12] Much of the debate on this question across the non-European world is about the implications and inspirations of their general theoretical schemes as well as the inferences drawn from various comments they made on the subject during their active literary and political careers. We are however concerned here about the more influential interpretations of Gramsci's thought addressed towards understanding the role of the intellectual in articulating 'the national question' across the global South where it has taken the compendium form of the 'colonial and national question' especially vis-à-vis theoretical understandings of nationalism and self-determination. While the debate on the national question lasted in the Second and Third International,[13] the related question of the role of intellectuals and other vanguardist forces in articulating revolutionary change was discussed. Vladimir I. Lenin (1870–1924), Rosa Luxemburg (1871–1919), Rudolf Hilferding (1877–1941), Joseph Stalin (1878–1953), Leon Trotsky (1879–1940) and Nikolai I. Bukharin (1888–1938) were eloquent voices in this regard. It was also during this debate that Lenin – working out his ideas from the immediate practical problems facing the revolution in a hugely multi-ethnic empire – highlighted the central question of political democracy as the kernel or keystone of Marxist analyses of nationalism. While this emphasis led him to formulate his famous thesis on the rights of all nations to self-determination,[14] his proposals were not directed towards constructing a general theoretical paradigm for nationalism, self-determination or the role of the intellectual across the colonial and postcolonial world. More so, as Partha Chatterjee (1986, 18) has observed, Marxists across the world have continued the arguments and discussions on these questions since the tumultuous period of national liberation movements that followed the 1930s. It is within this discursive space that one locates the interventions on Africa and the rest of the world.[15] Here, the earliest imagination of and reference to the role of the intellectual as a modern actor is historically fused with the colonial question in which the assertion of national identity was necessarily a form of struggle against colonial exploitation. While the colonial condition produced postcolonial subjects with mentalities harmonious and in tandem with the needs of the ruling classes of the imperialist countries, the role of the intellectual was defined not just in terms of liberating the productive forces across various colonial and postcolonial economies, but more fundamentally in terms of transforming the cultural – mental outlook of those populations – nurtured in the womb of colonial-imperialism, using the cultural eyeglasses imported from the West.[16] This role can even be better illustrated if we shift our gazes and sights from general theoretical treatments to the contexts of anticolonial and nationalist movements. I will now refer to the debate and works on Africa, a continent, where the articulation of anti-imperialist historiography was a central component of decolonisation and various nationalist struggles.

Mahmood Mamdani (1990) describes the intellectual as a broad and heterogeneous grouping whose social origin lies in the split between manual and mental labour, especially in all class-divided societies. It is also that social category which work combines at once mental conceptions and organisation of social processes and their theoretical application and explanation in society. It is the intra-class or sub-class category of the petty-bourgeoisie under capitalism that is simultaneously ideological and technical; and which ideological and technical orientations give rise to ideological and material distinctions amongst the various categories and ranks of the intellectuals. As members of society in custody of knowledge, they not only develop a technical specialisation but also points of view which are shaped by and which in turn shape the nature of struggles in society. According to Mamdani (1990, 2):

> It is both through their capacity to develop a material and social space autonomous of the political power, and through their point of view, that intellectuals become 'organic' to one or another broad social group. Thus the need to anchor the analysis of the intelligentsia in concrete historical and social processes.

Thandika Mkandawire (2005) defines intellectual work as the labour of the mind and soul, and describes intellectuals as persons who have played a major role in shaping ideologies, passions and societal visions. He explains the connections between these elements by illustrating the relationships between African intellectuals, nationalism and pan-Africanism, relationships which he describes as both fraught and symbiotic. As he puts it, while pan-Africanism is the context within which African nations have been imagined, nationalism informs the radical basis and context for intellectuality in the continent. To him, African intellectuals have impacted significantly on these whole processes by explaining and reconstructing the past, interpreting the present and mapping out visions of the future (Mkandawire 2005, 10–55). According to Abubakar Momoh (1999, 55), the primary condition for being an intellectual is the ability to tell the truth even if the truth harms your interest. As he surmises:

> The so-called objectivity and value-free claims of modern social science only allow for ideological obfuscation of class struggle, domination and

hegemony. A scholar with a sense of social responsibility cannot accept these positions... telling the truth is a moral issue and every class has its own morality. As Engels rightly submits, 'men (sic), consciously or unconsciously, derive their ethical ideas in the last resort from the practical relations on which their class position is based....'[17]

Ali A. Mazrui (2005) describes the intellectual as any person who is fascinated by ideas and has acquired and developed the capacity as well as skills to handle many of them effectively. According to him:

We can imagine intellectualism without pan-Africanism, but we cannot envisage pan-Africanism without the intellectualization of the African condition. It is not a historical accident that the founding fathers of the pan-Africanist movement were disproportionately intellectuals – W. E. B. Dubois, Kwame Nkrumah, George Padmore, Leopold Senghor and others (Mazrui 2005, 56).

Mazrui argues that intellectual endeavours on the continent have attained their full meaning and relevance mainly through the grounding of African intellectuals in the pan-African political projects and have become valorised through the actions of several other social actors. Hence the dissipations, the rise and worldviews of social movements, all of which have enormous implications for intellectual work across the regions. In marking the difference between the intellectual and other social categories within the knowledge economy, Samir Amin argues that the intellectual is not the technocrat serving the system, but the one that critiques the system, especially from without. According to him:

There are no intellectuals at the World Bank. And so the intellectual, or the intelligentsia, is not able to be a civil servant in such institutions. The responsibility of intellectuals is to remain critical of the system. This is why I prefer to talk about intelligentsia because it is not a question of academic titles nor of the technical capacity of a bureaucrat or a technocrat, it is a question of intellectual capacity to take positions which are by nature inseparable from politics. It is a position that is critical by nature. This means that intellectuals have a big responsibility. I do not believe that intellectuals transform the world. But I don't believe that the world can transform (sic) without some decisive help from the intelligentsia. For example we cannot imagine the French revolution, which was the great revolution of bourgeois history, without the Enlightenment. We could not have imagined the Russian revolution and the Chinese Revolution without the Third International, without the working class and the Marxist movement. In my mind we can also not think about the future without an intelligentsia which fulfils its role, which takes its responsibility (Dieng 2007, 1158–9).

While the study of intellectuals in and on Africa has attracted a lot of attention within the literature on African studies (Mamdani 1993, CODESRIA 1996, Makgoba 1999, Zeleza 2003, Falola 2004, Beckman and Adeoti 2006, Mkandawire 2006), in describing Ake as an organic intellectual, we have in mind a conception of Ake, who as a revolutionary-theorist and scholar-activist was committed to the service of humanity through his dedication to institution-building, knowledge production and transnational advocacy in advancing the material empowerment of the African people. As a calm, down-to-earth and resolute scholar, Ake personified – perhaps more than any other scholar of his generation throughout Africa – the combination of brilliant scholarship and revolutionary commitment.

Ake is to be functionally differentiated from another category of African thinkers, namely, those who were neither scholars nor theorists. In this sense, we must note that Ake was both a theorist and a writer, who being a scholar and an activist cannot be classified in the same mode of thinkers like Frantz Fanon, Julius M. K. Nyerere, Amilcar L. Cabral, Kwame Nkrumah, Patrice Lumumba and Ruth First, among others. Unlike Ake, these African nationalists and pan-African heroes were intellectual activists who emerged originally as unlikely candidates but later became leaders and spokespersons of their people. Their assignment as vanguards of the nationalist cause was historically imposed on them by the prevailing colonial realities of their time. In most cases, they emerged as revolutionary leaders in their time, mainly because they rejected the option of escaping from the realities and sufferings of their people, but elected instead, to 'return to the source' of their being through leading the various nationalist struggles and by reaffirming the rights of their people to take their own place in history. Through their written, often polemical works and other practical contributions to Africa's political transformation, they are appreciated as having contributed to the subject matter of African political thought. More than these heroes, however, Ake, being a scholar-activist was able to capture and speak more pungently to the realities of the African condition. And given his training as a revolutionary scholar and writer, he was much more theoretically rigorous, methodologically nuanced and therefore successfully systematic in his analysis of the continent. In Ake's group are Cheikh Anta Diop, Chinua Achebe, Kwasi Wiredu and

Oluwole Soyinka, some of who have been studied extensively in History, Philosophy and the Liberal Arts. Accordingly, while intellectual activists are here understood as engaged in instrumentalising knowledge, scholars take on knowledge production as a vocation or profession. Scholars are therefore vocationally confined to an area and are professionally dedicated to knowledge production, on a lifetime basis. The engagement of intellectual activists with knowledge production is however not usually on a fulltime career basis, but principally as an instrument, or as a means with which struggle is prosecuted towards a desired form of change. For scholars however, knowledge production is sacredly accepted as an unconditional assignment to which they are committed and dedicated. These illustrations should hopefully, help us appreciate more clearly, the differences between Ake as an activist, scholar and theorist and other modes of African thinkers who were neither scholars nor theorists, but nevertheless worked as activists and wrote some polemical-political texts during the anticolonial, nationalist and pan-African eras in African history.

Beyond his known achievements within the field of African studies where he served as a powerful critic and broke substantially new epistemological, methodological and theoretical grounds (Isaacman 2003), he also vigorously articulated strong anti-imperialist ethics of self-determination and other liberatory aspirations of the African people, especially as influenced by the responses to the challenges of the anti-colonial, nationalist and pan-African pasts. He contributed greatly to transnational knowledge production. His aim was to contribute towards modifying the strategies and trajectories of development on the continent. Given the deterritorialised forms assumed by most of the struggles in which he was involved, Ake contributed towards actualising democratic struggles on the continent. Through his published texts – most of which are multidisciplinary and constitute a form of social action – vibrant connections have been established which have had remarkably transformative impact across numerous global audiences and transnational spaces beyond Africa. He spoke truth to power and challenged colonial and postcolonial narratives that contest the multidimensional experiences of disadvantaged peoples of the world. At home, he was politically committed and socially relevant in national political struggles aimed at actualising the national and Niger Delta questions in Nigeria. For us, it was precisely through his involvements in these struggles – in institution-building, knowledge production, research networking, transnational advocacies, and at home, in the Niger Delta Environmental Survey (NDES) among other organs of the state in Nigeria – that Claude Ake acquired his organicity as a socially relevant public intellectual in Africa and beyond. His life and works have greatly inspired many generations of African scholars after him. These are major ways in which one understands Ake as an organic intellectual – at least in the limited understanding of this researcher – following the Gramscian, Marxian and Rodney's tradition of functionally representing his constituencies and also in speaking the truth to power. In his mode are Albert O. Hirschman, Edward W. Said and Samir Amin.

Biographical factors and early influences

Claude Ake's lifetime – from birth in his native home, Omoku, on 18 February 1939 until his death in an air crash on 7 November 1996 – spanned the periods of European colonial domination and political independence in Africa. His native home, Omoku, is located in the present day Ogba-Egbema Ndoni Local Government Area of Rivers State. He attended the Kings College in Lagos, where he passed the Cambridge School Certificate Examination with distinction and earned a scholarship to study Economics at the University of Ibadan. Ibadan. Nigeria, which was then known as the University College at Ibadan, an affiliate institution of the University of London (CASS 1997, 3). He graduated in 1962 with a First Class Honours in Economics and then proceeded to Columbia University in the City of New York, which awarded him a Doctorate (PhD) Degree in Political Science in 1966, with specialisation in development studies, political economy and political theory (Ake, Curriculum Vitae 1996, 1). An array of contrasting claims however surrounds the account of Ake's educational background, especially at his First Degree level. Among such claims, Sam E. Oyovbaire (1997, 48) maintains that:

> Ake's education was not, as the press has impressed upon the public, from King's College Lagos to Columbia University, or from London University to Columbia University, Carleton University, University of Dar es Salaam and University of Nairobi. I am not sure whether Ake was at London University as a student or professor. I know that he taught and did enormously valuable research at Carleton, Dar es Salaam and Nairobi, among many other centres of his scholarly sojourn. The more important fact of interest is that Ake attended the University of Ibadan for his undergraduate studies where he made an excellent and superior classification for the social sciences degree in political science. Somehow I feel, without imputing motives that the press has unwittingly ignored, omitted or played down the University of Ibadan in the making of Ake. I think I know the source of inadequacy of the press in this connection.

Yet, I think too that Ake would like to be identified with the University of Ibadan in his intellectual growth.

Although Oyovbaire tries to clarify the confusion of opinion surrounding Ake's educational background, especially at the first degree level, unfortunately, his contribution rather adds to the confusion. From all known biographical sources – oral and written accounts – none presents Ake as having studied Political Science at the first degree level, except Oyovbaire (1997), a claim that is not backed up by Ake's curriculum vitae. This is added to his inability to clarify the inadequacy of the press, which he noted regarding the accounts on Ake's institutional affiliation at the first degree level. Our intervention in this regard is that, following a detailed analysis of the facts about Ake's trajectory narrated in his curriculum vitae, and other insights gleaned from our oral interviews with some of Ake's contemporaries, Ake's career and scholarship are not as confusing as Oyovbaire and the press to which he alludes, have made them appear.

To be sure, Ake was actually educated at the University of Ibadan for his first degree, where he graduated in 1962. It was however known at that time, as the University College in Ibadan. This is mainly because the University of Ibadan was at that time an affiliate institution of the University of London in the United Kingdom (CASS 1997, 3). During this period, the degrees awarded by the University of Ibadan bore the institutional affiliation, logo and name of the University of London. It was not until after a few years, especially in 1965 that the University of Ibadan became an independent institution, awarding certificates, degrees and diplomas in its own capacity and right, with the full weight of the law. As such, given the affiliation of the University of Ibadan to the University of London as the main institution from which degrees offered in Ibadan were awarded, Ake's educational training at the first degree level actually spanned both institutions in a technical sense. Consequently, those who describe him as having attended either the University of Ibadan or the University of London for his first degree are admissibly correct in this qualified sense. However, in arguing that Ake studied Political Science at the first degree level in either of these institutions, Oyovbaire stands alone and is far from being correct. Rather, Ake studied Economics at the University of Ibadan and graduated with a First Class Honours Degree in 1962, and then proceeded to Columbia University in the United States of America where he studied Political Science, specialising in development studies, political economy and political theory, and graduated in 1966.

Our claims in reconstructing the contrasting claims on Ake's educational background are corroborated not only by the enriching insights gleaned from the discussions with some of his contemporaries, but also by his curriculum vitae and other documents made available to this researcher by the Centre for Advanced Social Science, a research centre founded by Ake himself. It however remains doubtful whether these sources were consulted by Oyovbaire and the press before advancing their positions on Ake's background. A careful reconstruction of such positions on Ake's educational background is however important, not only because it helps us set the records straight regarding his trajectory, but also because it helps us to advance our analyses and conclusions on the departed scholar from a well confirmed premise, free from controversies which might undermine the credibility of our conclusion. Having clarified this issue, we now narrate other aspects of Ake's background.

Ake had a rich and versatile teaching experience, beginning at Columbia University. New York, as an Assistant Professor, a position which he held from 1966–1968. In 1969, he relocated to Carleton University in Canada, where he stayed until 1977. While at Carleton University, Ake was a Visiting Professor of Political Science at the University of Nairobi in Kenya. This was from 1970–1972. From 1972–1974, he held a visiting professorial appointment at the University of Dar es Salaam in Tanzania. From 1975 to 1976, he was the Director of Research for the African Association of Political Science. From this point, Ake became involved in academic-intellectual struggles and advocated the need for endogeneity in knowledge production on Africa. In 1977, he left Carleton University and returned to the University of Port Harcourt, in Nigeria, where he established the Faculty of the Social Sciences, which he served as the pioneer Dean from 1977–1983. Within this period, that is, from 1977–1983, Ake served as an adviser to the Committee on the Maintenance, Protection and Use of Public Property of the Government of the Federal Republic of Nigeria. Also, from 1978–1979, he was the Chair to the Rivers State Housing Corporation, and in 1978, he was appointed by the United Nations Economic Commission for Africa (UNECA), as a consultant on Indigenisation. From 1983–1986, he was a member of the Board of Directors at the National Universities Commission in Nigeria (NUC) and a member of the Editorial Board of the Sage Series on Modernization and Development in Africa (Ake, Curriculum Vitae 1996).

By 1975, he became a member of the Editorial Board of the *African Studies Review* and a founding member of the *African Pugwash*. In 1979, Ake was a member of the UNESCO expert group on Social Science

Development in Africa, which met in October in Zaire. Later, between 1984 and 1986, he served as the Vice President of the Social Science Council of Nigeria, and in 1985, he became the Editor-in-Chief of the *African Journal of Political Economy*, now known as the *African Journal of Political Science*. In this capacity, Ake projected the journal as a platform for decolonising and endogenising the social sciences in Africa as a unified body of knowledge relevant for speaking to social realities on the continent. This, for him, is the alternative to the continent's dependence in the spheres of development and knowledge. His engagement with knowledge production is best understood as an epistemological project which spanned his entire lifetime. No wonder, even after his death, he had a seminal text posthumously published to his credit (see Ake 2000).

He was also a member of the Editorial Board of the *Nigerian Journal of Political Science*. He was an Associate Member of the Editorial Board of *Current Anthropology*, a world-class journal of the science of man, and a member of the Executive Committee, Association of Third World Economists, representing West Africa, in 1982. From 1981–1983, Ake served as the President of the Nigerian Political Science Association. Later in 1983, he was offered an appointment as a Visiting Fellow at the University of Oxford, and in 1984, he was appointed as a Visiting Fellow at the University of Cambridge in the United Kingdom. Between 1985 and 1988, he served as the President of the Council for the Development of Social Science Research in Africa, Dakar, Senegal, which was then an umbrella institution of the Social Science Organisation in Africa. Central to the Council's philosophy is the actualisation of an all-embracing African renaissance. To achieve this, it articulates the epistemological and other referential bases of Afrocentrism, and invokes the ontological connotations of Africanity. It strives to reclaim the humanity of Africans through decolonising knowledge and the very strategies of knowledge production on the continent. It harps on endogenous knowledge production as the most suitable framework for achieving such transformative aspirations. This is its option for transcending the epistemic heritages of Africa's problematic pasts. Knowledge production for this Council is therefore best understood as a recovery project. Through advocating a system of knowledge that derives the source codes for its epistemologies from the life forms and actual practices of its people, the Council projects the African voice as the most authentic expression of the African condition.

In 1988, he served as the Director of the International Development Research Centre in Canada, and in 1989, he was a consultant to the World Bank project on 'Sub-Saharan Africa: From Crisis to Sustainable

Growth', based in Washington, DC. In 1989, he was selected by the National Democratic Institute for International Affairs in the United States of America, as a member of the International team to oversee the Election in Chile (Ake, Curriculum Vitae 1996, 5). From 1985–1989, he was a member of the International Social Science Council in Paris, France. Between 1987 and 1992, he was a member of the Board of Directors of the Social Science Research Council, of the United States of America, one of two members who represented the rest of the world. From 1987–1993, he was a member of the International Institute for Labour Studies in Geneva, Switzerland. From 1990–1991, he was a Research Fellow at the Brookings Institution, in Washington, DC. In 1990, he was a consultant to the United Nations Development Programme.

From 1992–1993, he was a member of the Advisory Board of the UNHCR project on the 'State of the World's Refugees', based in Geneva, Switzerland. In 1992, he established the Centre for Advanced Social Science, a policy advocacy and research think-tank which is today described as his crowning glory. Also, in 1992, he was conferred the Nigerian National Merit Award and the Martin Luther Award for Community Service among others. From 1993–1994, Ake was a consultant to the United Nations Economic Commission for Africa on the Indigenization of African Economies. During the same period, that is, from 1993–1994, he was also a consultant to the African Development Bank (ADB), and gave a lead paper on the occasion of the annual seminar of the Bank in 1994. From 1993 until the period of his death in 1996, he was a member of the United Nations World Commission on Culture. From 1994, he was a member of the World Bank's Council of African Advisers and a member of the Executive Board of the African Capacity Building Foundation, a position which he held until his death. In 1996, he was a Visiting Professor at Yale University and was also a member of the Niger Delta Environmental Survey, from which he later resigned (Ake, Curriculum Vitae 1996).

As earlier noted, Ake's university education was within the North American analytic tradition at Columbia University in New York, which he joined as a postgraduate student in 1963 after graduating in 1962 from the University College in Ibadan, in Nigeria. He therefore began his career as a liberal scholar who was trained along the North American liberal heritage. Of his liberal intellectual background, Kelly Harris (2005, 74–5) remarks that, 'Ake was influenced by the dominant behavioural approach, which was dominant in political science throughout the 1950s and 1960s.

It was not until the late 1960s and early 1970s that the dependency theorists and post-behaviouralists began to offer significant challenges'.

During this period, two main features characterised Ake's career and scholarship. One, he came under the influences and works of core liberal Euro-American authorities (see Ake 1967a, 1967b). Examples of such authorities are many. These included Herbert A. Deane, L. Gray Cowan and Immanuel Wallerstein under whose tutelage his quest and research as a doctoral student began and was accomplished. Others included Gabriel Almond, David Apter, Douglas E. Ashford, Reinhard Bendix, Leonard Binder, Arnold Brecht, James Coleman, Robert Dahl, Ralf Dahrendorf, Karl Deutsch, Emile Durkheim, S. N. Eisenstadt, Amitai Etzioni, Sigmund Freud, Carl Friedrich, Ernst Haas, Richard Harris, Carlton J. Hayes, Frederick Hertz, Thomas Hodgkin, M. Hondmon, Samuel P. Huntington, P. Jacob, Morris Janowitz, Harold Lasswell, Hans Kohn, William Kornhauser, W. H. Lewis, Niccolo Machiavelli, Gaetano Mosca, Franz Neumann, Felix Oppenheim, Talcott Parsons, Lucian Pye, Carl Rosberg, George Simmel, Edward Shils, Herbert Spencer, Ferdinand Toennies, James Toscano, Sidney Verba, Max Weber, W. H. Wriggins and Aristide Zolberg.

Two, most of his works during this period, were also of very liberal ideological leaning. His research and scholarship took the form of theoretically exploring concepts and epistemes like (i) charismatic legitimation and political integration, (ii) modernisation and political instability, (iii) political instability and political integration in the new states, (iv) rights and utility as well as (v) the social contract theory and the problem of politicisation. For the most parts, Ake focused mainly on the theoretical treatment of the problem of political integration in Africa and other new states, as they were fondly called at that time. Examples of his works in this area are also many (Ake 1966, 1969, 1970). Thus, although he researched Africa, he did that mainly from a liberal perspective. His writings at this period reflected neither the Afrocentric engagement nor the neo-Marxist interventions in the debate on African studies, as we find in his later works.

Claude Ake's paradigm shift from liberalism to radical scholarship

Later, however, especially from the 1970s, Ake's posture as a liberal scholar was challenged by a number of developments which suggested an alternative paradigm to him. L. Adele Jinadu (2004) captured these developments within the context of an Afrocentric intellectual movement which emerged within the international social science community in the late 1960s and early 1970s. According to him, it was an intellectual movement which was defined by and which *raison d'être* was derived from its engagement with Africa's marginalisation in the world economy. It was also a form of intellectual-political struggle which interrogated the cumulative consequences of the historical developments within the world economy for African and world politics. This period was marked, largely by the world economic crisis, which was due mainly to the economic recession in the major capitalist countries, and for which an end was hardly in sight. In Europe and North America, the spectacle of the monetarist new right regimes of Kohl, Reagan, Thatcher and others were already growing. In Africa and other parts of the Third World, the rightward drifts of the imperialist countries had been accompanied by more pressures on the conservative, neo-colonial regimes and progressive states to adopt or favour more pro-capitalist strategies in combating underdevelopment. Accordingly, by the 1970s, about a decade after the attainment of formal independence by most African countries, the strangleholds of the international capitalist system on African initiatives had become more blatant, while political enforcements and influences had also become more overt. The Editorial of the *Journal of African Marxists* (1984, 2–3) observed with dismay the developments within Africa which characterised the emergence of this movement:

> From the early stages of the independence era it was argued by some radical nationalists and by socialists that the end of formal colonial rule was being turned against the African workers and peasants in that no comprehensive restructuring of the institutions and relations inherited from the colonial state was envisaged in the newly independent states. Indeed, it was felt that the spate of decolonisation settlements in many instances arose from a desire on the part of the imperialists to pre-empt popular struggles which would otherwise sweep away the pliable crop of nationalist leaders, thereby forcing onto the agenda more radical solutions on issues of internal development and relations with the major capitalist powers. The effect of this thwarting of true independence was 'neo-colonialism' – the outward trappings of independence, without the uprooting of the colonial state.

As Jinadu recounted, the intellectual roots of this movement lie in the radical reactions and tradition of the black African critique of colonialism and the international system, which date back to the 18th century, and which received powerful revolutionary reformulations and restatement in the writings of Frantz Fanon and Walter Rodney among others, in the penultimate decade of the decolonisation process. According to L. Adele Jinadu (2004, 1):

> More specifically, the movement crystallized itself within the conducive political environment, 'the dynamism that prevailed at the University of Dar es Salaam', to use Nabudere's expression, in the 1970s, with its magnetic attraction for a diverse array of leftist intellectual scholars from all over the world, at a time when the Cold War was raging and the liberation movements in Southern Africa were gaining increscent momentum.

Within this period, efforts were made to rethink the continued relevance of the neoclassical development approach, particularly the new role of the International Monetary Fund and the World Bank, which by virtue of being the collective voice of Western capital were able to dictate terms to Third World governments. Also questioned was the debate on neocolonialism, with the emphasis placed on the need to transcend its limitations, especially the dominant role which it assigned to external factors, almost exclusively. New approaches were therefore introduced which focused on the nature of African regimes, the crisis of neopatrimonialism, the character of the state in Africa and the ideologies that have informed its disastrous performances. African revolutionaries were thus encouraged to address their attention to the critical role of vanguard forces and the nature of state power in facilitating popular democracy (the Editorial of the *Journal of African Marxists* 1984, 3–6). Efforts were also made to provide platforms for critical debates, discussions and information with the aim of generating sound theoretical bases for political action by African revolutionary intellectuals and scholars.

The neo-Marxist debate at the University of Dar es Salaam

The most important factor or influence which significantly changed Ake's worldview and writings during this period was the great debate at the University of Dar es Salaam in Tanzania, in the 1970s, followed later, by his association with Terence Ranger, Walter Rodney and the writings of Frantz Fanon. During this period, the University of Dar es Salaam – just like most other postcolonial universities in Africa – coped with the problem of the contradictory nature of university education across the continent. The contradictions and discontinuities between the pre-colonial and colonial methods and patterns of education intensified, just as the emergent postcolonial components of formal education strove to retain their relevance to the changing needs of the society. Also within this period, the problematic interconnections between the inherited educational system and various aspects of the African society became pronounced, especially as the content, essence, language and structures of higher education on the continent became geared almost exclusively towards the production of high level manpower. Much limitation was therefore imposed on expatriate and progressive scholars in a society that verbally proclaimed its adoption of socialism while higher education remained determinately elitist as the core arena for producing government bureaucrats and the middle class in general. Various liberation movements struggled to establish themselves as popular ideological, military and political forces across the continent. Such liberation movements in Tanzania also sought for a philosophical framework with which to guide the decolonisation process. The debates on imperialism, socialism, social emancipation and underdevelopment attracted several progressive scholars who researched and taught in the university.

The University of Dar es Salaam grappled with several contending demands – the anti-colonial thrust of the freedom fighters; the bourgeoning demand for skilled manpower as well as the growing thirst for knowledge by the labouring masses. Scholars were also divided into those who wanted to consolidate and preserve university education as part of the historical process of civilising the African as well as those who insisted on questioning and re-examining its content, purpose and structure as a basis for reconstituting it – a division that remains permanent for as long as the funding for the university education continues to come from external sources. Also at that time, various research funding foundations in the United Kingdom and United States played a dominant role in curriculum development in the universities in Africa in a manner that directly gratified their desire to produce a compliant middle class. Following the decline of American as well as British foundations in the domestic affairs of these states, France, Germany, the Netherlands and other democratic states of Western Europe became active in financing agriculture, engineering and other faculties within the sciences across the continent. Consequently, while the requirement of skilled manpower met the need of the administration of the people, the needs of the main producers were not immediately met by the university. Remarkably also, while the educational needs of day-to-day reproduction across the continent were met through the transmission of agricultural knowledge and skills accumulated over centuries and conveyed through practical experience (Campbell 1991), the articulation and organisation of knowledge production within the postcolonial universities throughout the continent was based solely on a disciplinary mode borrowed and imagined from Western universities over the twentieth and twenty-first centuries (Mamdani 2011).

Although higher education generally plays a major role in the production and reproduction of knowledge as well as the social reproduction of all class divided societies, the centres of learning of pre-colonial Africa developed out of the need by the ruling classes in Africa to reproduce the ideology required for justifying their modes of economic exploitation and social divisions. Under colonialism, while the actual aim was to avoid the reproduction of what Lord Lugard had called 'the Indian disease' (Lugard 1911), namely, the development of an educated middle class that was likely to bear and spread the nationalist vision, the idea that Africans could not attain high educational standards was used as the pretext for not building universities in colonial Africa. As an alternative, the respective metropolitan powers provided the needs of the various colonial bureaucracies. Consequently, the first colonial universities across the continent – far apart from one another and few in number – Makerere in East Africa as well as Ibadan and Legon in West Africa, among others, were built during the death throes and dying days of colonialism, especially when the British saw the need to groom a crop of half-baked and poorly educated file-carrying pliable middle class. Until 1970, Makerere University in Kampala, Uganda, served the whole of Central and Eastern Africa as the University of East Africa. It also housed the East African Institute of Social Research where an abundance of intellectual energy was invested in studies of tribal change. Studies on nation building and plural democracy later came up against the fact that democratic traditions could not take root in a society where the history of extra-economic coercion and of force was central to the alienation of labour power. Not being able to transcend their suspicious and uncomfortable dispositions towards the educated African, other colonial powers – particularly the Belgians, the French and the Portuguese – resisted the pressures for higher education up to the era of decolonisation (Campbell 1991, 100). As Mamhood Mamdani (2011, 2) pointedly remarks:

> the development of higher education in Africa between the Sahara and the Limpopo was mainly a postcolonial development. To give but

one example, there was 1 university in Nigeria with 1,000 students at independence. Three decades later, in 1991, there were 41 universities with 131,000 students. Nigeria is not an exception. Everywhere, the development of universities was a key nationalist demand. At independence, every country needed to show its flag, national anthem, national currency and national university as proof that the country had indeed become independent.[18]

Following independence, while higher education has been articulated through a state-driven initiative and a market-driven vision respectively, social reproduction in the new state was confronted with the challenge of either continuing the colonial legacy of educating a select few to rule, or developing independent individuals and institutions and harnessing the knowledge and skills of the African masses as a basis for transcending the alienation and snobbery introduced and nurtured by the colonial system. The latter project required a society and state that accorded social transformation the pride of place. As widely acknowledged by most progressive opinions across the world, postcolonial Tanzania was remarkable for its attempt at charting a nationalist path to development beyond the classical neo-colonial path.[19] In doing this, the ideologies of *Ujamaa* and Education for Self-Reliance were the conscious efforts with which it struggled to break the shackles of the colonial educational system. A further energetic attempt to develop a system of universal primary education was the quantitative side of a broader project to decolonise education in Tanzania. Within this initiative, the University of Dar es Salaam, originally conceived of as just one of the postcolonial universities in Africa, became enmeshed in the debates concerning *Ujamaa* and socialist development following the promulgation in 1967 of the Arusha Declaration. It was first opened with a Faculty of Law in 1961. At that time, its first degrees were awarded through a special arrangement/ relationship with the University of London. Originally located at the centre of nationalist politics on the Lumumba Street. In 1964, the University was moved eight miles further. According to Horace Campbell (1991, 101):

> Similar to other universities in Africa at that time, the teaching staff was predominantly expatriate European and North American. After the overthrow of Kwame Nkrumah in 1966, Tanzania attracted an usually (sic) large number of expatriate scholars from other parts of Africa, from the Caribbean, and from Eastern Europe. Among the expatriates were those who considered themselves progressive and were supportive of the elementary initiatives of the Tanzanian society.

At that time, the university in Africa was cast in the image of a liberal institution. The very idea of scholarship and the university was widely seen as external to the larger society. The university then emphasised the sacredness of neutral scholarship, the separation of the ivory tower from the society in which it was located. It was not until 1966 when students, in reaction to the increasing demands being put on them to be committed to the society in which they lived and which paid for their studies, went on rampage. The occasion provided the opportunity for a lot of debate on the role of the scholar, the student and the university in a newly independent country which was not only underdeveloped, but also one of the poorest in the world at that time. During this period, the government of Tanzania produced – through its president, Julius M. Nyerere – a document on education titled, 'Education for Self-Reliance'. The accent was also put not just on the Tanzanian education system to produce 'high-level manpower fro development', but also on the commitment of those whom the education system produced (Swai 1981, 36–42).

This radical examination of the role of the university in Africa by these committed scholars contributed towards the formation of the Socialist Club in 1967, later transformed into the University Students' African Revolutionary Front (USARF), a large student movement which also produced *Cheche*, a journal devoted to the theoretical appraisal of the African reality and its stultification by imperialist domination. Questions of national liberation were hotly discussed, while the plight of Southern Africa was reviewed as well as the 'suspect politics' of visiting professors sponsored by the Ford, Rockefeller and other metropolitan foundations, exposed. Clashes with mainstream scholarship and pro-establishment agencies were rife. Later, both *Cheche* and USARF were banned, but the radicalism, once sparked, found its way into the TANU Youth League (TYL) branch on the Hill, and Maji Maji, its theoretical organ. The name '*Maji Maji*' was borrowed from the anti-imperialist war of 1905–07, during which most parts of Southern Tanzania rose up against German oppression and routed out its state apparatus (see Campbell 1991).

The Department of History at the University of Dar es Salaam played a commendable role in this regard. The University of Dar es Salaam's articulation of interventions and points of departure were also in tandem with other schools of thought developed across the continent during this period, especially in Dakar, Ibadan, Legon and Nairobi. Its niche area was central to the production of a post-nationalist historiography in Africa. This form of historiography sought to move beyond the bourgeois limitations of the Africanist historiography of the 1960s and pushed further towards the production of a form of historical knowledge which understands and presents the processes and production of Africa's history from the point of view of the peasants and workers' struggles. Postnationalist historiography in this sense does not refer to antinationalist historiography (Slater 1986, 249–60).

According to Yashpal Tandon (1982), in 1976, there opened a great debate at the University of Dar es Salaam which focused on class, the role of imperialism and the state in Africa. It took off on the heels of Issa Shivji's (1970, 1973) *Class Struggles in Tanzania*, and Dani W. Nabudere's (1982, 55–67) critique of the book. Other publications which also provoked the debate were Mahmood Mamdani's (1976) *Politics and Class Formation in Uganda*. The debate raised a number of important issues. It also suggested the need for absolute clarity, which was proposed by both the opponents and supporters of Shivji's book. It was later extended into other areas and brought forth contributions from scholars who were not initially involved (see Campbell 14–30). As Yashpal Tandon (1982, cover page) observes:

> In the Marxist-Leninist tradition the exchanges were sharp and uninhibited by bourgeois politeness or hypocritical applauses…. that debate, was not only important to Marxists in Tanzania but also to Marxists elsewhere in Africa and outside in their study of imperialism and the struggle against it.

The debate benefitted immensely from anti-imperialist struggles in India and Vietnam; the context of nationalism and the debate on development and underdevelopment in Latin America from 1945 onward. It also inspired the schools of thought in Dakar, Ibadan and Nairobi. Abdulrahman M. Babu describes the debate as a vigorous discussion of the most burning issues of the day – classes, finance capital, imperialism, monopoly capitalism and neocolonialism in the neo-colonies – issues which, according to Babu, had either been entirely ignored in Africa or had deliberately been subjected to oversimplified and therefore misleading investigations by opinion leaders, who themselves, had developed vested interests in the pro-imperialist status quo. As Babu (1982, 1) recounts:

> It is heartening that this excellent discussion by some of the finest brains in East Africa should have occurred at this moment when all of us need a clearer understanding of what is taking place under our very noses. Significant changes in our societies are occurring now and it needs a clear

analysis which subjects them to serious scrutiny in order to bring out into the open their underlying causes and tendencies (sic).

The debate brought together the works of Abdulrahman Babu (1982), Dani W. Nabudere (1977, 1982, 252–82), Yashpal Tandon (1982, 50–4, 154–71), Walter Rodney (1972) and other scholars. According to Babu (1982, 10):

> Finally, what is the purpose of these essays? They originate in response to the publication of three most important books to come out of East Africa. One of these is Issa Shivji's *Class Struggles in Tanzania*, one is Dan Nabudere's *The Political Economy of Imperialism* and third is *Politics and Class Formation in Uganda* by Mahmood Mamdani. These books have inspired a lot of thinking among East African intellectuals [unfortunately they could not reach the masses because they are written in English] and especially among those with Marxist inclinations

The purpose of these essays is obvious; Marxists do not engage in debates just for the fun of it as in school debates. Their principal task is to change the world. Their debates are about the correct understanding of the world around us. Once this world is understood then the task is to outline policies which will guide their struggle – to draw up the general line. This is arrived at by concrete analysis of the concrete situation in any given area. To do this they use the dialectical methodology, which is universally applicable, and they relate it to their concrete situation.

Of note in this enterprise was the role of Walter Rodney. Walter Rodney was one of the expatriate progressive scholars who worked in Tanzania during which period the radical intellectual tradition of the university was developed. He taught at the University of Dar es Salaam earlier in 1967 and later from 1969–74. In capturing Walter Rodney's contribution and impact towards Claude Ake's paradigm shift; the construction of a post-nationalist historiography; and the development of the neo-Marxist debate in Dar es Salaam, Tanzania, I draw mainly on my oral interview conducted in 2005 with Horace Campbell in Giza, Cairo, Egypt as well as Horace Campbell (1986 and 1991).

Rodney had completed his doctoral studies at the School of Oriental and African Studies at the University of London, at the age of twenty-four. His work on the Atlantic slave trade had already become a breakthrough in shedding new light on the impact of slavery on West Africa. Although he was briefly in Tanzania after his doctorate, he went to Jamaica to teach at the University of the West Indies, Mona campus. It was not long before the then Prime Minister of Jamaica, Hugh Shearer, described Walter Rodney as a thorn in his flesh (Swai 1981, 34). Shearer's uncomfortable disposition with Rodney's existence was informed by the vibrancy of the numerous lectures delivered by Walter Rodney to 'respected clubs'; the Rastafarians; various academic circles as well as other political and social groups in the country, eager to learn more about Africa, their ancestral home. Beyond its preoccupation with the past, history, especially as taught by Rodney, was for Shearer, a class affair. More so, Rodney's refusal to distort the teaching of history in line with the demands of the ruling bloc in Jamaica at that time, threatened the status quo greatly. In October 1968, Prime Minister Shearer expelled Rodney from Jamaica. On his return to Guyana in 1974, Burnham feared that what happened in Jamaica in the 1960s might occur in his own country. Consequently, notwithstanding his impressive curriculum vitae full of top-rated academic publications, Rodney was denied a teaching position at the University of Guyana. In 1980, following Zimbabwe's acquisition of formal independence, the country's first post-independence prime minister, Robert Mugabe, asked Rodney at the independence celebration in Salisbury, to remain in the country and establish an Institute of African Studies there. Rodney, however, declined the offer.

Although there were other offers from universities in the United Kingdom and the United States of America, he later returned to Tanzania in 1969 after being banned from 'Grounding with his brothers and sisters'.[20] His activities off the campus at Mona underlined his concern with the deprivation of oppressed classes as well as the oppression of subject populations across the world. From another account, it was not until his appointment at the University of Dar es Salaam that he worked for the first time, for any length of time to earn a living (Swai 1982, 38–52). Before that time, having been denied the right to work in Guyana, he was forced to grapple – more seriously than ever before – not only with the practical and theoretical issues of the revolution, but also with the biological issues of feeding himself and his family. At Dar es Salaam, Rodney contributed substantially not only to the articulation of radical historical practice, but also helped in building the Department of History into a world famous institution for the study of African history. As Bonaventure Swai (1982, 38–9) recounts, he contributed immensely to the forging of theoretical concepts and issues that continue to inspire very lively debates and serious discussions in the Department. Until 1982, the postgraduate programme established in the Department of History in 1973, followed the guidelines left behind by Rodney in 1974 when he returned to Guyana. The three

Historical Association of Tanzania Conferences convened in Morogoro in 1974, 1975, 1976 and the fourth held Dar es Salaam in 1977, followed very closely Rodney's recommendations set out regarding the actual shape which the study of African history should take. Also, the possibility of writing a socialist history of Tanzania to be titled, *Another history of Tanzania*, to replace an earlier book, *A history of Tanzania*, published under the auspices of the Department of History in 1969 was discussed. Rodney was an active contributor into this idea. Furthermore, he helped in establishing postgraduate studies and influenced the shaping of the curricula at all levels within the Department. The editors of the research bulletin (Tanzania Zamani 1974, 1) of the Department of History at the University of Dar es Salaam observed that:

> Partly as a result of some disillusionment with the difficulties of explaining the colonial experience in terms of African initiatives, partly as a result of the influence of socialist academics in this University, there has been some change in the preoccupations of the history department in the last few years. While religious history is still being investigated, processes of economic change and the growing impact of imperialist penetration have come to be regarded as more important in the 19th century and earlier, than state formation. On resistance, while the older view of resisters as troublesome and misguided conservatives is still stoutly opposed, the limited possibilities of resistance using weapons and tactics adopted is now stressed. On the economic and social impact of colonial rule, the processes of underdevelopment and class formation are being examined with a view to establishing the degrees of dependence (loss of initiative), differentiation, and selective impoverishment which resulted from the colonial economic system. On nationalism, it is now possible to look at the rise and triumph of nationalists as partly a result and not only as a cause of the process of decolonization, with the initiative taken away from the peasants and placed in the hands of the educated few.

Coming from the English-speaking Caribbean where the concept of African liberation had taken a deep root among the working people, Rodney returned to Dar es Salaam with the academic culture and intellectual traditions of the region. He also exhumed the confidence of a generation no longer dazzled by the vaunted Euro-American culture. He was a member of the generation of the New World Group – a small group of scholars that tried to transcend the contributions of Arthur Lewis, Eric Williams and others who tinkered with the ideas of cultural pluralism. His political development and education within the Dar es Salaam debates became the basis of several scholarly articles, essays and monographs.[21]

Beyond research and teaching, Walter Rodney participated in founding an analytic intellectual orientation known as the Dar es Salaam School. As Horace Campbell remarks, the books, debates, lectures, monographs and papers on class formation, decolonisation, delinking, disengagement, the emancipation of the oppressed, slavery, socialism and underdevelopment distinguished this university from several other African universities. In addition, there was a bold attempt to transcend the artificial divisions between the various disciplines within the humanities and the social sciences. The age-long mystifications of disciplinary boundaries and divisions into anthropology, archaeology, archival studies, demography, economics, geography, history, politics, psychology and sociology were exposed and transcended (Campbell 1991, 101–4). The preoccupation of the Dar es Salaam School with social transformation also greatly influenced Rodney's (1972) *How Europe Underdeveloped Africa*. At the centre of his concern were (i) the humanisation of the environment, (ii) the dignity of labour and (iii) the self emancipation of the toiling masses.

In his effort at transcending the contradictions of his professional training, he sought political involvement in the struggles of the working people as a basis for understanding the pre-conditions for the dignity of labour. One of his works in which he spoke to these issues, is his incomplete *History of the Guyanese Working People*, in which he emphasised the relationship between the humanisation of the environment and the self emancipation of the oppressed. The study was a theoretical breakthrough, which although was not produced in Dar es Salaam, was a logical outcome of his study of the technical conditions of the labour process in the plantation sector of colonial Tanganyika. Prior to the articulation of the philosophy of *Ujamaa* and the Arusha Declaration, Kenya, Tanzania and Uganda had attracted a large number of scholars who applied the modernisation paradigm towards researching and teaching economic, political and social change in Africa. The majority of these scholars operated from the standpoint that economic development was only possible with, and indeed started in Africa with colonialism. Rodney repudiated this position and demonstrated the inability of capitalism to develop either 'free labour' or even autonomous capitalist development in any colonial territory. While the Arusha Declaration of 1967 was a bold attempt at charting a new path for Tanzania, Rodney's works combined forces with those of other organic intellectuals on the continent, in confronting the modernisation school and other modes of analysis that had hitherto remained immune to alternative analysis.[22] According to Horace Campbell (1991:102–3):

His lasting contribution and that of Dar es Salaam School has been to demonstrate that capitalism led to historical (sic) arrest, backwardness and economic stagnation in Africa. But the awareness of blocked growth was not the same in the terms of the movement towards theoretical clarity for the path forward. To formulate the theoretical requirements of reconstruction remained the task of committed intellectuals. But this task was necessarily bound up with the freedom, skills, knowledge and intellectual culture of the broad masses in the process of becoming active agents in the making of their own history. For in relation to the fate of oppressed classes in a given country, Rodney believed that they must discover themselves in order to understand their historic mission in their own emancipation.

From another account, Rodney's contribution lies not just in having written many critical books on Africa, nor in having insisted on the necessity of intellectuals actively surveying – rather than superficially – the society in which they lived, but in having ensured that the dialectical unity between activism and radical scholarship is maintained. This, for many progressive intellectuals, was the most important contribution made by Rodney to the articulation of the African condition while in Dar es Salaam.[23] For Walter Rodney, there could be no such conception of history for its own sake. For him, history is best studied with the intent to advance and understand the living rather than the dead. Among the requirements in this endeavour, according to Walter Rodney, is the ability and capacity to be fair and impartial to both the past and the present. Herein, objectivity becomes an important aspect of historical writing.[24] History, in this regard, is not an antiquated exercise, and must never be ignored to become so. It offers among others, the account of our collective failure to achieve a decent society rather than a skewed record of past glories of conquest and empire building. While the past has entailed a dossier of creative achievements in humanistic pursuits and scientific discoveries, it has also not been free from the experiences of oppression, poverty and wars witnessed by a large spectrum of humanity. Consequently, while a study of such sordid experiences might not directly provide the blueprint by which to build a truly humane society, we cannot prepare for the future without accurately imagining and perceiving the material world we have made as well as the means used in making it. And to avoid being imprisoned by the past, we must understand these historical dynamics as a basis for transcending them. Rodney believed very strongly in this and also put it into practice. He saw the teaching of African history to be of paramount importance in liberating the oppressed both in Africa and the New World. By the time he was murdered in Georgetown, Guyana, on 13 June 1980, he had been involved not only in writing history but even more so in making it. As Bonaventure Swai (1982) recounted, it was one of Gregory Smith's bomb devices – handed to Rodney under the pretext of being a walkie-talkie intended to monitor the movement of the Guyanese forces of oppression harassing the opposition parties in the country – that terminated his life.[25] The origin of the device was traced to the National People's Congress in Guyana and the Central Intelligence Agency in the United States of America – both of which are united in maintaining the status quo in Latin America and the West Indies.[26] His elimination followed a series of harassment to which Rodney, his family and members of the Working People's Alliance had been subjected.[27]

At that time, coldblooded murder had largely become the most common weapon used by bankrupt regimes for silencing their opponents across Latin America, the West Indies and the Third World. The kind of politics propagated by Rodney and his Working People's Alliance had also become widespread throughout the Third World. According to Petras, Walter Rodney symbolised in several ways, a new generation of leaders in the Caribbean and Central America – intellectuals firmly committed to freedom, political and social democracy as well as radical egalitarianism (Petras 1980). The first generation of leaders in the Third World had told their oppressed populations to first seek the political kingdom and all its righteousness, with the promise that everything else would eventually be added unto it.[28] That millennium is yet to come. Curiously, the same generation of leaders continued to present themselves to the working masses as the new deliverers; the new Messiahs; the new prophets; even while failing to deliver the ends of popular expectation. To foreclose change and undermine resistance, they resorted to all forms of calumny, demagoguery and oppressive mechanisms of eliminating opposition. This group thus became understandably dangerous and opportunistic, claiming to be advancing 'indigenous socialism' while exploiting all kinds of tensions within their local societies as well as other high-sounding ideological slogans to which they are only marginally committed (Swai 1982, 33). The second generation of leaders, which Rodney represents, fought for equality, freedom and social justice across the global South (Rodney 1979, 33). It also demonstrated a sustained commitment towards accounting for the root causes of these tensions with a view to forging new alliances capable of further social solidarity among the ordinary people. Commenting on Walter Rodney's death, Petras (1980) underlines the dangers involved in articulating the material existence and interests of the toiling masses through revolutionary politics:

> Within the last year (1979) we have seen the assassination of Archbishop Oscar Arnulfo Romero of El Salvador and 15 professors from the University of San Carlos in Guatemala. Such people are faced with the choice of abandoning their homeland and the millions of their countrymen who are suffering oppression, or staying and risking death – perhaps at the hands of those who have the protection of the state. The list of unsolved murders of government opponents in South and Central America and in the Caribbean is long, and growing.[29]

On the impact of Ake's interactions with Walter Rodney on his scholarship, Okello Oculli remarks that Rodney had earlier written with commendable oral narration to what he calls the 'tumultuous intellectually battered, psychologically and emotionally hungry crowds in street corners in Jamaica, about the glorious histories of the Benin Empire, Songhai, Mali and the Oyo empires'. According to Oculli (1997, 29):

> Ake met his age mate, Walter Rodney, at a time when both brilliant men were groping for ways of seizing African post-colonial realities with their rare intellects. Rodney whose book would suggest his early contact with George Padmore's radical Work: How Britain Rules Africa (published in 1955), had made earlier contacts with revolutionary Marxist analysis of world history combining that with his research on the history of the slave trade on the West African coast, it was easy for Rodney to force Ake out of the liberal American social science rails. Ake's wrath after his moment of seeing the light is the burden of his work Social Science As Imperialism. The traditional scholar that he was, he felt the responsibility to expose, from within, the entrails of Western scholarship, its structures and imperialist political strategies (sic).

After having such an inconspicuous beginning, Ake later distanced himself from his earlier positions. Fanon's call to 'set afoot a new man' is most apropos for describing the nature of his radical departure, especially as seen in his subsequent writings in contrast to the earlier ones (Harris 2005, 76). From that period, Ake actually followed the works of Frantz Fanon, Fanonist scholars and others like Colin Leys and Samir Amin. He also advanced their contributions in many remarkable respects. Examples of his later works, written on the heels of this radical transformation are also many.[30]

According to Katabaro Miti (2006), the intellectual rendition at the University of Dar es Salaam in Tanzania contributed immensely to Ake's paradigm shift, especially from 1972–1976.[31] As Miti recalled, during this period Tanzania attracted several socialist scholars all over the world and the University system had a lot of academic freedom. He noted that there were always public seminars, which normally spanned between three to four weeks, and focused mostly on Tanzania's socialist experiment. To him, the debates and seminars suggested to most people the need to rethink socialism in East Africa and to reread the entire literature on Marxism. According to Miti, during this period, the Department of Political Science at the University of Dar es Salaam had the highest number of professors throughout the University – Claude Ake, Colin Leys, Dani W. Nabudere, Goran Hyden, Hamza Alavi, Issa Shivji, John Saul, Justin Rweyemamu, Mahmood Mamdani and Walter Rodney – were all in the University at that time. Not all these scholars were in the Department of Political Science in the University at that time, though. Dani W. Nabudere and Issa Shivji, for example, were in the Faculty of Law. Hamza Alavi was in Sociology though he was not a member of the University of Dar es Salaam academic staff. Justin Rweyemamu was in Economics. Walter Rodney was in History. Mahmood Mamdani was in the East African Economy and Society. Miti argued that Claude Ake was not the only scholar changed by the radical intellectual rendition.

Archie Mafeje (2006) argued that Ake's paradigm shift was influenced principally by the ideas of Black Nationalism.[32] He noted that from the period of his shift from the North American intellectual tradition, Ake was involved in intellectual – political struggles against imperialism and the military in Africa. Mafeje opined that Ake actually undertook another paradigm shift, namely, from radicalism to what he called mild liberalism, but also observed that the tragic circumstances of Ake's death did not allow us see how this was to be fully expressed. According to Mafeje, Ake's later texts are neither critical nor radical enough,[33] especially when compared with his earlier writings. Martin Doornbos (2006) entirely maintains the same position with Mafeje.[34] Mafeje cautioned that in critiquing Ake's second paradigm shift; we need to properly situate him within the context of the economic conditions and other pressures that underpinned his material and social existence. In doing this, Mafeje noted (2006); we will be able to appreciate the enormity of his contributions and the limitations of his organicity and praxis, as a public intellectual, especially towards the end of his life.

In explaining Ake's second paradigm shift, Adebayo O. Olukoshi, Bernard M. Magubane, Fantu Cheru, Mark Anikpo, Olujimi O. Adesina,

Samir Amin and Thandika Mkandawire pointed at the limitations characterising the global system of knowledge production.[35] As they illustrated, these realities define a constraining position for Third World scholars generally and African scholars in particular. The aspiration to secure academic positions in the West; the struggle to generate funding for their research; reproduce their material and social existence, and secure publication outlets for disseminating their research findings in various regions of the North, constrain their radical orientations greatly. Mkandawire submitted that the radical turning point in Ake's career and scholarship was actually the neo-Marxist debate at the University of Dar es Salaam in Tanzania in the 1970s. He recalled that Claude Ake, Emmanuel Hansen and other members of that group were the ones who later formed, not just the African Association of Political Science (AAPS) in Dar es Salaam, in 1973, but also the Council for the Development of Social Science Research in Africa (CODESRIA) in Dakar, in 1973, and other professional associations in the respective African countries.[36] Mkandawire reckoned that the Dar es Salaam School actually interrogated the critical question of how power is articulated and exercised in Africa as well as its implications for the manner in which society is constituted across the continent.[37]

Eme Ekekwe, a former colleague of the late professor at the Department of Political Science, University of Port Harcourt, Port Harcourt, Nigeria, argues that by Ake's tragic passage, Nigeria has lost its most brilliant social scientist ever. Ekekwe, who noted that he had known Ake since 1975 as one of Ake's graduate students at the Carleton University, Ottawa, Canada, commented that the fallen scholar stood for nothing but excellence in academics (Uwujaren 1996, 14–20). According to Eme Ekekwe (Uwujaren 1996, 19):

I knew Prof. Ake in 1975 when he taught me at Carleton. He was one of the most brilliant people I have ever met. In those days, many Canadians enrolled at the Political Science Department simply because of Ake.... Ake hated mediocrity and could be rigid on theories, most of which he often successfully proved. His book, which was originally written for his doctoral thesis, *A Theory of Political Integration*, was for many years the recommended text for political economy in many North American universities.

S. W. E. Ibodje, together with whom Ake founded the Department of Political Science and the Faculty of the Social Sciences at the University of Port Harcourt, Port Harcourt, Nigeria, also spoke glowingly about his departed senior colleague. As Ibodje (Uwujaren 1996, 15) recounts:

> Ake was hard to please in terms of academics because he demanded the best. To many he was difficult to get along with because his standards were very high, but mind you, he wouldn't expect you to do anything that he was not better at.

Mofia Akobo (Uwujaren 1996, 19), a medical practitioner based in Port Harcourt, who knew Ake for about three decades, also comments:

> He was a serious-minded, objective and committed person. He was also dispassionate about issues. He was highly independent minded. He drove other people the way he drove himself and I believe it is very difficult to find people who understood their subject matter as Ake did. The fact is: the world will miss him.

In the cover story in *The News* magazine (1996), the following remarks were made about Ake:

> He was internationally acclaimed as a scholar of repute. He belonged to the elite club of gifted Nigerian professors whose intellectual brilliance remains the only source of respect for the Nigerian academia. Ake was perhaps one of the deepest thinkers in the social sciences and a world class authority in political economy. His rich academic exploits in this area, earned quietly and almost unobtrusively invite superlatives even from the most cynical critics of his own brand of radical social science. He was an intellectual flower that bloomed with an ethereal sparkle. Not even the cult of mediocrity and anti-intellectualism so rife in the Nigerian academia could remove the shine from Ake. His genius shone so brightly that it was acknowledged at home by even the military, the target of most of his critical commentaries. In and outside the university, Ake has retained a puritanical devotion to his first love: teaching and research. At a time professors in Nigerian universities, clobbered by the general rot of their environment, had virtually stopped 'professing', Ake was still busy churning out one research paper after another at his non-governmental think-tank, the Centre for Advanced Social Science (CASS).

Nearly all his works are delivered with a brilliance and erudition that are uniquely Ake's. Though not a particularly charming personality, Ake was for his brilliance eminently popular amongst colleagues, students and the general public.

Claude Ake's death, 7 November 1996

On Thursday 7 November 1996, Claude Ake died in a plane crash in Nigeria. The airplane was flying to Lagos from Port Harcourt when it plunged into a lagoon outside of Lagos. There were no survivors. He was killed along with 131 other passengers and nine crew members in the Boeing 727 aeroplane, which crashed into a lagoon in a mangrove jungle 25 miles northeast of Lagos. The cause of this crash was described, especially by government sources in Nigeria, as unknown (see Adekanye 1996:563–4). Although the cause of Ake's tragic death remains uninvestigated and unknown, this chapter links it with the rot in Nigeria's aviation industry, and the negative features which characterised the state in Nigeria during the despotic years of military rule under the leadership of the late General Sani Abacha. Within that period, the political terrain in Nigeria was turned into a theatre of war, in which human life was unsafe, and was lost under circumstances linked with the state's complicity. These situations reflected the primacy of politics, which assumed its singularly negative turn in the desperate quest for state power and control, and the pursuit for power as an end in itself, by most African leaders.

The events which surrounded the circumstances of Ake's death were linked with his involvement and subsequent resignation from the Steering Committee of the Niger Delta Environmental Survey, which represented both the oil companies and the federal military government, under the late General Sani Abacha – a leadership widely known across the world for its lack of conscience, lack of respect for human rights, limited vision and tyrannical inclinations. As noted by the Yale Bulletin and Calendar (1996:1), before his death, Ake's final projects were focused on ethnicity and the roots of political violence in Africa and Nigeria. On 16 November 1995, following the executions of Kenule Saro-Wiwa and the other eight Ogoni by the state, Ake resigned his membership from the Steering Committee of the NDES. In a letter titled, 'Letter of Resignation', dated 15 November 1995, and addressed to Mr. Gamaliel Onosode, the Chairman of the Steering Committee of the NDES, Ake (1995(l)) reasoned out his position:

> In the light of the demise of Ken Saro-Wiwa and his colleagues, I have had to rethink NDES. For me agreeing to serve in the Steering Committee of NDES was a leap of faith. For if past experience is any guide, there is no reason to assume that the Petroleum industry in Nigeria is the least concerned about the plight of the oil producing countries including their susceptibility to environmental hazards and it was not reasonable to fear that NDES might be a cover-up (sic).

In the end I decided to serve and allow for the possibility that the Petroleum industry in Nigeria might have finally recognised the need to reconcile the profit motive with social responsibility. I have always felt that until this reconciliation is achieved, the oil producing communities will be increasingly alienated and hostile and all stakeholders will suffer in a rising tide of violent conflict. This is why I have been trying to initiate dialogue between them. The distinguished representative of the Oil companies in the NDES Steering Committee can testify to these efforts.

Continuing, Ake (1995(l)) observed that:

Unfortunately, the efforts did not succeed and conflict escalates with unfortunate consequences. It is clear now that NDES is too late and does not represent a change of heart. To begin with, it does not enjoy the enthusiastic support of the oil industry at large. Clearly there is nothing in the recent performance of the oil companies notably Shell, NAOC, Elf and Mobil to suggest that NDES is associated with increasing sensitivity to the plight of the oil producing communities. It is telling that as the tragedy unfolded in Ogoniland, Shell, whose perceived insensitivity engendered the conflict, in the first place did not intervene forcefully for conciliation. And when the disaster occurred, Shell expressed regrets but pointedly stated, according to the British press, that it was not considering any change in its current practices.

Considering the tragic enormity of recent happenings, and the crisis of conscience arising from them, NDES now seems to my mind diversionary and morally unacceptable. By all indications, what we need now is not an inventory of pollutants, but to look ourselves in the face, reach to our innermost sources and try to heal our badly damaged social and moral fabric.

Please be so kind as to accept my resignation.[38]

Following this, on 23 November 1995, he granted a public interview and issued a press statement explaining further the circumstances surrounding his acceptance to serve in the Steering Committee of the NDES. According to Ake (1995, 2):

It is with regret that I announce my resignation from the Steering Committee of the Niger Delta Environmental Survey (NDES), which took effect from November 16, 1995

I must confess that the decision to serve on that committee had been a difficult one to begin with, given the oil companies' past record of arrogance, insensitivity to the humanity of host communities and to environmental sustainability. But in the end I decided to serve, encouraged by Ken Saro-Wiwa, who argued that the NDES could be a window of opportunity for a constructive engagement.

Continuing, Ake (1995, 2) explains his role as a member of the Steering Committee of the Niger Delta Environmental Survey:

> As the designated 'representative' of the communities in the Committee, I tried to sensitise the Committee to community concerns and to develop a mechanism to facilitate communications between NDES in particular and the Oil Industry in general. This was reflected in the fact that at the stake holders' meeting in Port Harcourt on October 24, the Ijaw National Congress, Ogbakor Ikwerre, Ogba Solidarity, Ogbakor Etche, Movement for the Survival of Ogoni People, Oyigbo Forum, Bonny Indigenous Peoples Federation, Ndoni Community Association, Uzugbani Ekpeye and O'Elobo Eleme presented a common position paper on NDES and it was clear that the acknowledged success of the meeting was partly due to the fact that despite their doubts they too felt that something positive could come out of NDES.

He however regretted that these whole efforts did not achieve their intended expectations. Lamenting, Ake (1995, 2) noted that:

> Unfortunately, the realities intruded. It was clear that NDES did not have the enthusiastic support of the Oil industry. Apart from that, there was nothing in the posture and practices of the major oil companies, Shell, NAOC, Elf and Mobil, to signal the fact that NDES could be regarded as a forward movement. Rather as the agenda of NDES developed, it became difficult despite the good number of competent and well-meaning people on the Steering Committee, to expect much from NDES.
>
> I was already seriously considering resignation before the tragic turn of the Ogoni struggle culminating in the execution of Ken Saro-Wiwa and his colleagues. I do not think that the Oil industry in Nigeria, particularly Shell whose crude practices and insensitivity engendered the struggle in the first place, did enough to diffuse the situation.
>
> Their reaction to the tragedy was more unfortunate still. They have in effect been assuring everyone who cares to listen that nothing has changed and nothing will change. I cannot help thinking that even silence would have been better than such unfeeling belligerence. For, given the rising tide of resentment in the oil producing communities, this posture is bound to be catastrophic for Nigeria and self-defeating for the oil companies.

> These circumstances have left me no choice but to resign. For they
> have, to my mind, transformed NDES to an unwelcome division and
> rendered it morally unacceptable.

It was later noted by undisclosed sources that his decision to resign from
the Steering Committee of the NDES, particularly the press statement
which he issued, in which he publicised his resignation from the NDES,
endeared him to the anger and utter displeasure of the ruling military junta
in power in Nigeria at that time. From that period – until his death – it was
noted that he was placed under state surveillance.[39] There were insinuations
that his resignation and the press statement which he issued, not only
compounded the legitimacy crisis for the government, but also indicted
the federal military government greatly, through drawing the attention of
the international community to the huge moral crisis that characterised
the Sani Abacha administration. Hence the plot to assassinate or eliminate
him. The circumstances of Ake's death are not at the focus of this chapter.
These have been examined by scholars in other works.[40]

Conclusion

This chapter has offered a genealogical account of the biography and
theoretical orientations of the late Claude Ake. It presented him as
one of the most fertile and influential voices within the social sciences
community in Africa. As noted earlier, while the ideas of political leaders
in Africa provide a popular entrée to African politics, the exploration of
their contributions and profiles still remains a largely underdeveloped
genre (Clapham 1970, 1). This is especially the case with intellectuals and
scholar-activists on the continent. Yet, by challenging existing hierarchies
and oppressive institutions as well as truth regimes and the structures of
power that produce and support them, engaged scholars occupy a uniquely
critical position in the society. The world therefore has a lot to learn from
their contributions and failings as progressive social forces. Ake's profile
and works have been examined as a basis for filling this crevasse. As a
public intellectual, Ake had a long history of political activism which
preceded his career as a scholar and continued throughout his life. That
experience enriched his scholarship in speaking to an audience much
larger than the academy and also in transforming the terms of engagement
with knowledge production in Africa (Isaacman 2003, 14–20). In his
mode are Basil Davidson, Francis Deng, Joseph Harris, Susan Geiger and
Walter Rodney.

The chapter highlighted the nature of politics and social relations in colonial and postcolonial Africa. It underlined the developments and experiences in Europe which necessitated the capitalist expansion and penetration of the global South by the major imperial powers. It also discussed the character and mode of organisation of the colonial economies including the contradictions and contraptions which characterised the colonial society and state. In doing this, it situated the development and emergence of decolonisation struggles and nationalist aspirations within the context of the contradictions and crises of the colonial economies and state. Furthermore, attention was paid to the emergence and role of popular forces and the various social movements in the struggles for an independent Africa. The chapter therefore examined issues at the intersection of Africa's economic, political and social histories. These helped in capturing the political and socio-economic structures of the continent.

The central argument, which has been emphasised so far, is meant to demonstrate the fact that, while the nationalist past provides the background for understanding anti-colonial nationalism and decolonisation in Africa, the antecedents of intellectual and political struggles in colonial and postcolonial Africa, together with the African experiences of struggles in the pre-colonial era shaped Ake's scholarship and writings. These experiences, together with the intellectual renditions which accompanied the struggles for independence and local ownership of the social sciences in Africa, constitute the intellectual roots and sources of Ake's radical inspiration, paradigms shift and revolutionary inclinations. The study therefore showed Ake as a scholar who although was influenced by the realities of the colonial situation, was not limited to it.

By situating Ake's biography and theoretical orientations within the experiences and realities in Africa, the study presented his scholarship and works as products of such experiences rather than abstracting him from the complex social history within which he lived and worked. In this sense, the story of his biography is best narrated in a manner that centres among others on how he as an individual not only comes into existence but also makes sense of his existence and concretises that existence. The methodological implication of our approach is that Ake's life and writings, together with his consciousness and experiences must be evaluated through an interrogative analysis of the historical interplay of such interactions between the various productive forces and class relations which make up the entire social structure in Africa. This helps us appreciate not just how his ideas are constituted and represented, but also his contributions towards resolving the epistemological and other challenges confronted in the enterprise of knowledge production on the continent.

Notes

1. See also Trevor A. Campbell (1981, 49).

2. This was done by establishing his role in professional associations like the Nigerian Political Science Association (NPSA), the African Association of Political Science (AAPS), the International Political Science Association (IPSA), the Council for the Development of Social Science Research in Africa (CODESRIA) and research institutions like the Centre for Advanced Social Science (CASS), the National Universities Commission (NUC), the United Nations Economic Commission for Africa (UNECA), the Sage Series on Modernisation and Development in Africa, the Brookings Institution, and the United Nations University-World Institute for Development Economics Research (UNU-WIDER).

3. On the limitations of oral sources in narrating biographical accounts and history writing, see Sarah Nuttall and Carli Coetzee (1998), Luise White et al. (2001), Ciral Shahid Rassool (2004, 12–45 and 51–96), Leslie Wit and Ciral S. Rassool (2008).

4. By this word, reference is made to alertness, especially vis-à-vis Ake's disposition and engagement with the topical issues of his time.

5. Antonio Gramsci was one of the most widely respected Marxist philosophers of the twentieth century and by every means, one of the world's greatest cultural critics. Popularly known as 'the theoretician of the superstructure', Gramsci declined from following the dogmatic Marxian interpretation of the primacy of 'the material basis' of society over 'the superstructure'. He argued that ideas, intellectual production and language were not merely ancillary or incidental consequences of the factors of production, but had far reaching causal effects on their own in shaping society. Just like Tommaso Campanella (1568–1638), Gramsci and other Italian intellectuals who contributed to Western thought spent their lives and wrote their best works while in exile or prison. Tommaso Campanella wrote the first Italian "Utopia", *La citta del sole*, during his twenty-seven years of incarceration, while Gramsci wrote in prison the most important draft on the educational and political function of the intellectual –2,848 pages of handwritten notes – known as 'the prison notebooks' (*quaderni del carcere*). In these notes, Gramsci offers an analysis of Italian intellectuals, a guide

to an understanding of Italian intellectual history and a prophesy on the historical destiny of his message, particularly in relation to the critical question of how such message is perceived across the world. For further illustrations on Gramsci's biography and theoretical orientations, see Perry Anderson (1976).

6.   While this characteristically sexist language is typically Gramscian, his illustrations of the intellectual, however include men and women.

7.   He explains this by averring that, although everyone at some time fries a couple of eggs or sews up a tear in a jacket; we do not necessarily say that everyone is a cook or a tailor in that regard, or even on that basis.

8.   Gramsci used the concept of 'social group' as a subtle referent for speaking to 'social classes'. Having written his famous notes while in Benito Mussolini's prison, although the word 'group' is not necessarily an effective euphemism for 'class', however, to avoid using the word 'class' in a manner that its direct Marxist overtones would be immediately apparent, he carefully used 'groups' and strategically used the phrase 'fundamental social groups' to avoid ambiguities while referring to anyone of the major social classes–bourgeoisie or proletariat–in Italy. His writing was subject to close scrutiny by the prison guards. This made him create an elaborate new vocabulary. However, most of his new concepts are not entirely new. They are rather new words substituted for already existing and widely known concepts. Far from being entirely new, 'hegemony', for example, is in many respects, a recasting of the traditional Marxist concept of 'ideology'. There is considerable debate in Marxist discourse concerning the merit of these changes. Some authorities have argued that they are not simply new words but genuinely new concepts, while others take the view that the changes are had at the price of a loss of a sense of intellectual heritage. His deviation from doctrinaire Marxism won him a wide readership in *Cultural Studies* and *The New Left* throughout the United Kingdom. For an account of Gramsci's compelling theorisation of the role played by culture in politics and other lived essentialisms, see Ian Buchanan (2010, 208–10).

9.   For further illustrations on Gramsci's concepts of 'civil society' and 'political society', see Gramsci, *Selections from Prison Notebooks*, 3–33.

10.   According to Ian Buchanan (2010, 208–10), the banking crisis or credit crunch of 2007–09 illustrates clearly what Gramsci's analysis of the operations of hegemony looks like in practice. Taxpayers' money was

used by governments in the United Kingdom and the United States of America to prop up failing banks with the pretext that we would all be worse off if they were allowed to fail. This rationale was effective because, as Gramsci argued, the ruling class' control of the cultural means of production is carefully deployed as a legitimising veneer for this capitalist end.

11. In addition, he advocated 'popular education', namely, education for everyone at every stage of their lives. This, he says, holds much potential for exposing as well as reconciling the source of the reactionary nature of the oppressed and a promise of change.

12. There exists a body of notebooks by Marx on the Asiatic mode of production, in which he dealt with the colonial question in India and other non-European societies. There has, so far, been very little discussion on these notes.

13. For a review of the literature on this subject, see Partha Chatterjee (1986, 34). See especially footnotes 35 and 36 on that page.

14. For a list of Vladimir I. Lenin's works on this subject, see Partha Chatterjee (1986:34). See especially footnote 36 on that page.

15. I use the italicised expression, following Chinwe Chinweizu (1986), for referring to Africa and other non-Western societies.

16. For a seminal statement on the role of Third World scholars in advancing cultural decolonisation, see Ngugi wa Thiong'o (1985).

17. See Abubakar Momoh (1999, 55).

18. See Mahmood Mamdani (2011, 2). For further accounts on the historical context of higher education in Nigeria, see Adewunmi Fajana (1978) and Babatunde A. Fafunwa (1974).

19. Tanzania mainland was known as Tanganyika before 1964 when it joined with the island of Zanzibar to form the United Republic of Tanzania.

20. For an account of the reaction of the Jamaican government to Walter Rodney in Jamaica, see Ralph Gonsalves (1978). See also Walter Rodney (1969).

21. See for example, Bonaventure Swai (1981, 31–43, 1982, 38–52), Edward Alpers and Pierre-Michelle Fontaine (1982) and Horace Campbell (1983).

22. See Horace Campbell (1986, 103–5).

23. Following this radical rendition, Issa G. Shivji published *The silent class struggle* (1970) and *Class struggles in Tanzania* (1973); while Walter Rodney wrote *How Europe underdeveloped Africa* (1972).

24. See Walter Rodney (1972, 7–12).

25. See *Latin American Weekly Report* (1980) and *Punch* (1980).

26. See *The Guardian* (1980).

27. A statement from the Working People's Alliance in Guyana on the death of Walter Rodney (1980).

28. Kwame Nkrumah.

29. See Petras (1980).

30. See Claude Ake (1978, 1979).

31. An oral interview conducted with Katabaro Miti during the Social Sciences Conference in Johannesburg, South Africa, in September 2006. Katabaro Miti was at that time a Professor of Political Science at the University of Pretoria, Pretoria, South Africa.

32. An oral interview conducted with Archie Mafeje during the Social Sciences Conference in Johannesburg, South Africa, in September 2006.

33. For an example of such works, see Ake (1996).

34. An oral interview conducted with Martin Doornbos in March 2008 at the International Institute of Social Studies, The Hague, the Netherlands. This author was at that time a Visiting Fellow at the African Studies Centre, Leiden, the Netherlands. Martin Doornbos, an emeritus Professor of Political Science at the Institute of Social Studies, The Hague, is a right-wing intellectual. Also interviewed were Hairat Balogun and Joy Ogwu–both right-wing female intellectuals and past Chairs of the Board of the Centre for Advanced Social Science–were interviewed between August and September 2004. At that time, this author was a Visiting Fellow at the Centre.

35. These were interviewed during the Social Sciences Conference in Johannesburg, South Africa, in September 2006. Fantu Cheru and Samir Amin were interviewed by this author between September and

November 2008 at the Nordic Africa Institute, Uppsala, Sweden. The author was at that time a Guest Researcher at the Institute.

36. These included the Egyptian Political Science Association and the Nigerian Political Science Association.

37. The list of interviewees has been limited to those whose views are directly linked with the issues discussed here.

38. See Claude Ake (1995, 1).

39. Oral interviews conducted in August–September 2004 with Grace Okoye and Mariam Agiobu, joint secretaries to the late Claude Ake at the Centre for Advanced Social Science in Port Harcourt, Nigeria. At that time the author was a Visiting Fellow at the Centre.

40. For further notes on these, see 'Bayo Adekanye (1996).

41. Chapter four of this book is entirely devoted to an examination of this and other related questions.

African studies and the bias of Eurocentricism

Historical knowledge is always an interpretation of 'traces' of the past, used as evidence relative to the question being investigated. The quality of the historical interpretation and its communication depends on three factors: the amount of evidence considered compared to all existing evidence; the rigor with which the rules of logical historical critique are applied; and the reader's understanding of the logical and 'psychological' probability of the proposed interpretation – whether the proposed reconstruction appears 'reasonable' – and in the final analysis this last factor is evaluated by one's general vision of the world.

— Vansina, 1986, 28

Animating Africa within the field of African studies is presently deeply problematic. This is mainly because the power undergirding the construction of Africa within the field is welded within the epistemic modes of Western intellectual thought. Consequently, unless Africanism is decolonised from that epistemological mode, African studies remains a colonised field of enquiry. Its utilitarian value for the continent also remains ineffectual. Actualising the decolonisation of knowledge in this regard is no doubt an epistemological project. It is also a matter of intellectual and political struggles. This is mainly because the actual histories of the various disciplinary practices around which knowledge production takes place – on Africa – have a profoundly colonial genealogy. The task of working Africa's destiny out of that heritage is therefore a compelling task for African studies as well as postcolonial studies. How did Africa become the object of historical and scientific enquiries? Through what forms of rationality and historical conditions did the African subject become the object of a possible knowledge system? At what price and by whom is this objectification? Through what knowledge systems is subjectivity produced in relation to Africa and with what effect? How can African historical knowledge further African development? How might African studies serve as an instrument of liberation and progress rather than domination? These questions are central to our attention in this chapter.

This chapter examines the historical conditions prevailing in the production of African studies. Its inspiration was drawn from Partha Chatterjee's (1986, 10–11) critique of anthropology and its bias in its references to non-metropolitan cultures. It reflects on the political considerations underlining the production of knowledge on Africa as well as the social contexts of its consumption. In a major sense, it examines the archaeology of knowledge production on the continent.

Its methodological approach is profoundly Foucauldian. For Michel Foucault, as the investigation of that which renders necessary a certain form of thought, archaeology implies the excavation of unconsciously organised sediments of thought. And much unlike 'a history of ideas', it does not assume that knowledge accumulates towards any particular historical conclusion. It ignores individual histories – this largely explains why he was reluctant to write his own biography or have someone do it for him, although many have done so since his death – and prefers instead, to excavate impersonal structures of knowledge and establish their connections with the operations of power. As a task, it does not consist of treating discourses as signs referring to any real content such as madness. Rather, it treats discourses, such as medicine, as 'practices' that form the objects of which we speak. Closely linked with Foucault's archaeology of knowledge, are his notions of discourse, episteme and genealogy. He describes a discourse as signifying 'a practice' and understands an episteme as the underground grid or network of ideas that allows thought to congeal, constitute and organise itself in relation to a specified historical phase or subject matter. Each historical period therefore has its own episteme, which limits the totality of experience, knowledge and truth, and governs each science within a specific period. With genealogy, he underlines his attempt to reveal discourse at the moment that it appears in history as a system of constraint. While his notion of genealogy allows for historical change, it is neither bothered with describing neutral archaeological structures of knowledge nor is it preoccupied with finding a truth to history. It is rather interested in history as 'will to power'.

Genealogy compels Foucault to examine ethical, literary and other bodies of knowledge in relation to how such 'knowledges' might relate, for example, to the discourse on heredity or sexuality. This way, he tries to study the effects of such discourses – medicine, psychiatry and sociology – claiming to be scientific, on such practices as the penal system, as they first appear. He urges us to dispense with the habit of looking for an author's authority, and show instead, how the power of discourse constrains the author, his utterances and the text. Hence the Foucauldian term of transdiscursiveness, by which reference is made to how, for example, Friedrich Nietzsche (1844–1900), Sigmund Freud (1856–1939) or Karl Marx (1818–83) is not just simply an author of a book, but more seriously the author of a discipline, theory or tradition. To underline the regulative function of context,[1] and his point that subjectivity is not entirely considerable in philosophical isolation, he refers to the 'classical era' of the seventeenth and eighteenth centuries in Europe to show that madness is an object of perception within a 'social space' structured in different ways throughout history. In other words, just like other human experiences, madness is an object of perception historically produced under varying cultural contexts and social practices rather than simply an object of sensibility or thought which could be so freely analysed.

Two positions in Foucault's thought are central to our purpose here. One, for Foucault, history is not a predictable mechanism, but a problematic site of often random struggles articulated in a cruel world of master-slave relationships. Philosophy, according to him, is therefore, not a view of history which can achieve completion, but an endless task carried out against the backdrop of an infinite horizon. He does not understand subjectivity in philosophical isolation, but considers it as linked, intrinsically, with – and even produced by knowledge and power through – dividing various practices, where for example, psychiatry defines and divides the insane. Georg W. F. Hegel (1770–1831) had described reality as a continuous historical process. Drawing on his understanding of Hegel's philosophy of history – elaborated by Jean Hypolite (1907–68) – Foucault described reason as the sovereign of the world and submits that this way, the history of the world presents us with a rational process.

The second is the argument that the individual is the product of power. Here, he says power relations have an immediate hold upon the body – forcing, investing, marking, torturing and training it to carry out tasks; to emit signs; and perform ceremonies. The more organised and technically thought-out knowledge becomes, the closer we get to the political technology of the body. Interpellating power with knowledge, he says, no power is exercised without the extraction, appropriation, distribution and retention of knowledge, especially using the ideological apparatus of the state. In doing this, therefore – through combining literary skills with painstaking historical enquiry – Foucault became the curious instigator of a method of historical inquiry which has had profound effects on the study of discourse, history, knowledge, madness, power, subjectivity and the penal system among others. Hence the term Foucauldian.[2]

Closely linked to the Foucauldian insight deployed here, is Mahmood Mamdani's (2011) admonishment on the need to (i) identify and question the assumptions driving the very process of knowledge production on our subject matter and (ii) think critically through the ensuing as well as underlying questions rather than rushing into any solution. To follow Mamdani's intervention in this sense would be to ask: What are the grounding concepts that enable one think about 'the self' in relation to 'the other' – within the humanities and the social sciences – and their relationships with the constellation of power? What are the foundational concepts of the humanities and the social sciences in Africa and how are they related to the exercise of power across the global South? What does it mean to think about the state in Africa given that the very foundational grounding concepts and the modern ideas of power – together with the modular forms around which prevailing theoretical understandings of civil society, democracy, justice, liberty, nationalism, the nation, the nation-state and the state – across the continent are based on the imaginations drawn from the West? Applied to Claude Ake's works, it is also important to ask: How does Ake aid our understanding of the complex relations of power in the very conception of knowledge production on Africa? To what extent does his corpus help us question the colonial foundations of the dominant knowledge systems and their links with the constellations of power vis-à-vis the operations of the state in Africa? How relevant are those texts for recreating the imagination of the African subject using a knowledge-driven liberatory project? What prospects do they offer us, for rethinking Africa's future beyond the early colonial desire and vision of westernising the continent?[3]

These are deeply contentious questions in which considerations of the type of researcher most suitable for undertaking research on the continent, becomes crucial to history writing. According to Johann Gottlieb Fichte (1762–1814), what sort of philosophy one chooses depends entirely on what sort of person the individual is (Landau et al. 2011, 176). As Jan

Vansina (1986, 28) has argued, the vision of Africa projected across various quarters is crucial for judging the reasonableness of the historical evidence deployed and the accompanying interpretation. This point should be noted at least because the dominant perceptions of the African past are largely conditioned by Western epistemological categories. Similarly, the prevailing ideas, around which development and governance are framed on the continent, have a certain intellectual and material force driving and underlining them; and when these are not properly challenged, become very fierce representations of power in rather counterproductive manner. The disposition by European thought for Eurocentricism and its accompanying epistemological violence should not be surprising. As Arthur Schopenhauer (1788–1860) has submitted, most times, man takes the limits of his own field of vision for the limits of the world (Landau 2011, 186). As the debates on Africa have their ways of becoming compelling, research funding within the field is increasingly justified by underlining the contribution it can make towards solving looming development problems. While this is no doubt related to the general understanding that scientific research must contribute towards improving human existence, the expectation entails several epistemological and practical considerations which are not only at the centre of African studies, but also speak to the power-driven ordering of the field. Viewed from such a standpoint, the dominance of African studies within the epistemic mode of Western intellectual thought, is mainly a manifestation of a serious problem, namely, that of the underlying power relations in producing knowledge on the continent, established as a post-Enlightenment legacy of European intellectual history, strategically placed as the epistemic and moral foundation for a supposedly universal framework of thought which perpetuates, in a real sense, a colonial domination.

The production of historical knowledge on Africa is a markedly political question (Slater 1986, 249–50). This is due mainly to the duality in the nature of knowledge itself. While knowledge of the past furthers our understanding of the present and continues to condition our imagination of the future, social science knowledge is not just a product of contemporary social reality – and in some cases a reflection of it – but also contributes to the molding of that same reality. In this sense, it represents a political intervention that contributes to the forces determining the movement of a particular present toward a particular future. The integration of Western epistemology into its discursive production conditions African historiography within the western knowledge system greatly. As a result, animating Africa within African studies is deeply problematic.

This is mainly because the power undergirding the construction of Africa within African studies is wielded within the epistemic mode of Western intellectual thought. While the content and course of the field are conditioned by the continent's political history (MacGaffey 1986, 47), the major approaches used within it are deeply rooted in Euro-American epistemology. This is due, among other reasons, to the failure of the neo-Marxist epistemological break, which never really materialised.[4] Consequently, unless Africanism is decolonised from that epistemic mode, African studies remains a colonised field of enquiry. Its utilitarian value for the continent also remains ineffectual. This is the main argument of this chapter. Drawing on Jean-François Lyotard (1924–98)'s *différend*, it argues epistemologically, that the performance and production of African studies is based on antagonistic claims as well as conflictual premises by Africans and Africanists. To illustrate, African scholars and their Africanist counterparts share neither the same responsibilities nor the same existential constraints in knowledge production on the continent (Jewsiewicki 1986, 9–17).

How is it that the African subject becomes the object of both historical and scientific enquiry? Through what forms of rationality and historical conditions did the African subject become the object of a possible knowledge system? At what price and by whom is this objectification? Can we possibly return to – or at least map the genealogies and lineages of, through painstaking historical inquiry – the actual 'zero point' in the course of African history when the continent was suddenly separated from modern understandings of development, progress and reason? In other words, how is it that Africans have historically become the object and subject of economic, legal, philosophical, political, scientific and social discourses and practices? What does it mean to say that Africa begins to function as a site of a possible discursive formation and practice? To follow Foucault in this instance is to ask, what forms of reason; and which historical conditions led to this? Through what knowledge system is subjectivity produced in relation to Africa? Through which knowledge system is subjectivity produced in relation to the African subject and with what effect?[5] How can African historical knowledge further African development? And how might African studies serve as an instrument of liberation – as a lever of progress?

In one of his philosophical works, Jean-François Lyotard (1924–98) uses the term 'différend'[6] for speaking to a form of dispute utterly irresoluble through consensus as the parties involved speak radically contradictory and heterogeneous languages (Macey 2000, 235–7). He describes the postmodernist outlook as one characterised by an attitude of incredulity towards metanarratives. By this, he refers to openly expressed disbeliefs in the grand narrative or ideology underlying modernity and the Enlightenment project. According to Lyotard (1983), modernity tends to suppress 'différends', an expression with which he refers to irresoluble disputes in which neither side can accept the claims or terms of reference of the other (Stuart and Van Loon 2009:96). His illustrations of this term are many. These include, first nation inhabitants disputing the property claim of their territory's colonisers without surrendering their own claims in the process. The black Americans, the native South Africans and the Australian aborigines are examples of such groups. Two, when France declared Algeria a part of its entity, it created a 'différend' between that claim and the Algerian aspiration for independence that could neither be judged nor met within the existing system of justice.

From another perspective, 'différend' arises when a conflict takes place in such a manner that the offended or wronged party is unable to find the means of representing itself. Lyotard uses the extreme relativist position adopted by the Holocaust-denier Robert Faurisson in which, according to him, the only person who can testify to the existence of gas chambers is the individual who actually died in one. Most importantly, a 'différend' cannot be possibly resolved. At best, a partial resolution can be achieved or negotiated (Buchanan 2010, 300–2). That experience resulted inevitably in the Algerian war of independence. Lyotard contends that, unless identified 'différends' are democratically recognised, resolved and respected, humanity drifts into an authoritarian and brutish society in which other less powerful and subaltern voices are silenced by dominant or supremacist forces. He illustrates this position with the experience of most first nation inhabitants in the new world who find themselves dispossessed, ignored and marginalised by their colonisers.

Jean-François Lyotard's 'différend' is certainly different from Jacques Derrida's 'différance', a word he made up in French for describing the process by which meaning 'slips' in the act of transmission. For Derrida, structuralism is both authoritarian in manner and is also based on questionable philosophical premises. He argues that the standard conception of meaning in the West depends on an assumption of 'a metaphysics of presence', which suggests that the full meaning of a word is held to be present to the speaker or writer in their mind, as they use it. Structuralism thus demands that meaning be present in artefacts and should only wait to be recovered by the art of analysis. Derrida's theory of meaning, however, pictures it as a rather transitory and a far less stable phenomenon. According to Derrida, words always contain within themselves traces of other meanings beyond their assumed or even primary meanings. He considers it much better to transcend logocentrism and speak of a field of meanings – one that, critical enough can never be bounded since it is underlined by a surplus of meanings at any point in time – rather than a precise one-to-one correspondence between word and meaning. With this amorphousness, Derrida dismantles the idea of forming totalities.

'Différance' is a central component of Derrida's deconstruction. On its part, deconstruction – a philosophy which very self-consciously sets out to deflate philosophical pretentions about our ability to order the world – is arguably the most influential branch of poststructuralism and without any doubt, one of its strongest sceptics, especially as practised by Derrida, its leading exponent. His work has been widely described as a major attack on the principal structuralist progenitors, particularly Ferdinand de Saussure and Claude Levi-Strauss. With deconstruction, Derrida proposes a movement, shift or transition from system-building to system-dismantling. His major concern is to direct our attention to the several, often inadvertent, gaps in our systems of discourse and thought, which we can hardly successfully disguise, however well we try to.[7]

As this chapter illustrates, given the opposing claims around which knowledge production on the continent takes place, the articulation of African studies constitutes a 'différend'. This is the main argument pursued in this chapter. It is acknowledged that African studies exists as a legitimate field of academic enquiry and pursuit, just like Asian and European studies, among other global spheres of area studies generally. It is also conceded that the contributions directed towards understanding the continent transcend continental boundaries as well as disciplinary and nationality lines. Nevertheless, in addition to its lack of commitment, and barring a few exceptions, the pursuance of African studies by non-Africans distorts and misrepresents, rather than furthering the understanding of social reality on the continent. I am not generalising this assertion, but the dominant Africanist approach on Africa is guilty of the misrepresentation and negative image-making of the continent. While a few exceptions exist to my position in this regard, it is to the dominant Africanist approach on the continent that I refer. It is the bias of Eurocentric historical theories in their application to non-metropolitan cultures that has led to the search for alternative intellectual perspectives everywhere in the world through the development of counter-hegemonic knowledges and narratives from the South, a practice which counters the portrayal of postcolonial histories as a history of lack or as a history that falls short of true history.[8] According to Peter C. W. Gutkind and Immanuel Wallerstein (1976):

> The historiography of modern Africa has been a battleground of so-called Eurocentric versus so-called Afrocentric interpretations and we have passed from early crude versions of each to a state of sophisticated and subtle arguments about analytical primacy. This intellectual battle of course reflects a wider social battle. At a certain point in time, both Europe and Africa – large zones of each – came to be incorporated into a single social system, a capitalist world-economy, whose fundamental dynamics largely controlled the actors located in both sectors of one united arena. It is in the reciprocal linkages of the various regions of the capitalist world-economy that we find the underlying determinants of social actions at a more local level.

From its inception, the performance of African studies has taken place within the context of an epistemic mode that proclaims the universality of the Western outlook.[9] Some Western theorists on Africa have claimed that there is nothing like African philosophy. Not only is the right to knowledge production on Africa arrogated by Europe and more broadly the West, but also the very idea of discourse production through the monopoly of discourse formation as a historically produced and performed practice. Hence the questions: 'Who is actually qualified to speak on Africa? Who is elected to speak for the continent?' 'By whom is this election?' In other words: 'Who has the most authentic voice on the continent?' 'How is the continent to be best constituted, constructed and represented?' The answers provided to these questions, together with the ideological battles around which research is conducted on the continent – explain the rupture between African scholars and their foreign counterparts – especially given the arrogant deployment of the discursive power in recent years by the Africanist communities.

Modern historical method developed in Europe within a context wherein the historian was a part of the society described (Vansina 1986, 28) with written African history emerging primarily outside the continent. As Michel Foucault has demonstrated, knowledge and power are mutually complicit. This reality should not be surprising. After all, the dominant global systems of social control historically developed simultaneously with the human sciences since the 17th century Enlightenment. History and philosophy themselves have been accomplices in this complex power play of dominating others by marginalising them. While institutionalised knowledge is the instrument of power that pathologises the criminal, the mad and the sexually abnormal or erotic, official histories filter, prioritise and select what constitutes acceptable knowledge and consciously exclude other interpretations and meanings. This way, the dominant histories of philosophy only serve to legitimise those models of progress entirely consistent with the hegemonic interests and the ideological positions of the world's dominant classes. European thought thus appropriates outside material – in representing Africa – and justifies this practice by its reference to the universal validity of scientific thought. Consequently, the prevailing perceptions of the continent together with our understandings of its pasts are conditioned by the epistemological categories developed and established in the eighteenth and nineteenth centuries largely by various colonial administrators, missionaries and travellers. As knowledge production is strongly linked with the operations of power, one can hardly expect a capitalist society to produce – on its own – an epistemological outlook underwritten by a socialist worldview on knowledge. Europe thus monopolises the categories of knowledge production on the continent; while the power relations within the field continue to produce asymmetries contiguous with the dynamics of North–South hierarchies underpinning the interactions between Africa and the West.

It is these asymmetries and hierarchies of power – understood here as a 'différend' – that this chapter seeks to question. Drawing on Africa's specific experience, it is developed as a critique of post-Enlightenment traditions of European historiography in their references to non-metropolitan cultures. The aim is to question and ultimately transcend historically dominant imperial-centred analyses of African history. To achieve this task, it draws on the field of African studies as a basis for rethinking such questions as the relation of knowledge to power and their implications for imagining development and for understanding 'the self' on the continent.[10]

Following the introduction, this chapter is divided into four sections. The first considers the Enlightenment as a universal project throughout the heritage of world civilisations, especially given its achievements and benefits for humanity throughout the world. It discusses the major post-Enlightenment intellectual agenda or project for the world, namely (i) the universalisation of Western intellectual thought and tradition, (ii) its inflation with power, (iii) the development and universalisation of a system of knowledge anchored on and driven by the epistemic mode of Western intellectual thought, and (vi) the relegation and subjugation of all other non-Western agencies and knowledge systems. The second discusses the academic discipline of anthropology as a confirmation of the operations of Eurocentricism across various disciplinary practices. The third examines the field of African studies as another illustration of Eurocentricism, while the fourth provides the conclusion. On the whole, the argument that is advanced is meant to emphasise the need to articulate and construct anti-imperialist historiography within the field of African studies as a material precondition for autonomous development, from the perspective of knowledge production on the continent.

The Enlightenment as a universal project

As a grand narrative, the Enlightenment was a universal project in all spheres of human activity. Our description of the Enlightenment as a grand narrative follows Jean-François Lyotard's deployment of the term as a discursive referent for speaking to such ideas or notions adjudged as relevant enough for legitimating certain social actions or practices. An example of this is revolution, since the French Revolution has served to legitimate large scale programmes of social change. The Enlightenment has, in this sense, served to legitimate a movement towards secular reason.

No single intellectual force during the past three centuries has so transformed the world like Western science and the technology that has flowed from its understanding of nature. Between approximately 1700 and 1850, extraordinary changes occurred in Western civilisation. With Europe becoming a great exporter of ideas and technologies, these developments immensely transformed human experience across Europe, the Americas and the rest of the world. While the sixteenth and seventeenth centuries witnessed a remarkable change in the scientific view of the world, the impact of science could make itself felt first in Europe and later in other worlds only as the conviction spread that change and reform were both desirable and possible. Coming into force mainly after 1700, the attitude, capacity and eagerness to embrace change – particularly change inspired and justified on scientific grounds – represents a major intellectual heritage of that age. Notwithstanding the widespread interest – throughout the world – in non-traditional methods of healing, the impact of Western science on every area of human existence remains dominant and phenomenal. Of all the movements of modern European thought, the most influential have been the scientific revolution and the Enlightenment. The scientific revolution was the process that established the new view of the universe. From being considered the centre of the universe, the Earth was now seen as just another planet orbiting around the sun. The sun itself became one among several millions of stars – a transformation that led to a vast rethinking of moral ideas and religious matters especially in relation to scientific theory. The scientific method also became so impressive and influential that it set a new standard for evaluating knowledge – first in the West and later – throughout the world.

Symbolising an intellectual current, the Enlightenment was the name given to the era of critical and intellectual ferment that flowed across Europe, North America and beyond in the late 17th century and continued through the century that followed. Its leading exponents – a diverse range of thinkers, the philosopes, in France – combined confidence in the human mind inspired by the Scientific Revolution with faith in the power of rational criticism to challenge the intellectual authority of revealed knowledge and tradition. While the major Enlightenment philosophers shared no coherent intellectual programme, they believed that humanity could comprehend the operations of 'physical nature' and mould it to the ends of material and moral improvement. Drawing on the Scientific Revolution of the 16th and 17th centuries as their inspiration, these thinkers advanced the rationality of 'the physical universe' as the standard against which the customs and traditions of society could be criticised and measured – a criticism that penetrated every corner of contemporary society. Resulting also from that experience, the spirit of improvement and innovation came to characterise Western society – an outlook that later became one of the most important European cultural exports to the rest of the world. At that time, the church wielded its influence over society through static priestly castes that sought to monopolise knowledge and thought. It insisted on orthodox explanations and actively discouraged the articulation and spreading of independent thinking as well as unconventional ideas, insisting that, today's beliefs must always be consistent with yesterday's.

Asserting the primacy of reason, Nicolaus Copernicus (1473–1543), a Polish astronomer; Tycho Brahe (1546–1601), a Danish astronomer; Galileo Galilei (1564–1642), an Italian scientist; Johannes Kepler (1571–1630), a German astronomer and others demonstrated the falsity of the church's teaching that the Earth was at the centre of the universe. Isaac Newton (1642–1727) had – through inferences made from observations – come up with a complete explanation of motion; from that of a cannon ball through the air to a planet orbiting the Sun. These advances in experimental science in the later part of the 17th century – with their compelling explanatory and predictive power – led to the triumph of empiricism over Cartesianism, the system of the French philosopher René Descartes (1596–1650). Descartes had held that all knowledge acquired through the senses was unreliable, and all that is knowable must be deducible from the basic and irrefutable premise, 'I think therefore I am'. The major principles of empiricism, most of which contradicted those of Cartesianism, were enunciated by John Locke (1632–1704), an English philosopher, in his (1690) 'Essay concerning human understanding' – in which he argued that humans generally have no innate ideas, but derive all knowledge from experience, drawing on 'reflection' and 'sensation', the summation of which he understands as constituting 'reason', especially 'as contradistinguished to faith'.

Its roots lay in the Renaissance; English intellectual and political culture as well as the heritages of the scientific revolution. As a cultural movement of the Renaissance, humanism laid the foundations for the Enlightenment through its emphasis on the dignity and reason of man. During this period, Michel de Montaigne and other humanists wrote essays in which they questioned the prevailing ideas of their time, especially in relation to the exercise of power and the operations of religion. In 1688, the English king James II was overthrown and replaced by William III. This and other political reforms inspired François-Marie Arouet (better known as Voltaire, 1694–1778) and other French philosophers in advocating religious tolerance – preferring the English legal system and its constitutional monarchy as alternatives to French absolutism. Also, in 1734, Voltaire published his *Lettres philosophiques*. It was immediately banned. Although there is no consensus concerning when exactly the Enlightenment began, it is however, not thought to have began before the publication of René Descartes' (1637) *Discourse on the method of rightly conducting one's reason and of seeking truth in the sciences* (*Discours de la methode pour bien conduire sa raison, et chercher la vérité dans les sciences*) – in which the famous slogan, 'I think, therefore I am' (*je pense, donc je suis*) was deployed for emphasising the centrality of reason. While a direct line of intellectual descent exists from those movements to the science and social criticism of the present day (Buchanan 2010, 151; Crofton 2011, 104–7), the spirit of the Enlightenment persists wherever modern science and technology are pursued and their effects felt.

One notable attribute of human history is the acceleration in the pace of change. While modern humans are agreed to have appeared first about 100,000 years ago, from about 7000 BCE, when they migrated from Africa to other parts of the world – during which they adapted to new climes and lived by fishing, hunting and gathering – right into the twentieth century when invention, research and scientific discovery became institutionalised in corporate, government and university laboratories (Craig et al. 2008, 6), several achievements have been made in terms of human understanding of the physical universe. While the foremost advance in technology during this longest span of human existence was the discovery of rough stone tools, and later, the transition to smooth stone weapons, from about 7000 BCE, innovations began. Humans learned to till the soil; domesticate animals and make pots for food storage. A few millennia later, bronze was discovered and the river valley civilisations formed along the Nile, the Tigris-Euphrates, the Indus and the Yellow River. Cities developed. Writing was invented. Societies divided into castes, classes and ethnics, specialising into farming, governmental, military, priestly and trading roles. They also expanded and became increasingly populous, powerful and richer. The last millennium BCE, witnessed two remarkable developments. One was the emergence of the philosophical and religious revolutions that would indelibly mark their respective civilisations, namely, monotheistic Judaism from which would later develop the world religions of Christianity and Islam in the Middle East, Buddhism and Hinduism in southern Asia as well as the philosophies of China and Greece. This took place during 600–300 BCE. The second was the rise of the iron-age empires – the Roman, the Mauryan along the Ganges, and the Han in China – during the centuries that straddled the end of the century. Following the fall of these early empires, swift changes took place. For about a millennium, Europe and Byzantium fell behind, while China and the Middle East led in technology and the arts of government. But by 1500 Europe had caught up, and after 1700, it led the world. Although India had invented Arabic numerals, while Arab thinkers inspired the Renaissance, it was Europe that produced Nicolaus Copernicus (1473–1543) and Isaac Newton (1642–1727). The nineteenth century marked the invention of the locomotive, the steam engine, the steam ship, the telegraph, the telephone and the automobile. After that came electric lights, the radio, and in the century that followed, the airplane. In the twentieth century, invention and scientific discovery became institutionalised in corporate, government and university laboratories. Much larger amounts of resources were committed to research at the institutional site of the university. By the beginning of the twenty-first century, man had walked on the moon; deciphered the humane genome, and unlocked the power of the atom.[11]

With the Enlightenment, humanity has thus reached the highest point in the history and revolution in thinking. At least, so we are made to understand by the West. Its leading exponents included John Locke (1632–1704), an English philosopher who popularised the idea of 'the social contract' between a government and the governed and championed empiricism – the belief that knowledge is ultimately derived through the senses; Charles Louis de Secondat, Baron de Montesquieu (1689–1755), a French philosopher who showed how various systems of government as well as the operations of the law varied from society to society – thus informing the concept of cultural relativism;[12] Voltaire (1694–1778), the French philosopher who popularised the ideas of John Locke and Isaac Newton – championing modern notions of liberty and toleration;[13] David Hume (1711–1776), a Scottish philosopher who – continuing in the empiricist tradition – rejected the existence of innate ideas, examined the psychological basis of human nature and applied an extreme scepticism to everything from supposed miracles to the very idea of cause and effect, which he described as an appellation of 'constant conjunction' rather than being premised on the existence of a system of 'a logical inevitability'; Denis Diderot (1713–1784), a French philosopher widely known as a strong opponent of Christianity and a sustained proponent of materialism (see Parrott 2011, 255–61); Jean-Jacques Rousseau (1712–1778), a French philosopher who – as a champion of the primacy of individual feeling and radical opponent of rationalism – held the view that human nature is innately good but was defiled and spoiled by the corruption inherent in human society;[14] Adam Smith (1723–1790), a Scottish philosopher who espoused the idea of free trade as against monopoly and regulation;[15] and Cesare Beccaria (1738–1794), an Italian legal theorist who advocated the abolition of capital punishment and torture, and inspired many countries to reform their penal codes.[16] Most Enlightenment thinkers looked up to three English philosophers – Francis Bacon (1561–1626),[17] John Locke (1632–1704) [18] and Isaac Newton (1643–1727)[19] – for inspiration as their patron saints and torch bearers, aided by an explosion in printing and the widespread use of the French language, these thinkers appropriated the advances in science as a basis for changing the way people thought about government and society, thus replacing injustice, superstitions and tyranny with modern understandings of legal equality, reason and tolerance (Hart-Davis 2007, 270–1).

Between 1751 and 1772, Denis Diderot and Jean d'Alement published the *Encyclopédie, ou dictionnaire raisonne des sciences, des arts et des métiers*. This was the most important repository of, and the most influential tool with which Enlightenment thought and values were spread throughout the world. It was a 28-volume document that boasted an impressive array of authorities, including Charles S. B. Montesquieu, Voltaire, Jacques Turgot and Jean-Jacques Rousseau. As a magnum opus, its 11 volumes of engravings and 17 volumes of text contained 72,000 articles and more than 2,500 plates. As one of the defining works of the Enlightenment, 'the

Encyclopédie' assembled, catalogued and disseminated the depth of human knowledge – in philosophy, politics, religion and science – in accessible and clear prose with the aim of educating public opinion by 'changing accepted habits of thought' based mainly on revealed knowledge. Given its anti-Catholic and anti-religion stance, and more so, with its emphasis on reason, 'the Encyclopédie' was banned twice, especially in Spain, where the Catholic Inquisition objected to its content. Its survival thus relied only on the support of the state censor. A rather effective – though surprising – way through which its ideas were spread was through the deployment of satire. Charles S. B. Montesquieu championed this trend with his (1721) 'Lettres persanes', in which he depicted European and French customs through the eyes of Persian visitors, thereby poking fun at the Church, Court and French society. Voltaire perfected and took this further in his (1759) 'Candide', in which he rendered the account of a naïve young man's adventures, by exposing the hypocrisies of the attitudes and institutions that he encountered.

From 1750, a 'republic of letters' was formed in Paris in partnership with literary salons and 'the Encyclopédie'. A major target of attack by most Enlightenment thinkers, during this period, was the Church. While some saw it as one of the repugnant obstacles to reform, arguing that politics and religion must be separated as a basis for states to be progressive, others rationalised the need for religion in order to uphold the social order – thus an irreconcilable conflict emerged. Spread by satirical novels and prints, anticlerical sentiments were fuelled by unending anger at the abuse of power as well as corruption by the Church. In the process, freemasons lodges sprung up across Europe as secular spaces for disciples of the 'Cult of Reason' to congregate and exchange ideas. The second target was royal absolutism. In France, the king and his ministers often stood in dispute with 'the parlements' – French law courts dominated by the aristocracy. Montesquieu successfully transformed the political debate by proposing – in his (1748) 'Spirit of the laws' – a limited monarchy based on a three-way division of powers between the executive (the king), the judiciary and the legislature (the parliament). At this period, most thinkers believed that a rational and scientific approach could be applied to any subject matter. Adam Smith's analysis of capitalism in his (1776) *Wealth of nations*, invented the new science of economics. Benedictus (or Baruch) Spinoza (1632–1677) in his (1670) *Theological-political treatise* and (1677) *Ethics*, described liberty as the essence of government; while Immanuel Kant's (1781) *Critique of pure reason*, presented a more scientific approach for understanding knowledge and philosophy.

From the 18th century to the present, Enlightenment thinkers have provided a pattern for intellectuals who wish to make their societies rational, scientific, secular and therefore 'modern'. And, through Europe's dominance of the world – made possible through colonisation, economic productivity, the deployment of military power and state building – the Enlightenment model has become dominant throughout the world. Societies and state systems worldwide are now adjudged modern or otherwise, mainly to the extent that their economies are industrialised and market-oriented, and their societies scientific and secular. Harping insistently on 'reason' as the underlining basis of a productive economic life as well as 'the weapon' for reform, Enlightenment thinkers deployed reason against Christianity and the influence of the church in European politics and societies. However, while this holds sway in the West, the disposition to extend this practice to other religions in the world – outside the West – has informed the perception that religion and science are inherently conflictual. It has also underlined the tendency to consider less scientifically advanced societies as intrinsically culturally backward. The apogee of all these has been the development of a Eurocentric outlook articulated through the modernisation paradigm, which popularises the Western cultural experience as the universal model to which humanity throughout the world must approximate and conform.[20]

The heritage of the Enlightenment has therefore been complex. This is especially the case in the area of political thought. One strand of Enlightenment political thought that often drew upon the English political experience contributed to constitutionalism and modes of government in which the authority and power of the central government stand sharply circumscribed. For example, Montesquieu influenced the Constitution of the United States of America greatly as well as other numerous constitutions which that document later influenced. Another strand, found in Voltaire, contributed immensely to the growth of enlightened absolutism and other monarchical governments, seen as capable of formulating and imposing rational solutions to political and social problems as a basis for overcoming various competing interests. Reflection on the new form of the state that was emerging produced the great age of political theory, which includes the work of the major thinkers from Niccolo Machiavelli to Georg F. W. Hegel (Gamble 1981, 14). From Rousseau, another strand of Enlightenment political thought, leading to the socialist concern with the inequality of wealth and a desire for radical democratic government, was also developed (Craig et al. 2008, 676–705). On the whole, the Enlightenment helped to establish and foreground the values of modern liberal democracies. In doing this, the consent of the people was established as the sole basis of a government's authority (Rousseau 1762). It also provoked both radical change and a growing criticism of its ideas. Increased demand for political participation and representation paved the way for the American and French revolutions. Their founding fathers incorporated many of Montesquieu's political ideas, including the separation of power, into the Constitution of the United States of America. Egalitarianism, equality, freedom, justice, liberty and other modern political ideas that continue to animate political discourse in Western liberal democracies and political thought throughout the world, trace their roots to the Enlightenment.

By the second half of the 18th century, Enlightenment ideas had become so widespread that few failed to share confidence in the 'Cult of Reason'. However, the 19th century Romantic Movement emphasised emotion, imagination and a love of nature over industrial progress and reason. Following the devastations and horrors of the Second World War, the United Nations was founded in 1949 to resolve international relations, again, drawing on the Enlightenment idea of the equality of all humans as well as universal citizenship. The self-interest of modern nation states, particularly the major world powers, has however, often come first, and sometimes undermining the essence of the United Nations as a global organisation.

Curiously, the seventeenth and eighteenth centuries, whose ideas facilitated the Enlightenment also witnessed the rise of European colonial empires and the establishment of overseas plantation economies based on slavery. Thus, while much of what has been best about the Western cultural legacy to the global culture derives largely from the Enlightenment; and while some of the most admirable principles of Western culture – such as the global advocacy of democracy and human rights – can be traced to the Enlightenment, Europeans' treatment of non-Europeans; their warfare against each other in this era, together with their continuing humiliation of non-metropolitan societies during the colonial and postcolonial periods, have all belied the very principles of the Enlightenment. The Enlightenment has thus given birth to a post-Enlightenment order full of ambiguities, contradictions and contraptions for different regions of the world.

The post-Enlightenment period has therefore been bleak for non-European societies generally and the postcolonial world in particular. The foundations of these unequal conditions date back to the centuries-long advances experienced by Europe and North America – made possible by their leading role in colonisation; economic growth and industrialisation; the development of military might and state building – on the one hand as well as past and continuing imbalances and setbacks – brought about chiefly by the contradictions and contraptions of colonial and global capitalism – that cripple the aspirations by Africa, Asia and the rest of the world for commercial and economic development; advancement in their intellectual and material cultures, democracy and political stability and industrial expansion. Consistent with the post-Enlightenment agenda, there has therefore, been a universalisation of the achievements, heritages and legacies of the Enlightenment period. This has been possible through the universalisation of Western intellectual thought and its accompanying tradition; their inflation with power; the relegation as well as the subjugation of all other non-Western knowledges through the projection of the Western outlook as the most authentic worldview for imagining and reconciling the self to the modern.

The historical achievements and developments recorded by African and other civilisations have been dismissed by the overarching developments of the Enlightenment period. There now exists an unprecedented domination of the world's economy, intellectual life, military and political histories by the legacies of a small segment of the world's population.[21] As Albert M. Craig et al (2008, 846–7) have observed, whether by adaptation, outright imitation, rejection or syncretism, humanity throughout the world has had to contend with the power – economically, intellectually, militarily and technologically – of the West:

> The vitality of so many of the cultures and traditions that bore the brunt of the Western onslaught has been striking. Arab, Iranian, Indian, African and other encounters with Western material and intellectual domination produced different and often very creative responses and initiatives. These have borne full fruit in political, economic, and intellectual independence only since 1945, although most began much earlier. For example, modern Islamic reform and resurgence began in the eighteenth century, although it has only recently become a major global factor. Indian national, as opposed to regional, consciousness developed from the late 18th century onward in response to British imperial and colonial domination, even though it led to national union and independence only after the World War II. Ironically, exposure of the indigenous elite to European political and social philosophies gave future leaders of colonial independence drives vital intellectual ammunition with which to develop ideologies of self-rule. Creative thinkers like Mohandas K. Gandhi (1869–1948) merged these European philosophies with ideas drawn from their own cultures

to create distinctive new ideologies that could inspire sympathizers from the West as well as their own indigenous followers to oppose European imperialism and oppression of all kinds. African nationalist leaders such as Julius Nyerere (1922–1999) and Jomo Kenyatta (1889–1978) similarly found creative ways to merge European nationalist models with indigenous cultural ones.

Certainly one result of the imperial-colonial experience almost everywhere has been to sharpen the cultural self-consciousness and self-confidence of those peoples most negatively affected by Western dominance. The imperial-colonial experiences of the Third World nations may well prove to have been not only ones of misery and reversal, but also of transition to positive development and resurgence, despite the problems that plague many of these nations.

In the area of intellectual thought, the post-Enlightenment agenda has brought with it, the relegation of non-European agencies and the subjugation of all other non-Western knowledges – an attempt which continues to receive one of the fiercest counterattacks from postcolonial scholars throughout the world. Two examples are in order, to foreground our contention in this regard. These concern the presentation of 'extroversion' as the 'nomothetic' and the deliberate but unkind erasure of what is uniquely African from the collective global memory.

One, as Olujimi O. Adesina (2006) has observed, Anthony Giddens defines sociology as 'a generalising discipline that concerns itself above all with modernity; with the character and dynamics of modern industrialised societies.' This is added to the attempt by most texts in the field to trace the emergence of the discipline to Auguste Comte, the nineteenth century French philosopher and identify Emile Durkheim, Karl Marx and Max Weber as its founding fathers. Such approaches deny uniquely African contributions, a position not only in sociology but also in other social sciences disciplines. For example, Ibn Khaldun (A.D. 1332–1406/A.H. 732–808) had written his three volume magnum opus, *Kitab Al 'Ibar* in 1378 AD. In the first volume, the *Muqaddimah*, Ibn Khaldun sets out the conceptual framework and methodological bases for adjudicating between competing data sources, all of which are self-consciously sociological. As Mahmoud Dhaouadi (1990) and Sayed Farid Alatas (2006) have shown, Ibn Khaldun outlines his 'new sciences' of human organisation and society 'ilm al-umran al-bashari' and 'ilm al ijtima al-insani', which were rejected by the extroversions of Westernisation. Drawing on Adesina's (2006) estimation, this had occurred for about 452 years before the first volume of Auguste Comte's six volumes of *Cours de Philosophie Positive* was published. In the same work, Ibn Khaldun articulates the concept of 'asabiyyah' for explaining the normative basis of group cohesion; its decomposition and reconstitution; and the different ways in which it manifests at different levels of social organisation among different groups. Again, following Adesina's (2006:6) estimation, this had occurred about 515 years before Emile Durkheim's (1893) *De la Division du Travail Social* and its accompanying idea of social norms was published. Unfortunately, in spite of these instructive and pioneering efforts by Africans, one hardly encounters any modern sociology book available to students even in African universities mentioning Ibn Khaldun or even discussing any of his works. Carefully and deliberately, the value of Ibn Khaldun's works has been repudiated by Eurocentricism on the grounds that (i) they are riddled with excessively religious thinking, which supposedly diverges from the modern context of reason and secularism; and (ii) that they do not focus on the operations of 'modern societies'.

Two, in addition to the erasure of uniquely African contributions from the global system of knowledge production, there is also the denial of systematic knowledge to the continent, following the Hegelian logic and tradition. While not substituting erasure for an uncritical adulation, the point at issue here, is to highlight the immanently Eurocentric and racist inclination to create binary opposites between ignorance and knowledge on the one hand as well as magic and science on the other. Within this structure, while dubious magic and ignorance are presented as the signifiers of Africa and the East generally, the West is privileged as 'the source' of all legitimate significations as well as scientific knowledge. By extension, Africa is reduced to raw material production, while Europe specialises in the production of capital goods and finished products. This practice is consistent with the ideological reduction of the continent to a source from which data are generated and exported to Europe, wherein various theories are produced for advancing the frontiers of knowledge. This way, the aim is to ensure that theories are perpetually imported into Africa from the West in a global system dominated by the operations of Western power. According to Abubakar Momoh (2003, 41):

> In all books on post-Newtonian science that exist, virtually all those mentioned as scientists that made discoveries are Europeans. Nowhere is Benjamin Banneker (1731–1806) or Jan Ernest Matzeliger (1852–1889) mentioned. German philosophy is widely acknowledged to be a major influence on modern western philosophy. Yet when works are written on German philosophy nothing is said about the Ghanaian philosopher,

William Amo, who was a Professor in a German University and whose views were well respected by philosophers such as Immanuel Kant.

Anthropology, international relations, philosophy and political science are four major academic disciplines whose histories and continuing practices drive home our argument. The historical development of anthropology as an academic discipline illuminates the problem of the relation of culture to history vis-à-vis the totalising universalist conception of culture and knowledge, an epistemological violence established in the post-Enlightenment period of European intellectual history – already alluded to, so far in this work – which places Europe and North America at the centre of all legitimate significations, with the rest of the world considered as backward and inferior. As Partha Chatterjee (1986, 10–7) has argued, the development of anthropology illustrates the longstanding connection between culture and knowledge on the one hand and their dialectical relationship to power on the other hand. Put crudely, anthropology was developed by and in the West mainly to account for the East's lag in culture and history in relation to the West. The leading inspiration here is Hegel's (1975, 150) philosophy of history. Within that discursive practice, history is understood as moving from the West to the West and in fact, the East exists outside both history and literature. Anthropology was thus developed as the requisite academic discipline first, to account for the non-existence of the East in history and literature, and second, to insert the East into the footnotes of world history and literature at the limits permitted by the West. Within that arrangement, while nationalism is understood as a cultural signifier, anthropology is deployed to study the operations of cultures and their performativity across various alien spaces. Its primary focus is chiefly on the Blacks, the Negroes, the savages and other alien cultures across the world. In South Africa, for example, since this logic would naturally adjudge and affirm the whites as being already civilised – as being parts of history and literature – anthropology would thus focus on accounting for the lack and lag of the Blacks. Understood against the backdrop of its barbarism and nativism, 'the Eastern other' is considered to be radically different from the West; yet anthropology claims it can be understood. Herein lies its major Eurocentric and racist contradiction, not just in its outlook as a discipline, but especially in terms of the structuring of its thoughts and writings on the East.

While the Enlightenment was a clearly bourgeois revolution, anthropology was developed as an intellectual offspring of Western imperialism. Its contradictory roots in Enlightenment visions of the human are also not deniable. The dialectical connections between the humanist visions of the Enlightenment; its lofty ideals and role as the foster parent of imperialism, have been established in other works.²² Our point here, is to argue that, it is mainly through the operations of power in its discursive constitution and production, that anthropology becomes the special science for understanding 'the other' – as a special specie of 'the homo sapiens' best understood in terms of its difference and aspiration to become Western – a gaze which the East is too powerless and weak to return. Without much ado, this is a major psychological and social legacy of colonialism on African and non-metropolitan populations throughout the world. For the most part, European colonial cultures tended to equate 'blackness' with impurity and inferiority, a psyche which shaped the perception and self-view of most colonial and postcolonial populations. Consequently, in struggling to 'escape' from such traumatising view of 'the self', the strategy adopted by most of such colonised subjects is to 'reject' 'blackness' in all its appearances and ramifications. In so doing, such people take on the 'assumed superiority' of the metropolitan cultures. The inferiority associated with 'being black' thus impels many colonised populations to adopt the 'mother country's cultural standards' and aspire to a 'western existence' by adopting 'a white world outlook'. By accepting and internalising such defeatist constructions of 'the self' as imagined by the other – and failing to imagine or think their destinies and existence beyond the West – postcolonial subjects have had no historical alternatives but to approximate the given attributes of modernity and progress – enthroned by the West – even when that process of approximation means their continued subjection under a world order which only sets their tasks for them and over which they have no measure of control. This is what Fanon (1952) meant when he noted with dismay that, 'For the black man there is only one destiny. And it is white'. There is therefore, no sense in recounting this development without placing in a proper historical perspective the role of colonial anthropology.²³ It is also in that sense that, the Enlightenment constitutes and reproduces itself as a specific anthropology best understood as a mode of existence and a system of thought, the meaning of which is a problem of continuing historical analysis (Mafeje 1976, 309–10).

Unfortunately, while the Enlightenment has successfully universalised its anthropological viewpoint – becoming the fertile ground for instituting the 'civilising mission' during the eighteenth and nineteenth centuries – this period and viewpoint marked the apogee in the operations of European colonial expansion. Its philosophies also rationalised military conquest, political subjugation and the economic exploitation of weaker states across the East spearheaded by the major European powers. While the individual details of these experiences have varied from country to country – with various writers developing different notions of critique underlying their operations – their historical and theoretical nuances have more often than not, largely coincided.

The academic discipline of international relations also offers an instance for understanding the operations of Eurocentricism. Although the disciplinary history of international relations reflects the contingent historical situation that gave rise to it, the discipline has remained – since its inception – largely oriented towards explaining the Western world, and at best, understanding the rest of the world from the perspective of the West, thereby marginalising the world outside the West. While this constitutive image of the discipline is a product of the operations of power as well as a deep sense of superiority and historically consolidated privileges, the deployment of myths of cultural origins about Europe's ascendancy has served to account for its acclaimed progress and a difference appropriated for distinguishing the West from its non-Western other. In particular, the claim about development in the West understood as driven by factors entirely endogenous to it, has led to the utter disregard of the contributions of other regions of the world. This perceived superiority informs the fundamental assumptions as well as operational premises on which the discipline is hinged. To wit, the emphasis on the operations of the great powers, together with an overriding understanding of the European state system as the ideal universal state form – by diplomatic historians, economists, international lawyers and philosophers – have been inscribed into the field since its earliest development.[24]

The years after the First World War were followed with contemplations and reflections about the causes of the war and the need for measures to avoid future humanitarian catastrophes. This led, among others, to the establishment of the first chair in international politics at the University of Aberystwyth in Wales, endowed by Lord Davies (see Hobson and Hobden 2002). In the years after this development, the field of international relations attained increasing formal institutionalisation across the Western world, most notably in the United Kingdom and the United States of America, where the discipline assumed different intellectual traditions. Yet, it remained insensitive to the world beyond the West. This historically narrowed focus has been further consolidated by the skewed historiographies from which authorities within the discipline have continued to draw in articulating their theoretical positions. The idea of drawing from the varied repositories of world history as a basis for genuinely reorienting the discipline to the world at large has been carefully ignored. Consequently, although 'the international' in international relations and 'the world' in world history would suggest that this discipline would not be reduced to the interactions among the states within the Western world together with the heritages and histories of the Western world, this has been and remains the ontological focus of the discipline, together with its idea of world history. This narrowed understanding of the substantive constitutive elements of the discipline underlines its failure to develop an inclusive world historiography that accommodates Africa and other regions of the world. It also reinforces the continued exclusion of the civilisational contributions, heritages and voices from the global South from its narratives (Nkiwane 2001).

In philosophy, modern understandings of the discipline are unabashedly European. From Chantal Mouffe in Belgium; Simon Critchley in England; Jean-Luc Nancy in France; Peter Sloterdijk in Germany; Slavoj Zizek in Slovenia; down to Judith Butler and Wendy Brown in the United States of America; almost all the active and important philosophers are products of the European philosophical genealogy. The philosophy they practice also enjoys the highest degree of globality and self-conscious acceptance without which no alternative thinking can be presumably universal (Dabashi 2013).

In the same mode, European philosophy is considered as 'philosophy' while African or Asian philosophy is described as 'ethnophilosophy' – just as European thinkers are 'thinkers' while their counterparts from South Asia are labelled 'South Asian thinkers'. As Hamid Dabashi (2013) puts it 'if Mozart sneezes it is music … but the most sophisticated Indian music ragas are the subject of ethnomusicology'. Jacques Derrida, Jacques Lacan, Louis Althusser, Michel Foucault and their legatees across the European intellectual pedigree are regarded as philosophers, while Achille Mbembe, Chinua Achebe, Emmanuel C. Eze, Henry O. Oruka, Ngugi wa Thiong'o, Okot p'Bitek, Souleymane B. Diagne, Taban L. Liyong, Valentine Y. Mudimbe and Wole Soyinka in Africa – as well as Akeel Bilgrami, Akhil Gupta, Amitav Ghosh, Arjun Appadurai, Ashis Nandy, Dipesh Chakrabarty, Gayatri C. Spivak, Homi K. Bhabha, Partha Chatterjee, Ranajit Guha, Sudipta Kaviraj and Sumit Sarkar in South Asia – are classified as ethnophilosophers.

Within political science, theoretical constructions on the state employed for analysing socio-economic formations across the global South are largely based on deficit analyses which reproduce the ideal-typical

Western vision of statehood, the 'gemeinschaft-gesellschaft' as the actual universal state form. This is especially the case in Africa where statehood is often entirely denied the continent. Postcolonial societies are thus increasingly defined in terms of their dysfunctionalities using a set of theoretically determined state attributes and functions which deliberately deny the functional and historically specific articulations of postcolonial societies. Such deficit analyses of the state in Africa have provided justifications for the continent's cultural, economic and political dominance by the West. Such approaches are appropriated for legitimising various humanitarian, military and technological interventions in rebuilding collapsed and failed states on the continent according to *en vogue* notions of modern developmental practices. They also reinforce nineteenth century colonial discourses which construct Africa as the West's absolute other. The orientation of such dominant (mis)conceptions of the state is to blur and undermine rather than rendering visible the specific historical functionalities of postcolonial socioeconomic formations.[25] Thus, for all of the major approaches within the discipline, there is only one real society – Western – that can be considered a deserving model for the modern state within the social sciences. For a long time, too, radical rhetoric hid its impotence by searching for an alternative political and theoretical model. Notwithstanding the various strands of socialism – Chinese, Cuban and East European socialism – the modern operations of knowledge have had no major alternative conceptual tools with which to imagine an epistemology that would not be rooted in the Western 19th-century understandings of the world. Consistent with the Enlightenment tradition, the social sciences consider societies in black Africa as a laboratory for studying Western evolution. With this perception of Africa as a laboratory both for understanding the past and future of social change, African realities are not only considered to be of secondary importance, more seriously, social change across Western societies is considered to be the legitimate creator of those special conditions underlining the development of African studies as a field of enquiry (Jewsiewicki 1989, 5–10).

Given this premise, it is hardly thinkable to discuss the Enlightenment or 19th century British liberal thought without accounting for the place that the idea of race occupies in its discursive production. To ignore it altogether would be to omit the actual epistemological ground on which liberal thought is built. Its centrality is illustrated, among others, in the idea of tutelage in liberal imperialism, an idea implicitly founded on a theory of race, articulated in the 'not yet' of history – a subtle locution for 'never'. Within that discursive space, race was the foundational social fact of Empire – an idea embedded more in practices than in discourse – and a foundational category of thought that made other perceptions possible. The highest point in the articulation of the 'not yet' of history as the racial sub-text for a perpetual deferment of the possibility of independence across the colonies, was the year 1857, a year widely acclaimed as one of the most important events in modern Indian history and universally acknowledged to be the single most important anti-colonial uprising in modern history. Otherwise, why was it necessary for the British to postpone independence for the future – through the promulgation of self-rule as a political solution in 1858 – when several people have died to make it clear that they wanted it in 1857? Clearly, 'race' functioned here, as elsewhere, as the unstated term through which the gradualism of liberalism reconciled itself to the permanence of Empire and thus accommodated the notion of incorrigibility, assuming the failure of all correctional efforts. This viewpoint helps one understand how someone like John S. Mill saw himself as possibly reconciling two apparently irreconcilable positions – democracy at home, despotism abroad. To wit, he saw no conflict between his hobby of theorising about liberty and his day-job as the overseer of the Indian Empire. It was clearly John S. Mill and other liberal thinkers of his ilk who managed to believe two contradictory and divergent positions at the same time (see Ghosh and Chakrabarty 2002, 148–52).

While imperial thought developed as a direct offshoot of liberalism, the place of race in liberal thought cannot be factually denied. The idea of civilisation itself was a racist idea, although its articulation produced significant differences in the way in which the Europeans related to, and treated the so-called 'primitives' on the one hand, and the supposedly 'civilised' peoples, whom the imperialists acknowledged as having experienced a prior and superior 'civilisation' on the other. The calibrated scale of 'civilisation' was an Enlightenment phenomenon. For the most part, the Enlightenment was remarkable in its universalisation of different versions of the idea of equality, a practice which allowed the colonised to charge the colonisers with self-contradiction – of making a travesty of their principles of human equality. It exhumes the dilemmas at the heart of European thought, introduced by 17th and 18th century ideas about the human – about international law, ownership, property and the tension stemming between the universal applicability that liberalism claims for itself and the unacknowledged racism that runs throughout its script. The civilisational calculus was thus subordinated to the racial. To acknowledge this point is to appreciate the ambivalence introduced into 19th-century European thought – an ambivalence underlined chiefly by the tension between the universalist aspects and declarations of science and the particularist emphasis on race – and from which stems the heinous perceptions of primitivism with references to African and other non-Western cultures.

By premising race at the centre of imperial and liberal thought, the real struggles – together with the sites of those struggles – between the East and the West were radically shifted and transformed from the coercive to the persuasive apparatuses of empire, so that the only grounds available for any possible resistance would be within the terms of the conquerors. This was achieved mainly by (i) compelling the colonised into a fragile acceptance and precarious accommodation of colonialism, (ii) through the absolute disintegration of their worldview and (iii) by ensuring that the colonised neither imagines any other construction of reality vis-à-vis themselves nor possesses any alternative investment in rethinking the implications of the cultural acceptance of empire beyond the colonisers' worldview.[26] Understood this way, racism is not just an exclusivist or supremacist ideology but, is more seriously founded on certain ideas that relate one to biology, evolution, nature and science – a specifically post-Enlightenment ideology whose resilience is underlined by its incorporation of certain elements of scientific thinking, but originally aimed at duping non-metro -politan subjects through the projection of development and reform as inseparably tied to the essence of Empire. While the Enlightenment provided the enabling condition for institutionalising colonial or modern racism across various colonial societies – with our ability to perceive and recognise it enabled and limited according to the varying degrees to which we are, or are not true Enlightenment subjects – this practice has continued even in the contemporary times in which aggressive capitalist expansionism is carefully cloaked in the language of economic progress and political reform across much of the global South.

As Partha Chatterjee (2011, 4–11) has argued, although the epic moment of modern political theory largely began in seventeenth century England, the conceptual innovations that enabled the discursive construction of that abstract time-space – and successfully secured it against the incursions of the real world of politics – appeared mainly during the turn of the nineteenth century. During that period, although all the major European countries had had the experience of conquering and ruling over vast territories in the Americas, the European empires back home did not seriously pose the problem of incorporating the forms of government as well as the systems of law and property relations of the indigenous American populations within a European political order. The latter were in essence, not regarded as having any credible political experience or society worth integrating into the emerging imperial formations. Eric Hobsbawm's description of non-Western societies as 'backward' and 'pre-political societies' was thus widely in use at that time. In particular, the indigenous societies of the Amerindians were understood as examples of Hobsbawm's pre-political depiction of human condition to be superseded as a basis for the desired and well-ordered civilised, commercial and political societies to emerge. European colonial settlements across Africa and Asia had been organised according to the most modern European normative principles of the time.

Since the indigenous political institutions of the defeated Oriental kingdoms could not be entirely ignored or set aside – for understandable historical and political reasons – in managing the African and Asian societies conquered during the eighteenth and nineteenth centuries, such societies were given a new place within the emergent European imperial order. In articulating the decided relations, a system of double standard, based on what Edmund Burke (1788/1991) describes as a skewed plan of geographic morality – by which the conduct of men in their private affairs and public exchanges were neither governed nor judged by their relations to the Great Governor of the Universe nor by their relations with their fellowmen, but by their standing in specific climates as well as their degrees of latitudes and longitude – was instituted. With Britain standing out in this practice, during the course of the history of the emergence of its modern empire, several deviations were noted in the application of British norms across its colonies. In the contexts of India and Nigeria, the spirit of equity, justice and lenity – that characterised the operations of the law vis-à-vis every British subject – were only selectively applied to the natives and other colonial subjects. The fact that such indigenous societies had their own constitutions, laws and legitimate dynasties; and the idea that the European colonisers ought to have respected their customs and institutions did not seem to matter much to the various European colonial powers.

This was articulated through an ambivalent posture by the colonial state based on 'the rule of colonial difference' (Chatterjee 1994, 14–20). This reflected 'the ambivalence of colonial rule and the contradictory nature of its discourse' (Bhabha 1994). It also underlined the role of the colonial state as the agency that brought the modular forms of the modern state to the colonies and also ensured that its normalising mission was never fulfilled therein. To illustrate, since the principal justification for the modern regime of power is that by making social regulations integral to the self-disciplining of normalised individuals, power is made more effective, humane and therefore productive, there are three possible positions with regard to the universality of this argument:

> One is that this must apply in principle to all societies irrespective of historical or cultural specificities. The second is that the principle is inescapably tied to the specific history and culture of Western societies and cannot be exported elsewhere; this implies a rejection of the universality of the principle. The third is that the historical and cultural differences, although an impediment in the beginning, can be eventually overcome by a suitable process of training and education. The third position, therefore, while admitting the objection raised by the second, nevertheless seeks to restore the universality of the principle. (Chatterjee 1994, 17–8)

Within this practice, although back home, the respective colonial powers were democratic and conformed with the entire features and requirements of modernity in their home countries, only a perverted version of such modern practices was entrenched in the colonies. Even though the imperialists all shared the belief in the self-evident legitimacy of the principles which should universally govern modern regimes of power, it was however, surprising that until the earlier half of the twentieth century, a persistent theme in colonial discourse was the steadfast refusal to admit the universal applicability of those principles to the colonies and later postcolonies. Universal notions of fundamental human rights, which were applied to every citizen in the West, were denied to Africans, Asians and other native populations. In addition to the ineffectuated nature of colonial and postcolonial institutions was the demand that such institutions must embrace 'imperial innovations' as a condition for approximating modernity.

Thus, in colonial Africa and South Asia, notwithstanding the provisions of the rule of law, legal procedures differed significantly in their application to the colonised and Europeans. Built into the operations of the rule of law across various colonial societies were the grounds for its own future subversion. This is because it was founded on an implicit, though unwritten understanding that, the rulers were – if not entirely above the laws – certainly subject to a different species of law than those applied to the ruled. Successive post-independence regimes have been adeptly astute to adapt this implicit exception for their own purposes. While the historical and continuing implications of such conceptual innovations and practices are yet to be sufficiently accounted for – with the empirical deviation of prevailing institutions and practices in a particular country from the universally desired norm the basis for declaring the exception[27] – such structuring of norm and exceptions has underlined virtually all justifications of colonial empires during the nineteenth and twentieth centuries. According to Partha Chatterjee (2011, 10):

> The puzzle posed by postcolonial political theory – by Uday Singh Mehta, for example – of liberal democratic governments in Europe holding overseas territories under their despotic rule, thus apparently contradicting their cherished normative principles, dissolves when one realizes the power of the norm-exception construct. Thus, John Stuart Mill, one of the greatest liberal political theorists of all time, while making an extended case for the universal superiority of representative government, specifically argued that it could not apply, at least not yet, to dependencies such as India and Ireland. The latter were exceptions; hence there was really no contradiction in Mill's normative liberal theory. He recommended a paternal British despotism for those countries until such time as their peoples became mature enough to govern themselves. Of course, neither Mill nor any other liberal could suggest an impartial way of deciding when and if such a stage had been reached. Apparently, there was no alternative but to rely on the good sense of the paternal guardians to grant self-government to their wards. Or rather, the only alternative was to acknowledge the right of a subject people to announce its attainment of maturity by rebelling against its masters – a right somewhat incompatible with liberal doctrines of good colonial governance.

From the nineteenth century onward, a consideration of postcolonial politics against the backdrop of Western normative theory – using what Partha Chatterjee (2011, 11) has described as the two senses of the norm – has encoded the basic political strategy of relating the normative to the empirical. This way, in deploying 'normalisation' as a theoretical key to the end of political strategy, while the norm-deviation structure would establish the empirical location of any particular social formation at any given time in relation to the empirically prevailing average or normal, the corresponding normative framework could then provide, by means of a norm-exception structure of justification, the ground for applying policy to intervene and bring the empirical average closer to the desired norm.

In response to such globally driven intellectual currents and struggles, which seek to perpetually canonise and reify the operations of imperial historiographies and therefore give little or no agency to non-Western cultures, postcolonial societies have returned the fiercest volleys of counter-attacks deployed largely through various epistemic and moral critiques of the normative standards upheld by Western political theory; and improvised through numerous practices that deviate from the universally acclaimed forms.[28] In struggling to decenter the absolutising inclinations and legacies of Western political theory and redefine the normative standards underlining the operations of modern politics in the light of the considerable accumulation of new experiences and practices most clearly understood in terms of their exceptions, attention has been drawn to an abundant repository of alternative sources.

While the progress of the industrial revolution has been widely acclaimed, not much is known about the connections between the contribution of Negro slavery and the West Indian colonies to it, within the corpus on English economic history. Yet, slavery contributed greatly to the development of British capitalism. In a study based on an examination of the relationship between early capitalism as exemplified by Great Britain, and the Negro slave, Negro slavery and the general colonial trade of the seventeenth and eighteenth centuries, Eric E. Williams (1944/1994) provided an account on the contribution and role of Negro slavery and the slave trade in developing the capital which financed the industrial revolution in England. In it, he showed what the New World owes to the Negro, the victim of slavery and the slave trade, for its development; particularly in its pioneer stages; and England for its rise from a small power to the world's greatest empire (Rogers 1945). Thus, contrary to what the West would have us believe, several economic and political institutions of the modern West were not endogenously produced but in active dialogue and interaction with the colonial worlds across various regions of the East. The idea of universal citizenship, to be sure, was first posed in the age of revolutions during the Haitian revolt by black slaves (Trouillot 1995). Relatedly, the consciousness of emancipation that inspired the idea of equal citizenship in the modern state – especially as elaborated by Georg W. F. Hegel among other philosophers – was a direct product of an engagement with the compelling challenge posed by the Haitian revolution (Buck-Morss 2009, 22). The modern factory, as a central institution of the industrial revolution, was invented as the foreign trading station of the European merchant companies. Similarly, the joint stock company – another pillar of modern capitalism – was first developed as an institution of colonial trade, in which the English East India Company was the most successful pioneer (Chaudhuri 1978, 22). While these instances can be extended and multiplied to include institutions such as the bureaucracy, diplomacy, crowd control, emergency relief, international law, penal administration, surveillance and a host of other aspects of the operations of modern government,

> The point is not merely to insist upon an acknowledgement that the institutions of economic and political life in the modern West have a historical genealogy that extends into the formerly colonial world. It is to explore the further implication of that history for the authoritative status of the normative claims of Western political theory for our contemporary world. If we know that the principal hegemonic strategy for establishing the universal claims of the normative standards of Western political institutions is to combine a norm-deviation paradigm in the empirical domain with a norm-exception paradigm in the policy domain, what has been the consequence of decolonization and the emergence of postcolonial thinking for the continued relevance of this strategy? (Chatterjee 2011, 23)

Other examples abound on African and non-Western philosophers whose works have been erased on similar grounds by the power-driven impulses of modernity and the West in the post-Enlightenment period, so that, the academic discipline of anthropology and the works of Ibn Khaldun are just a few illustrations of such instructive and pioneering efforts from Africa dispossessed of the value of their intellectual labour and contributions to the global system of knowledge production. Other examples of indigenous non-metropolitan developments in thought include the works of Usman Dan Fodio in northern Nigeria and Ifa corpus, the oracle of divination within Yoruba oracular discourse. What has been even more appalling and disturbing in this regard has been the eagerness with which humanity across the East has so readily welcomed such practices. On the whole, the attempt to over glorify and romanticise the contributions and legacies of the Enlightenment, not just by the West, but also by populations across the East, has foreclosed the prospect for autochthonous development in the East. Articulating his critique of such a disposition with reference to India, Amitav Ghosh (2002, 156–8) recently queried:

> Why should we so reflexively assume that the reformist spirit in 19th-century India derived its strength primarily from Enlightenment sources? We know that long before Bentinck, the Mughals as well as many major and minor Hindu rulers did everything in their power to discourage sati (I am referring here to Catherine Weinberger-Thomas's research in *Ashes of Immortality*). We know similarly that anti-hierarchical thought in India goes back through the bhakti period to the Buddha and Mahavira.

Why should we so completely disavow the liberatory potential of these traditions? (E.g.: Why should we assume that Dr. Ambedkar was making a deathbed compromise rather than stating a deeply-felt belief?) Why should we assume also that the egalitarian impulse in 19th-century India derived its power primarily from the Enlightenment (when indeed, all the exegetical material goes against this)?

To take this further: in making these assumptions are we not also accepting certain fundamental (but unstated) beliefs about colonialism? Are we not implicitly conceding the argument that imperialism was, in at least one of its aspects, an enterprise of social reform?

In fact, the British did everything they could to reinforce the hierarchical aspects of Indian society – indeed they introduced hierarchies of their own. That is why I think we should not reflexively assume that the egalitarian and liberatory impulses of 19th-century Indian society came solely or even primarily from Enlightenment roots. That there was an admixture of influences is undeniable: indeed it is to be celebrated. But inasmuch as Indians appropriated certain aspects of Enlightenment thought it was against the will and weight of the Empire, and it would have happened (as in Thailand and Japan) whether there was an Empire or not.[29]

Thus, the position that the Enlightenment – in its combination with capitalism – was special and unique in the way in which it helped to make 'equality' and other admirable modern concepts of the human vision, into universal categories of secular life; entrenched them into every aspect of human activity and built them into all general measures of exchange – is a one-sided thesis that deliberately denies non-metropolitan agencies and contributions to the making of global modernity. It is based on a shallow reading of African cultures and non-metropolitan histories generally. In the next section, the field of African studies is examined to drive home our point on the operations of Eurocentricism within various disciplinary practices and fields of study as a post-Enlightenment agenda. It is also discussed as an instance of an anti-imperialist and non-hierarchical dialogue that harps on the originality and uniqueness of the African voice in articulating the complexities and perplexities of the African condition.

The field of African Studies

Suppose we come across someone who looks to us subordinated and oppressed but who does not give us any signs of being in that state, at least signs that we would recognize? How do we know then that this person has actually developed ways of forgetting that state or not representing that state to himself or herself? How do we know that ours is a truer representation of the 'deeper' facts of their life? Why could not we allow for the possibility that they have developed ways of living – life-forms – in which our very questions are of lesser relevance? (Ghosh and Chakrabarty 2002, 165)

As we have tried to argue in the cases of anthropology, philosophy and political science, the field of African studies – just like Asian and Latin American studies – historically developed as a post-Enlightenment attempt to study non-Western societies from the perspective of an area studies approach based on Western standards. It began with the anthropological activities carried out by early adventurers, imperial administrators and missionaries before and after colonisation and the capitalist expansion across the continent. During this period, area studies was originally construct-ed and contrived as part of an epistemological attempt by the West to control backward regions of the world using the ideology of developmentalism and the notion of the plural society. To instantiate this point, it is worthwhile to examine the context and experience of South Africa – a country where the development of African studies dates back to the earliest part of the twentieth century.[30]

From its inception, African studies in South Africa was directly linked with the operations of the state and its policy on the native question.[31] The University of Cape Town – the first university in Africa to establish a school that would focus on African studies – played a major role in that regard.

African studies at the University of Cape Town began in the early part of the twentieth century when missionaries such as W. A. Norton suggested – to state officials – the need to have a Chair of Bantu philology established in the Cape. According to R. Gordon (1990, 17), Norton was a missionary affiliated with the Church of England 'who was on friendly terms with several Cape Town professors' and also assisted his fellow missionaries to 'overcome barriers of misunderstanding by providing them with proper language training'. Although the University of Cape Town saw a role for itself in providing resources for formulating and implementing the native policy, Norton's efforts were interrupted following the formation of the Union of South Africa and the First World War, which shifted focus away from the shared interests between the state and the university.

After the War, Norton revived debates around 'the scholarly study of the indigenous African population' and successfully convinced relevant authorities in academic and government circles of the importance and urgency of the issue as a basis for developing 'a solid native policy'. Earlier in 1916, in an address to the South African Association for the Advancement of Science, he stated, 'Many a fatal mistake not only in dealing with individuals but also of general policy might have been avoided by a grounding in ethnology and comparative religion' (Norton 1916, 21). In 1917, in a published paper titled, 'The need and value of academic study of native philology and ethnology', Norton (1917, 18) presented 'the study of the language of the natives as the best index to their psychology'; and queried that it was absurd for a South African university to ignore 'the customs and languages of five-sixths of the population'.

In response to Norton's efforts, the government approved the creation of a chair in Bantu Philology in 1917. Although this chair was occupied by Norton, it was suddenly frozen as part of the state's wartime economy drive. In 1919, following the conclusion of deliberations by a government committee of inquiry set up to address 'problems whose solution is necessary for the future safe development of a country in which white and black are to live side by side' (Phillips 1993, 27) and to which Norton gave evidence, the Union government endorsed the idea of establishing a school at the University of Cape Town. In 1920, Norton presented a plan of the school to government (Ntsebeza 2012, 4).

The vision was that the school would be 'a sizeable faculty presided over by a dean, teaching in languages as far afield as Swahili, and with research interests in such diverse subjects as the ethnology, religion and psychology of African peoples' (Van der Merwe 1979, 62–3). A comprehensive, two-professor School of Bantu Languages and Life at the University of Cape Town with a 3000 pound per annum grant – guaranteed for five years – was also recommended (Phillips 1993, 22). In April 1920, Norton – who was at that time 50 years of age – was appointed chair of Bantu Philology. He immediately recommended a change of name to 'African' as a way of expanding his chair beyond the Bantu-speaking zones. The second chair was named Social Anthropology rather than Ethnology – the name suggested by the government committee of inquiry. In December 1920, the initial budget of 3000 pounds approved by the government was cut by half. As Lungisile Ntsebeza (2012, 4) recalls, Norton was initially appointed as a professor of Bantu Philology, but for financial reasons was eventually appointed a lecturer in Bantu Languages and Literatures. It was not until 1921 that the position was converted to a professorship of Bantu Philology. The other chair of the School went to Alfred R. Radcliffe-Brown – a 39-year-old Cambridge graduate – 'unanimously appointed' to the chair in 1921 – just one year after Norton's appointment. However, as

Chair of Social Anthropology, Radcliffe-Brown was also the head of the school. He was a popular teacher who drew large numbers of students.

Two points stand out clearly from South Africa's experience. One, the articulation and operations of apartheid were made possible not only through the institutions of cultural technologies, based only on the modern regime of power and techniques of governmentality, but also by a system of knowledge – in this case African studies – that not only makes apartheid and colonialism possible, but also keeps the continent as a central part of the North's periphery even in the post-apartheid and postcolonial periods. Bernard S. Cohn (1996) and Christopher S. Bayly (1996) make this point in their references to India. On South Africa, Lungisile Ntsebeza (2012, 4–5) points out that:

> The genealogy of the concept of African studies at UCT cannot be divorced from the colonial strategy of ruling over the indigenous people. The role that Radcliffe-Brown and by extension anthropology played in this regard is of particular interest. According to Gordon, there was clear complicity between Radcliffe-Brown and the colonial project, something which, according to Gordon, had far reaching implications for the discipline of Anthropology and its implication not only in the colonial project but also in the elaboration of the apartheid project in the 1940s and later. Gordon cites Paul Rich (1984) in noting that General Smuts personally invited A. R. Radcliffe-Brown to establish the social anthropology course at the University of Cape Town in 1921, leading to the establishment of the first distinctly South African anthropological journal, Bantu studies. Fortes remarked that 'at the time' there was not a single full-time professorship of anthropology in any British university', suggesting that the first full-time professorial position in the British system was awarded to Radcliffe-Brown at UCT.

Two, interaction between the various actors performing African studies has historically been ridden with tension. Again Lungisile Ntsebeza (2012, 5) underlines this with respect to Norton and Radcliffe-Brown in South Africa:

> Relations between Radcliffe-Brown and Norton were apparently not at their best. Norton's main interest, Phillips seems to suggest, was research, rather than teaching. His courses never attracted more than one student a year, something that was not appreciated by both Beattie, the principal, and his colleagues. He enjoyed collecting 'native lore and history' from the elderly, which he wrote up and published as 'intellectually lightweight papers' between 1921 and 1926. On his part, Radcliffe-Brown despised the work of Norton as the following quote

shows: '(A) trained anthropologist with no knowledge of the languages will do work of infinitely more scientific value than an untrained man with a perfect knowledge of the language. Radcliffe-Brown wanted the chair of Philology to go. This eventually happened in 1923. Although Norton resigned with effect from 1 April 1925, he was forced to leave on the day of his resignation. This, according to Phillips, spelt the decline of African languages at UCT, with the school being a school of languages only in name.

Frustrated by unsuccessful attempts at struggling to extract funds from unimpressed colonial bureaucrats,[32] Radcliffe-Brown also resigned in 1925 to take up a newly created chair in social anthropology at the University of Sydney in Australia.[33] Nevertheless, the school – despite the numerous changes made to its name – remained under the intellectual and political control of the white minority government. Its purpose was also limited to 'equipping government and informing it about appropriate strategies for ruling Bantu people' (Phillips 1993, 167). It was not until the 1940s that the foremost attempt at Africanising and decolonising African studies at the University of Cape Town began with the appointment of A. C. Jordan in 1946 as a Lecturer in the Language section at the then School of African Studies, University of Cape Town. Jordan had by then published his classic, *Ingqumbo yeminyanya* (The wrath of the ancestors), and later became the first black African to be awarded a doctorate in African Languages by the University of Cape Town (Ntsebeza 2012, 8–9).

The details of A. C. Jordan's efforts at Africanising African studies at the University of Cape Town and the resultant frustrations are best suited for another research discussion. It bears repeating, however, that subsequent attempts in this direction were not free from encumbrances and hindrances. The most recent in our account draws on the eventual turn of events during the dramatic developments of the late 1980s and early 1990s – developments which ushered in political negotiations for a new democratic South Africa and the establishment of the A. C. Jordan Chair in African Studies at the Centre for African Studies at the University of Cape Town – an attempt interpreted by Martin Hall (1998, 87) as part of a 'drive to reverse isolation and connect South Africa to its continent'. The major context of this period was the anticipated demise of apartheid and the imminent black majority rule by the African National Congress. The Centre for African Studies was still grappling with what African studies would entail in post-apartheid South Africa.

Although the selection committee expressed commitment in appointing a black person as Director of the Centre with the aim of setting the

University on 'a new path' entirely different from its past experience in terms of African studies, it did not follow through with its stipulated intention. Notwithstanding his towering international profile and the fact that he met all the objective requirements set by the committee, Archie Mafeje was denied the position. He was not even interviewed (see Ntsebeza 2008, 36–43; 2012, 13). Mahmood Mamdani's appointment to the A. C. Jordan Chair of African Studies and as Director of the Centre in the second phase of the selection process[34] – originally conceived as a corrective measure but proved to be a regretted appointment, as Lungisile Ntsebeza (2012, 13) puts it, 'based on a limited knowledge of the person' – rather opened a new round of combative conversations between Mamdani and other senior role players at the University over what a centre for African studies should be in the context of post-apartheid South Africa (see Mamdani 1996; 1998). In response to the conflictual exchanges elicited by his provocative and scathing critique of African studies and the resultant hostile interactions, Mamdani resigned at the University of Cape Town and took up an appointment at Columbia University in New York.[35]

Under the leadership of a new Director – Harry Garuba – the Centre for African Studies 'gradually deteriorated' and became the subject of consideration for 'disestablishment' (Ntsebeza 2012, 15). The Centre's declining performance continued until September 2012 when Lungisile Ntsebeza was appointed as the A. C. Jordan Professor of African Studies and Director of the Centre for African Studies with approval to appoint two research fellows of African Studies.[36] To surmise, although there are striking connections and similarities with the South African example, the overall pictures across the continent vary and do not entirely follow the South African path or trajectory.[37]

To clarify, although the early years of African studies at the University of Cape Town were symptomatic of the wider colonial power relations, the continued problems encountered with the Africanization of academic posts at the University cannot be cited as typical of the recent situations across Africa. Almost all post-independence African universities Africanised their staffing immediately and have never looked back. No doubt, apartheid distorted higher education in a malign and massive manner in South Africa; but this cannot be taken as representative of present-day African higher education in general. Even within South Africa, there has been the racial rebalancing of the South African student body within the space of twenty years – 1994 to 2014. The student population almost exactly mirrors the national demographic; academic standards – at least in its leading universities – are increasingly high, while debates and intellectual engagements are continual and intense. For anyone working on African studies, South Africa must now be seen as being at the centre, no more at the fringes, marginalities or periphery.

Following the spate of anticolonial nationalisms and the decolonisation struggles which took place across Africa, Asia and Latin America after the Second World War in 1945 together with the rise of the East-West ideological Cold War, the importance of African studies and area studies generally expanded in the United States of America as part of the intellectual demands and policy requirements of projecting and strengthening American power in a post-war world in the throes of an ideological polarisation as well as an expanding arms race. Its emergence within the higher educational system in Europe was tied to the attempt at accounting for the lack of development in hitherto pre-capitalist societies in non-metropolitan societies and the projection of the colonial system as the only credible alternative for the development and modernisation of their economic, political and social institutions and structures. In other words, while the preoccupation with the question of development – which became central to policy and political attention in the period of early and late colonialism – was central to the development of African studies and area studies in Europe (thus forming part of the post-1945 development agenda that emerged as one of the responses to the growing nationalist pressures during late colonialism),[38] the question of generating research information for formulating foreign policy objectives and strategies towards developing countries, was central to the development of area studies in the United States of America.

Thus, for the most part, the earliest academic journals within the proveneness of area studies began first as colonial newsletters – across the colonies operating within the bureaucratic systems throughout the colonies – with which the European powers articulated and rationalised their imperial positions. Such journals were used for explaining the factors and reasons underlying the lack of development in backward and traditional societies across the global South. They were also used for elaborating Eurocentric options for development into these societies. Later, during the period of nationalist struggles, when anti-colonial newspapers were published by nationalist groups across the colonies, such journals also served for defending the criticisms levied against the colonial state by the nationalists in the colonies. They were later transformed into academic journals by established institutions of learning in their respective home countries.[39]

Later, African studies developed into a distinct field of enquiry with significant collaboration with disciplines in the humanities and the social sciences. While centres and departments of African studies proliferated across the continent and beyond, universities and other institutions of advanced studies launched degree and non-degree programmes. In Europe and North America, African studies not only interfaced varying degrees with development cooperation and development studies. It was also largely financed through the aid budget set aside for Africa and other overseas territories by European and North American economies. It was therefore not surprising that the fortune of the field fluctuated with the level of development assistance. Reductions in aid support thus directly impacts on the resource endowments available for African studies and consequently its research outputs and productivity. Similarly, the crises of development cooperation assistance have thus been interpreted as crises of African studies. In situations where the development assistance community has been confident about the future, the Africanist community has felt the same way, while pessimism about the impact of development assistance on the continent has equally nurtured Afro-pessimism in African studies. This was especially the case in the 1990s.

Without belabouring an obvious fact, this historical reality about its development underlines the disposition of the major bilateral and multi-lateral development cooperation in Europe and North America providing African researchers with funding assistance on the one hand, and pushing their own conceptual concerns and frameworks as well as striving to provide direction for aid policies and research on the continent on the other. In the years following the end of the Second World War, African initiatives and research have been entirely ignored not only in the determi-nation of global policies generally, but also in the formulation of policies towards the continent. External Africanists have rapidly assumed the function of interpreting the world to Africa and representing the continent to the outside world. Thus, the asymmetries between the knowledge on the continent and the power driving such knowledge have been reinforced, while the capacity and independence of Africa's research community for cross cultural and non-hierarchical dialogue have been greatly undermined. These situations continue to elicit counter reactions from intellectual communities across the continent to appropriate and transform African studies into an emancipatory project beyond the initial conception of its original Euro-American progenitors. This section discusses the Africa-driven interventions within African studies as an anti-imperialist intellectual project and examines the implications of such efforts for the liberatory aspirations of the African people and the status of the field.

The fundamental problem in the academic literature on African studies lies in the questions of where and by whom knowledge is produced on the continent as well as where and by whom it is read across the world. These questions have been variedly posed from a plethora of disciplinary and regional perspectives (Chabal 2005; Coquery-Vidrovitch 2006). They have also brought to the fore, the compelling and critical question of the role of Africa and Africans in the discursive production of African studies – a question that has continued to agitate the global discourse on African studies since the 1960s and has provoked a tensed debate on the future directions and possibilities of development for the continent. While the contexts and immediate concerns of the debate have varied over time, the issues carried into it have also been coloured by specific disciplinary orientations as by the changing fortunes of the continent itself; the dominant trends in the Euro-American Africanist community that studies the continent as well as the changing strategic considerations of Western development cooperation and foreign policy establishments (Olukoshi 2006).

The history of African warfare is perhaps the last bastion of the known kind of distorted Eurocentric scholarship that characterised African studies before the 1960s. Richard Reid (2007) makes this point effectively and there is almost no need restating the argument. Nevertheless a recapitulation of its central component is in order. Within that discursive space, African populations were widely considered as savage and warlike tribes pursuing irrational bloodlusts. The practice of proper war was considered absent due to technological backwardness and the arcane obstacles presented by seemingly endless custom and ritual. The aim here, once again, is to deny African and other non-Western historical agencies and arrogate modern contributions to the art of war as an exclusively European genius (Hobson 2012).

For understandable historical reasons, the colonial archive is the major repository from where evidence is drawn for writing African history. However, this archive is marked by its preoccupation with representing power. Thus, while the colonial archive cannot and should not be ignored – as an establishment site in which imperial power constructs the picture of how it wants society to live and be seen as well as decides what version of the state's history it privileges for projection – the actual task of African and area studies generally, is not to begin and end with those narratives provided by the colonial archive, but to proceed to critique them and ultimately replace them with alternative narratives that represent the experiences and voices of the people.[40]

Central to history writing is the question of evidence – especially in the form of historical documents – and the related question of how one treats the chosen evidence. What evidence does one concentrate on? What evidence does one ignore? What are the implications of working with a particular set of evidence? And, what are the implications of ignoring other sets of evidence? These are contending questions of continuing relevance for history writing on any society. Such questions will also continue to attract the attention of authorities and experts in the field for many more years to come. While scholars cannot write history without using their imagination, to properly write history, it is compelling to go beyond the evidence provided by those in power. In the case of Africa, since the 'colonial' is a clearly limited site and deeply problematic space, the challenge of African studies – in this regard – is to write African history beyond the evidence provided by the colonial archive and transcend pre-vailing Eurocentric constructions of the African past. Following Michel Foucault, to do this, is to explore history as a problem with the aim of questioning and uncovering the assumptions undergirding what we know about Africa, rather than gullibly accepting history – in this case African history – as a predictable mechanism existing in a content and form context, a story telling format, or even as the account of antagonists versus protagonists, already produced by the West. While the examples of alternative evidence and sources referred to here include oral sources,[41] the essence of researching African studies is to advance an understanding of Africa that transcends the predicaments into which the colonial past has condemned its populations. Doing this demands epistemologically questioning the knowledge systems around which Africa's historical existence is constructed by the West. The Africa-driven research within African studies represents a decolonisation initiative in this direction. Examples of these interventions are examined here below.

Following the 1960s – the decade of African independence – the first major decolonisation struggle within African studies was to Africanise the curricula and reorient the dominant narratives on the history and prospects of the state in Africa from their imperial tenor and tone. The active participation of Africans and the understanding and utilisation of African languages were emphasised as central components to the rearticulation of African studies. For the first time since colonisation, Africans showed commendable signs of appropriating the capacity to represent themselves within and beyond various academic disciplines (Jewsiewicki and Newbury 1986, 7).

In history, the development of anti-imperialist historiography sought to radicalise African history through rewriting the historiography of landmark moments in the continent's ancient and modern experiences.[42] For a long time before this intervention, African history as a course was taught in African schools as African folklore. There was severe debate as to whether there was anything called African history. All that was taught throughout Nigerian schools and universities during the colonial and early post-independence periods was European history. Most Nigerian students who studied history at these periods were limited to European history. It was not until the end of the civil war in 1970 that African history was formally introduced into the curricula of Nigerian schools and universities. African philosophy was never taught in any Nigerian university until the 1980s. One of the greatest achievements of the Ibadan School of African history was thus the introduction of African history as a teachable curriculum throughout Nigerian universities. Following this achievement, *Tarikh* emerged as a frontline journal for disseminating research on African history.

In literature, a lively debate centred on the relevance of indigenous languages and orature occurred. In philosophy, extensive studies were carried out on indigenous systems of knowledge and thought. Various African stakeholders took a frontline position in the attempt at underwriting an African influence and presence on the performance of African studies.

The major spur for the success of this struggle was the establishment of postcolonial universities across the continent. The establishment of such universities – Makerere in East Africa as well as Ibadan and Legon in West Africa – provided the focus for a new school of academic historians. In Nigeria, for example, Kenneth O. Dike, as professor and first Nigerian Head of the Department of History at the University of Ibadan, Ibadan, Nigeria, served as the first President of the Historical Society of Nigeria – founded in 1955 – and became the leading inspiration for Ibadan school of African history. Through the influence of their pioneering works, A. E. Afigbo, E. A. Ayandele, Jacob F. A. Ajayi, Kenneth O. Dike, Obaro Ikime and Saburi Biobaku – all of the University of Ibadan, Ibadan, Nigeria – exercised intellectual leadership within that school. Their works also became some of the leading models for constructing the new anti-imperialist historiography of the continent. Dike was noted to have established the National Archives of Nigeria in 1954 to take custody of all public records in Nigeria (Alagoa 1986, 189–96).

The first generation of African scholars was concerned with proving that Africans have their rich repositories of cultures and that African history is a viable academic discipline. We owe that generation of African scholars a lot. In that category we must include such luminaries as anthropologists like Archie Mafeje and Maxwell Owusu; geographers like Akinola Mabogunje and Simeon Ominde; historians like Adu Boahen, B. A. Ogot, Jacob F. A. Ajayi and Kenneth O. Dike; language authorities like A. C. Jordan; literary giants like Chinua Achebe, Christopher Okigbo, Ezekiel Mphalele, Ngugi wa Thiong'o, Okot pBitek, Ousmane Sambene, Oluwole Soyinka and political scientists like Ali A. Mazrui, Billy J. Dudley, Claude Ake and Martin Kilson in the African diaspora. That generation made a lasting impact in professional worlds hitherto dominated by European expatriates. It reinterpreted the colonial period of African history as one in which Africans struggled to exercise a will of their own independent of the actions and policies of the colonial authorities. At a time when Africa was most misrepresented, it also gave African studies an energised sense of direction and a lead in what is today called 'local ownership' (Nyong'o 2004).

It worked hard to counter the prevailing hierarchical and racist discourses about the continent within the Euro-American academies. This decolonising project embraced insights from other disciplines. It also enjoyed commendable collaboration with and support from Basil Davidson, Claude Meillasoux, Lennart Wohlgemuth, Thomas Hodgkin and other eminent Africanists across the world. The efforts of members of this generation led to the emergence of various schools – in Dakar, Dar es Salaam, Ibadan and Zaria – that challenged received wisdom about the continent's past. Thus, within the first three decades of its existence – the 1950s into the 1970s – African studies was marked by an intense struggle to assert itself as an entirely new field across the continent.

While the development of African studies took root during its early years as a new and radical area of specialisation, and was rapidly distinguished from conventional historical preoccupations as they existed, by the 1980s and the 1990s, the crisis of higher education and the simultaneous drain of talents from universities in Africa to European and North American centres of research and teaching accelerated. There thus began a new round of discussions on the future of the field. These discussions were enriched by the large number of new generation of highly qualified African scholars that entered into the production of African studies in the West. Such reflections recurred alongside several efforts targeted at transforming the continent as a basis for defining the central issues and also for mapping the terrain of such struggles.

As Adebayo Olukoshi (2006, 534) recounted, following the East-West Cold War, as Western foreign policy concerns reorganised towards the end of the 1980s, the initial global decline in area studies produced a distinct set of challenges and concerns about the changing focus and future of African studies. In response to such developments, some institutions, especially in Europe and North America merged African studies with Black studies, while others entirely closed down their programmes in the face of dwindling funding opportunities. Arguably, the post-Cold War decline of African studies was not unconnected to the irrelevance of much of the policy as well as research outputs of the leading Africanist community to the policy establishments in the West.

In fact, as Stephen Ellis (1996) and Crawford Young (2004) have argued, the post-Cold War period witnessed a noted decline in attention and focus on Africa. This much is attested to by the historical literature on the continent. During the decade of African independence, which coincided with the apogee of the Cold War, the new state became a battlefield for the capitalist and communist blocs; and the two global ideological blocs also competed, maximally for the affiliation of the state in Africa, or minimally to pre-empt any possible alignment with the other bloc (Cooper 2006, 159–61). By contrast, the 1980s was marked by a shift in focus away from the continent. Two factors explain this shift away from the continent. Internally, symptoms of structural crisis were already evident in rather pronounced proportions across Africa. The major factors identified as the sources of this crisis were policy options which concentrated all development activities in the state. Added with the combination of economic mismanagement and adverse global trends, far from a development-oriented integral state, what emerged on the continent was an extravagantly personalising power, exemplified by the rapturous encomium paid to political leaders and state officials. This ushered in a paradigm shift in development economics, with the Washington Consensus taking shape within the international financial institutions and much of the donor community touting the supremacy of the market. Margaret Thatcher and Ronald Reagan aggressively advocated an anti-state ethos. This restoration of neoclassical economics to intellectual hegemony forced African countries seeking aid and loan assistance to comply with the reform demands defined by the neoliberal agenda.

Externally, the attention of the major power blocs was attracted to developments within their home countries. In particular, while the major capitalist countries became engrossed with the Gulf War in the Middle East, the Soviet bloc was faced with a deepening economic crisis. As a corollary, the 'new thinking' associated with Mikhail Gorbachev nurtured reluctance for aid commitment towards Africa.

However, following September 11, 2001 and the rise of the 'War on Terror', African studies and area studies generally, which had previously suffered worrisome neglect by the major global policy establishments, were immediately resuscitated. Western geopolitical and strategic calculations rapidly demanded a renewed investment in knowledge production about Africa and other distant and hitherto ignored regions of the world. In particular, the continent's contradictory demographic composition – its abundance of strategic natural resources, its history of civil wars and internecine conflicts, its huge Muslim populations and a host of other disturbing flashpoints – informed the reasoning concerning the huge economic, security and other policy implications of ignoring the continent within the global and more precisely the Western knowledge-driven agenda.

Beyond Africa, the response by the United States of America to the events of September 11, 2001 – including the war in Afghanistan and Iraq – brought upon the world an unprecedented understanding of human history in a global context. While the concepts prevailing in the academic community are usually not solely of an academic or scientific relevance (Nnoli 1978, 1), prior to the attacks on New York and Washington and the subsequent intervention by the United States in the Middle East, most people had understood globalisation and world history as mere academic concepts. However, with these developments, they now understand them as realities shaping our everyday experience and existence. The immediate pressures of the here and now as well as those of the foreseeable future compel us to seek a more certain and expansive understanding of the past and the entire world holistically and integrally. Most importantly, the idea of globalisation is now a pressing reality on the lives of all nations affecting the domestic security of their citizens; their deployment of armed forces; the environment and increasingly their standards of living.

The acknowledgement that we have now reached a new era in world history in which no active citizen or educated person can productively escape the necessity of understanding the past in global terms; the realisation that the historical experiences together with the moral, political and religious values of the different civilisations of the world in the past can impact on – and indeed actively shape the course of the future – and the supersonic emergence of China as a much weightier player in the post-

Cold War and post-September 11 world, and as its quest for resources began to translate into extensive forays into Africa and its construction of various geostrategic alliances across the continent, all explain the revival of African studies and area studies scholarship throughout the world.

Regretfully, notwithstanding the efforts made by Africans towards decolonising African studies, the field remains deeply hierachised between Africans and their Africanist counterparts. Questions impinging on the epistemological orientation of the field continue to be posed within historically determined asymmetries of power underlying North-South relations. While such questions are important in terms of the weight of their implications, when posed by Africans they are glibly and lightly dismissed as a one-sided claim to an entitlement culture anchored on an imagined ideology of authenticity and nativism which inexorably results into parochialism. Africa is yet to be accepted – like the West – as a living subject of history whose peoples in their daily struggles for freedom and progress, are the true makers of their destinies. As yet, also, the pursuit of African studies by Africans, has not achieved the production of non-hierarchical North-South dialogue. More so, the underlining motive propelling research within the field is meant to serve non-African needs, especially that of decoding Africa and Africans for the world and not vice versa.

The dominant perception of Africa as a lifeless object, whose populations – governors and governed alike – constitute a permanent enigma for which the Africanist is the only expert and legitimate interpreter, remains. Given these realities, the task of working Africa's destiny out of its inherited Eurocentric mode of cognition remains an uncompleted project.

Two positions are clear from our examination of the field of African studies. One, far from being subservient, the intellectual tradition of African scholarship has historically been and continues to be largely progressive and radical, especially in terms of its orientation. It has not been defined entirely by conventional and obedient discipline-based academic study. Rather, being shaped by and having responded to significant challenges and inspirations in the eras of anticolonial, nationalist and pan-African struggles for freedom and self-determination, it has been a critical tradition premised on an ethic of freedom and a search for the ideational basis of that freedom. It holds itself accountable, not to any particular class, gender, institution or regime, but to the collective imagination and interests of the ordinary people. By challenging and subverting the constraints of dominant as well as received disciplinary approaches and paradigms; it seeks to be politically responsible and socially relevant in more than a liberal or neutral sense. It is therefore, guided by an ethic that simultaneously challenges and requires scholars in the continent to be grounded in and identified within the broader landscape of Africa's democracy and liberation movements.

Two, while the ethical foundations of this scholarship have been conceptualised, framed and understood by the considerations of endogeny, epistemology, identity, methodology and ontology, and, while Africa's radical intellectuals have engaged and pursued anti-imperialist ethics of self-reconstitution for the people, the liberatory dividends and other promises of the anticolonial pasts and nationalist eras are far from being delivered (see Mama 2007). Consequently, the bias and negative imagery of Eurocentric historical theories in their application to Africa has continued, as has the search for alternative intellectual perspectives and the development of counter-hegemonic knowledges for discursively reconstituting the continent.

Conclusion

It remains to reflect on the theoretical assumptions underlining our formulations. To wit, what are the implications of critiquing the operations of Eurocentricism within the field of African studies and knowledge production on the continent generally? To conclude the critique of Eurocentricism is not necessarily to have the last word in this regard. Such an expectation is at best a mirage. It seems to me much less appropriate to talk about finishing the critique of Eurocentricism. This is mainly because history itself is continually in the making and there is always a lot in the telling and retelling of the past. History writing therefore, can neither assert any finality nor impose fixities. It cannot also insist on any oracular form. Since problems will perpetually continue to arise, to finish the critique of Eurocentricism is therefore, to continuously put to question the very epistemes within which Eurocentric assumptions are produced across various disciplinary spaces in relation to non-metropolitan cultures. In Jacques Derrida's (1978) formulation, to advance the critique of Eurocentricism is to continuously embrace the necessity of using the master's tools as a basis for dismantling the master's house. This suggests using Western epistemes as intellectual bases and premises for critiquing the operations of imperial thought or Western power, especially in their application to non-Western societies.

More seriously, to overstretch the idea of finishing the critique of Eurocentricism within African studies is to follow Derrida uncritically. Derrida (1978) argues that to actually finish the critique of Eurocentricism, one must write one's destiny and existence beyond it as well as out of it. This is not entirely possible. For example, if it is patriarchy that produces the female–male dichotomies; animating feminism or fighting for womanhood, one is simply operating within the epistemic mode of patriarchy. Under such a circumstance, not much epistemological transformation is possible. Similarly, if it is racism that constructs and produces the human as black, coloured and white, as one struggles to animate blackness, one is simply valorising and working within the epistemic frameworks constructed by racism and thus reinforcing racism rather than subverting it.

To question and subvert the operations of imperial thought, especially in relation to the post-Enlightenment construction of binaries – Black/White, East/West, female/male – distinction is not to entirely surpass or hope to permanently transcend the underlining contradictions, but to continuously historicise and problematise – in other words, continuously put to question – the very representations and structures of power that deny the capacity of subordinated populations to express their freedom and represent themselves within the prevailing system of injustice. With reference to African studies, this should be done in relation to Immanuel Kant's answer to the question, 'What is the Enlightenment?' (1991)[43] While the aim should be to come to terms with those scripts that produced us, in doing this, taking the African seriously while accounting for the crudeness of one's formulations within the field, is the unfinished task of African studies.

African criticisms of the West often ignore the fact that the very canons and epistemes deployed in advancing such critiques are produced within the epistemic frameworks of Western intellectual thought. This should not be surprising. As Dipesh Chakrabarty (2000, 6) has made clear, although European thought has a contradictory relationship to Africa and other instances of non-metropolitan cultures, it is nevertheless indispensable for developing the social sciences and knowledge production generally on the continent. This is the relationship existing between the East and the West. Notwithstanding the inadequacy of Western social sciences in accounting for the transformations taking place across Africa, scholars on the continent cannot develop their vocations without drawing from the paradigms emanating from the West. Eurocentricism thus produces us as irredeemably universalists. This dependence is a major legacy of the post-Enlightenment thought for postcolonial societies generally.

Intellectual thought in the East, therefore betrays a characteristic element of self-contradiction. An urge to emphasise the differences of indigenous knowledge, local and national culture from that of the West conflicts with a simultaneous aspiration towards modernity definable only in terms of the post-Enlightenment rationalism of European culture. Nationalism thus sings the glory of the national culture as it is simultaneously anguished by a perceived backwardness of the nation. The axioms and frameworks of knowledge that nationalist thought employs are no different from those employed by colonial rulers (Chakrabarty 1987, 1137–8). Intellectual thought in the continent thus unwittingly accepts and adopts the same essentialist conceptions based on the distinctions between the East and the West; the same typology created by a transcendent studying subject and hence the same objectifying procedures of knowledge constructed in the post-Enlightenment age of Western science (Chatterjee 1986, 38). Far from being independent, intellectual thought and knowledge production on Africa therefore exist within a borrowed and constrained framework. This dilemma is a product of the history of the East and somehow, the reality about its destiny. Hence the Derridean position in postcolonial theory that colonialism led colonial and postcolonial societies into irretrievable pasts and paths.

The acquisition of formal sovereignty by postcolonial societies in the latter half of the twentieth century appeared to have affirmed their determination not to allow the imperial powers continually point to an empirical deviation from the norm and declare an exception in relation to the universal normative standard. Following independence, however, successive postcolonial regimes have adopted the same norm-deviation as well as norm-exception paradigms for governing their populations. Popular politics has also revolved around the same paradigms, thus inviting governmental authorities to declare an exception and suspend the norm in their case. Under these circumstances, the questions that pervade postcolonial politics in Africa and other regions of the South today are: What exactly constitutes the exception and the norm? Who should actually declare them? Who is best elected to speak for these societies? And, is it possible to imagine and think of modern politics outside the norm-deviation and norm-exception paradigms (Chatterjee 2011, 25–6)? These questions are hardly thinkable today outside the domain of the universal conception of the modern. In the next chapter, we discuss Claude Ake's scholarship and works as an instantiation of some of the Africa-driven interventions within the field of African studies.

Notes

1. For Jacques Derrida, as much as for Michel Foucault, context plays a major regulative role in determining meaning.

2. On the archaeology of knowledge, see Michel Foucault (1973) and Chris Horrocks and Zoran Jevtic (2009).

3. Although some of the questions posed in this paragraph have been raised earlier in chapter one of this book, they particularly have further relevance here. Hence I have raised them here again.

4. For an articulation of this position, see Bogumil Jewsiewicki (1987; 1989, 1–5).

5. These questions are compelling given Edward W. Said's (1978) argument that there is no discursive basis for problematising independence or even for speaking about subjectivity in Africa without colonialism.

6. This is literarily translated to mean a dispute; an injustice or a wrong; which cannot really be resolved mainly because there is no external point of view from which the opposing claims put forward can be judged.

7. For a detailed understanding of 'différance', see Jacque Derrida (1967; 1978). On 'différend', see Jean-François Lyotard (1979; 1983).

8. See Partha Chatterjee (1994, 30–4) and Archie Mafeje (2000, 66–71).

9. For a critique of the Africanist disposition in this regard, see Abubakar Momoh (2003).

10. A foremost – and by no means the only – attempt in this direction is Archie Mafeje (1976).

11. For an expansive account of these achievements and early civilisations as well as how they fit into the sweep of history, see Albert Craig et al (2008, 4–45).

12. Charles S. B. Montesquieu's (1748) *Spirit of law* (*Esprit des lois*) is the main work in which this position is famously articulated.

13. François-Marie Arouet, better known as Voltaire, was especially known for his satirical novella *Candide*. He described freedom as entailing the ability 'to reason correctly and know the rights of man'. According to him, when these rights are well known, they are possibly well defended. In his (1734) *Philosophical letters on the English*, Voltaire discussed the works of John Locke (1632–1704) and Isaac Newton (1643–1727) and expressed admiration for British liberties – in contrast to the autocracy of the ancien régime in his native France. See Ian Crofton (2011, 104–5).

14. Jean-Jacques Rousseau championed the primacy of individual feeling and strongly opposed rationalism. In his (1749) *The arts and sciences*, and his (1755) *Equality*, arguing that social progress had helped to corrupt human nature, Rousseau challenged basic Enlightenment beliefs and railed against inequality and moral decadence. In his

(1761) *La Nouvelle Héloïse*, and *Emile* (1762), Rousseau tapped into a profound vein of *sentimentalism*, which soon made him the doyen of the chattering classes. See Adam Hart-Davis (2007, 270–1).

15. In addition to his demonstration of the economic advantages of the division of labour, Adam Smith also upheld the role of self-interest in the creation of a new wealthier society.

16. In his *Crimes and punishments*, Cesare Beccaria (1764) expounded the principle behind the modern operations of criminal law.

17. Francis Bacon was famous for his development of the scientific method based on experimentation and observation.

18. John Locke contributed immensely to the development of empiricism – hinged on the acceptance of knowledge based on direct experience. He was also central to the development of the political theory based on the social contract.

19. Isaac Newton (1643–1727) is widely known for his unifying scientific discoveries and laws.

20. A famous articulation of the modernisation thesis is Walt W. Rostow (1960).

21. For a seminal critique in this direction, see Fredric Jameson (2002).

22. See Archie Mafeje (1976). For an earlier account on this position, see Talal Asad (1973).

23. For further illustrations on this position, see Roger Sanjek (1993).

24. For example, pay attention to J. M. Hobson (2004), G. Bhambra (2007), B. Shilliam (2009), A. Acharya and B. Buzan (2010) and R. Duchesne (2011).

25. See Frankfurt Research Centre for Postcolonial Studies (2011).

26. For illustrations on this analysis and how various African and Asian populations realised that 'the accommodation and received constructions of their pasts' had no connection with their actual realities, see Amitav Ghosh and Dipesh Chakrabarty (2002, 160–3).

27. For an account on how such practices have continued into postcolonial histories, see 'Colonial difference as postcolonial difference', in Partha Chatterjee (1994, 32–4).

28. I understand 'normative Western political theory', following Partha Chatterjee (2011, 3) as the corpus of writings, chiefly in English, French and German, representing liberal thought and currently dominating the academy and general public discourse in all contemporary democracies throughout the world. On the appropriation of morality in the articulation of postcolonial politics, see Raymond Geuss (2008).

29. Amitav Ghosh's (2002, 156–8) query here, is directed at Dipesh Chakrabarty's (2000, 4) position that: 'The phenomenon of 'political modernity' – namely the rule by modern institutions of the state, bureaucracy, and capitalist enterprise – is impossible to 'think' of anywhere in the world without invoking certain categories and concepts, the genealogies of which go deep into the intellectual and even theological traditions of Europe. Concepts such as citizenship, the state, civil society, public sphere, human rights, equality before the law, the individual, distinctions between public and private, the idea of the subject, democracy, popular sovereignty, social justice, scientific rationality, and so on all bear the burden of European thought and history. One simply cannot think of political modernity without these and other related concepts that found a climatic form in the course of the European Enlightenment and the nineteenth century.' These concepts entail an unavoidable – and in a sense indispensable – universal and secular vision of the human. The European colonizer of the nineteenth century both preached this Enlightenment humanism at the colonized and at the same time denied it in practice. But the vision has been powerful in its effects. It has historically provided a strong foundation on which to erect – both in Europe and outside – critiques of socially unjust practices. Marxist and liberal thought are legatees of this intellectual heritage. This heritage is now global... Modern social critiques of caste, oppressions of women, the lack of rights for laboring and subaltern classes ... and so on – and, in fact, the very critique of colonialism itself – are unthinkable except as a legacy, partially, of how Enlightenment Europe was appropriated.

30. My analysis of the South African experience, in this work, draws on Lungisile Ntsebeza (2012).

31. The 'native question' in South Africa was posed by the dilemma of a foreign minority ruling over an indigenous majority. This question preoccupied the colonialists and became a subject of much serious discussion when moves were afoot for establishing the Union of South Africa in 1910. For a detailed account of this question, see Mahmood Mamdani (1996).

32. On the year of his assumption of duty in 1921, the government grant was further cut by half from 3000 to 1500 British pounds. See Ntsebeza (2012, 6).

33. As R. Gordon (1990, 22) recounted, Radcliffe-Brown left the School in a disturbing state of disarray – without any meaningful succession plan – under the leadership of his erstwhile research assistant, A. J. H. Goodwin, who became an acting professor and two postgraduate students as temporary replacements. By 1933, eight years after the resignation of Radcliffe-Brown, the then Principal of the University of

Cape Town, Sir Carruthers Beattie, was to confide to his old friend C. T. Loram as follows: 'At present I look upon the school as our worst effort. We were unfortunate in many ways in getting Radcliffe-Brown – a careerist – and Norton – a fool. I have taken on my job for another three years. One of the objects will be to pull this school together or get rid of it.'

34. Mahmood Mamdani was appointed as the A. C. Jordan Professor of African Studies at the University of Cape Town in September of 1996 and then as Director of its Centre for African Studies in early 1997. See Mahmood Mamdani (1998, 1).

35. See the contributions in the 1998 issue of *Social Dynamics: A Journal of African Studies* 24(2).

36. Following Lungisile Ntsebeza's appointment into these positions, this author was also appointed as A. C. Jordan Fellow of African Studies at the Centre for African Studies, University of Cape Town.

37. For detailed accounts on the influence of colonial attitudes in the development of African studies in Nigeria, see Jacob F. Ade Ajayi and Tekena N. Tamuno (1973), Pierre L. Van den Berghe (1973) and Bolanle Awe (2000, 79–95). For examples on other African countries, see the contributions in the 2014 special section of *Social Dynamics: A Journal of African Studies* 40(2), on 'African studies and knowledge production in the universities in postcolonial Africa'.

38. As Adebayo Olukoshi (2006, 536) noted in the particular case of African studies, such responses included the formal establishment of (i) centres and institutes of African studies in Europe and North America, (ii) development cooperation institutes, and (iii) university colleges, with their pioneer staff including a significant number of former colonial district and provincial officials.

39. Several examples suffice here. *African Studies* published in England by Taylor and Francis on behalf of the University of the Witwatersrand, Johannesburg, South Africa, formerly known as *Bantu Studies* is a notable example.

40. An example of such imperial accounts is the British depiction of King Hintsa – and other indigenous South African rulers – as treacherous and unreliable savages. For a detailed account of such misrepresentations, see Premesh J. Lalu (2009).

41. On the validity of oral sources for history writing on Africa, see the works of members of the Ibadan school on African history. See in particular, Kenneth O. Dike (1958). On the limitations of oral sources for history writing generally, see Sarah Nuttall and Carli Coetzee (1998), Luise White et al (2001), Ciral Shahid Rassool (2004, 12–45; and 51–96) as well as Leslie Witz and Ciral Shahid Rassool (2008).

42. Examples of some early works which sought to deconstruct the operations of imperial historiography on the continent include Kenneth O. Dike (1958), E. A. Ayandele (1966), J. D. Fage (1969), Martin J. Legassick (1974), M. Kaniki (1980) and Henry Slater (1981). For a much recent account on the same theme, see Premesh J. Lalu (2009).

43. Kant's essay under this title was first published in the *Berlinische Monatsschrift* in December 1784.

The contribution of Claude E. Ake

Wherever colonisation is a fact, the indigenous culture begins to rot and among the ruins something begins to be born which is condemned to exist on the margin allowed it by the European culture.

— Steve Biko 1973, 200

This chapter examines Claude Ake's contribution to the African debate on South-driven initiatives on (i) endogenous development, (ii) nation-building, (iii) political integration and (iv) state reconstruction. In drawing on Ake's works on these issues, I focus mainly on homegrown discourses on Africa's pathway towards actualising autonomous capitalist or socialist development as well as the responsibilities of African social scientists in their engagements with their crafts in this regard. This is distinct from the idea of embracing neo-modernisation prescriptions. In the overall quest towards attaining the much needed epistemic autonomy within the social sciences community in Africa, examining homegrown discourses is a compelling initial step. Its merit is its commitment towards valorising the scholarship of relevant African thinkers on such themes. Without any doubt, Claude Ake is an important figure within the social sciences community in Africa whose works deserve such scholarly attention. This is the task of this chapter. Following this introduction, the chapter is divided into five sections. The first considers Ake's contribution to the theme of endogeneity in knowledge production on Africa. The second discusses his corpus on nation building in Africa. The third evaluates his works on political integration in Africa. The fourth examines his thesis on state reconstruction in the continent, while the fifth provides the conclusion.

On endogeneity in knowledge production

This section discusses Claude Ake's contribution to the enterprise of knowledge production on Africa. Given his advocacy of the need to reconstruct existing disciplinary fields following uniquely African critiques and interpretations, the chapter presents Ake's works as a corrective intervention to Eurocentricism and advocates the practice of 'cross cultural nonhierarchical dialogue' in which neither the North nor the South is taken as the epistemological paradigm or universe against which 'the Other' is measured and pronounced inadequate. It examines his critique of the Western social sciences in their application to Africa. One of his major works, *Social science as imperialism: The theory of political development* (Ake 1979) is discussed in the light of his critique of expatriate social sciences and his conception of the conditions for recreating and reinventing the social sciences in Africa as a unified body of knowledge relevant for speaking to social realities on the continent. As such, the making of Ake's career and scholarship as well as the other developments and issues which influenced different aspects and periods of his thought are matters that will not be treated here. These have been examined in chapter two of this book. Instead, his contribution to endogenous development using endogenous knowledge and the social sciences in Africa in particular, through his critique of the Western social sciences as well as the limitations of his efforts in that regard are the focus of analysis in this chapter. The aim is to establish some of Ake's contributions and insights that are relevant for the autochthonous transformation of the state in Africa.

There is a marked difference between endogenous knowledge and the quest for endogenous development. Endogenous knowledge is a philosophical exploration and is concerned with autochthonous considerations regarding African knowledge systems – at epistemological and ontological levels. In several instances, such as Benin, Nigeria and South Africa, what is often characterised as endogenous knowledge is usually meant to refer to indigenous knowledge systems. In the fields of medicine and organic chemistry, for example, explorations in endogenous knowledge would involve exploring the bio-chemical structures and curative efficacies of local herbal and medicinal therapies. Philosophically, such ventures into endogenous African knowledges would be concerned with their epistemological efficacies as part of much wider philosophical explorations.

On the other hand, endogenous development – the preoccupation of Claude Ake – refers to Africa's autonomous efforts at development, grounded in its endogenous culture and local resources; representing a marked shift from the current situation to a desired state, especially one rooted in the intangible and tangible aspects of the continent's local resources. In the language of the Lagos Plan of Action (1980), this entails ensuring that Africa can actually internalise its engine of growth. While the intangible resources – including endogenous knowledge – may be deployed in the process of driving endogenous development, this is not necessarily the case. It was also not a preoccupation for Claude Ake. Furthermore, while the concerns and sensibilities that drove his works – like much of his contemporaries – were inspired by distinctly African viewpoints, his corpus can hardly be described as an exploration in endogenous knowledge. In addition to Claude Ake, Joseph Ki-Zerbo, Paulin Hountondji and Olujimi O. Adesina are important authorities in interrogating the epistemological imperatives of endogenous knowledge and its significance for endogenous development across the continent. Their works have also been largely concerned with the issue of endogeneity in the social sciences in Africa. It was Joseph Ki-Zerbo who established the critical link between endogenous knowledge and endogenous development. Paulin Hountondji (1997) sought to grasp in philosophical terms the constituents and relevance of endogenous systems in Benin. It was Hountondji who contrasted such intellectual efforts with extraversions, namely, Africa and African social scientists being locked up in subordinate positions of suppliers of data within the global system of knowledge production. Building on Archie Mafeje, Joseph Ki-Zerbo and Paulin Hountondji, it was Olujimi O. Adesina who made the distinction between endogenous knowledge – as source codes – and endogeneity – as a mode of social sciences practice and as an imperative for the social sciences community in Africa – if it is to secure its needed epistemic autonomy. The idea of taking one's local – ethnographic – data seriously, on its own terms and sufficiently to engender epistemic ruptures in the dialogue with the global social sciences – was developed by Adesina (2002; 2006) over the years.

As we noted in chapter one, Claude Ake was one of the first generation of post-independence African academics trained in the United States of America, meant to be the intellectual shock-troops of the United States' project across the continent. His doctoral dissertation – from Columbia

University in 1966 – published as *A theory of political integration* (1967) is as mainstream from the right as it could get. His middle scholarship signalled by his second book, *Revolutionary pressures in Africa* (1978), was in a sense a rejection of his early scholarship and an atonement for his ideological naivety. It reflects his 'voluntary re-education' at the University of Dar es Salaam in the 1970s. *Revolutionary pressures in Africa* is in many ways a work of apprenticeship in Marxist scholarship – overtly tentative and trenchant. By contrast, *The feasibility of democracy in Africa*, published posthumously in 2000 by CODESRIA, Dakar, presents a confident and mature scholar with a magisterial command of his subject matter. It reflects Ake's late scholarship.

Epistemologically, Ake's works are broadly Marxian – at least his post-Dar es Salaam productions (Arowosegbe 2010).[1] To that extent, such works are best located within the wider post-Enlightenment European discourse. Put together, they constitute an articulated negation of imperialism in the same way that Marx's works represent a negation of capitalism. Nevertheless, such works are broadly located within European archives. Far from being a critique of Ake. Rather, it is about making a distinction between much of the anti-colonial literature or postcolonial scholarship on Africa and what would count for ventures in endogenous knowledge at an epistemic level. Paulin Hountondji's (1997) distinction between African philosophy and ethnophilosophy is perhaps a useful illustration of this distinction. For Hountondji (1997) African philosophy is constituted by the philosophical works of African philosophy scholars. What he calls ethnophilosophy – content rather than authorial – or sometimes more generously referred to as philosophical literature – will be later understood as aspects of endogenous knowledge (Hountondji 1997). The problem, however, is that aspects of what Hountondji conceives of as African philosophy could be works of extensions, mimicry and repetitions of philosophical outputs from the European intellectual archives and may have nothing to do with the African archives. In other words, they could involve African philosophy scholars enunciating Western philosophical treatises.

Another illustration of this position could be gleaned from Samuel Huntington's (1993, 1996) Clash of civilisations. For the dominant Western imperial powers, especially the United States of America, the Cold War was a battle fought within the same civilisation. Hence the adversaries were mutually intelligible. In the post-Cold War context, Huntington's thesis is that the conflicts will be between impulses, narratives and values that derive from different civilisations. Applied to this study, Ake's politics and works – as with the Marx inspired Cold War adversaries of the West – are intelligible to his imperial adversaries, in the same ways that the Mau Mau or Maji Maji rural uprisings were not. These would be distinct politics and value systems animated and shaped by different barbarisms or civilisations – as they were presented at the time – endogenous knowledge, belief and value systems. Without diminishing the value of Ake's scholarship, these are compelling considerations, which any serious scholarship on Ake ought to acknowledge. Valorising Ake's scholarship should not involve an uncritical adulation or a repetition, which might rather insult his criticality and openness to vigorous debate. Besides, extending the values of scholars' works ought to involve a critical engagement with their body of works.[2] The final clarification here is that, endogenous development is not the only area of focus of Claude Ake's works. Covering a complex range of issues, the scope of Ake's corpus is broad. Such issues have also attracted numerous attentions within the African and Africanist communities.[3]

Ake's concern is with the gamut of efforts meant to adapt and develop within the African contexts – development, policymaking and research institutions – what he refers to as the 'universal principles of science'. Although I do not disagree with his overall position and sentiment on this; what I dispute are his universalist claims for what are essentially Western sense making and technologies of science. As such, although they are located in an emancipatory politics and scholarship, Ake's works are best understood as using the European library for speaking and writing back to Empire from a uniquely African viewpoint. Epistemologically, doing that does not qualify his scholarship as an exploration in 'endogenous African knowledge'. In the broader sense, one needs to understand him as using the weapons of the adversaries for confronting them as well as for liberating oneself. While such works are driven by distinctly African location and sensibilities; their epistemic premise is clearly Marxian. Ake's problem with the Western social sciences is what he characterises as their 'imperialist character and dimensions'. His proposition is to exorcise the attitudes of mind which they inculcate. However, rather than ignoring or transcending Marxism, the alternative, for Claude Ake, is provided within the Marxist epistemic framework.

The major issue which he engages here is the question of how knowledge appropriated and developed by Africans on the basis of their historical experiences can be valorised for empowering the state in the pursuit of democracy and development (Ake n.d., 2). The pertinence of his intervention is timely, especially now when the continent's intellectual and political leadership has declared itself in search of a suitable framework for achieving an all-embracing continental renaissance. His *Social science as imperialism: The theory of political development* (Ake 1979) radically questions from the perspective of colonial and postcolonial societies, the profound epistemological transformations which 'the advent of theory' supposedly brought about. Dealing with the Western political science scholarship on the developing countries and the literature on political development in particular, Ake engages with one of the most pernicious albeit subtle forms of imperialism – imperialism in the guise of scientific knowledge and establishes its practical significance for development (Ake 1979, i–iv).

He takes a critical stance toward Continental theoretical discourses from Africa's point of view and exposes the Eurocentric assumptions undergirding the most avant-garde writings to emerge on the continent from the developed world.[4] He advances a critical reconstitution and rethinking of our fields' intellectual genealogies in ways that depart from the constricting narratives of disciplinary origins and originality received from the West. Focusing on the theory of political development, he opposes those Western versions of history which claim for themselves totality of knowledge on Africa. Yet, in keeping with social scientific ideals, he also reveals his own commitment to uncovering an apparently deeper level of truth. He demonstrates with copious evidence how the models earlier imported from Europe – Marxism, a belief in modernity and progress, a commitment to revolution as forward-looking, linear developmentalist transformation – are now increasingly in doubt.

His aim was not to reshape 'the modern African left' through transcending the classical university-based African Marxism of the 1960s and 1970s – as some scholars are wont to suggest, although this was achieved to some extent. Rather, his task was to contribute towards recreating 'the social sciences in Africa' as a unified body of knowledge relevant for speaking to social realities on the continent. On the ideological character of the theory of political development, Ake says its central position within the Western social sciences scholarship is not fortuitous (Ake 1979, 60–98). He traces its emergence to the winning of formal independence by the colonies in the atmosphere of the Cold War – a development – which some felt would jeopardise the vital interests of the colonising powers. In these circumstances, Ake argues, the interests of the major Western powers required the preservation of the fledgling peripheral capitalist states which they had nurtured from the penetrating influence of the Soviet Union. Corresponding to the need to preserve the West's hegemony across the world, the theory of political development thus emerged as the ideological tool for maintaining the existing world order under changing conditions that preserve liberal democratic values as the political correlate of capitalism. Ake says given its historical context and continuing partisan character, the theory of political development and more broadly, the Western social science scholarship 'in its application to postcolonial societies' is 'bourgeois ideology' (Ake 1979, i–iv). It has no scientific status. It is neither applicable to the South nor useful for understanding it.[5] At best, he says it merely fosters capitalist institutions and values; and legitimises the consolidation of the dictatorship of the Third World bourgeoisie, who are the willing allies of international capitalism (Ake 1979, 60–1). Given its orientations and value assumptions, he says, it studies Africa after the images of the North. It shows the persistent gaps and lacuna that the continent must overcome to finally reach 'the promised land of democracy and development; of economic prosperity and social progress'. This way, Ake contends, it constructs the continent's history in terms of 'a historical lack' by underlining what more is perpetually needed to make democracy work – industrialisation, institutionalisation, modernisation, the development of the civic community, civil society, social capital – and other recipes which seek to replicate in the political sphere (Rostow 1960). Ake deals with these issues with instructive effects.

According to him, it is incorrect and supercilious to claim that some ideas need to be treated as universally worthy and that their spread across the world is purely positive. In validating this position, he illustrates several strategic moments when particular interests of popular politics mobilised as community interests expose the limits of political universals that liberalism poses as sacred. In doing this, he offers an exposition of his transcontinental epistemological engagement with the questions of democracy and development in Africa. In his critique of members of the Princeton Series on Political Development, Ake tackles the liberal claim that the nation-state as the most legitimate form of the political community has been instrumental in creating some positive values – such as citizenship and the equality of rights – and making them acceptable and applicable across cultural and historical boundaries (Ake 1979, 12–59). According to him, while the modern nation-state recognises the nation as the only homogeneous and legitimate form of community, actual politics across the world gives rise to various heterogeneous collectivities that do not necessarily conform to the sovereign demands of the nation-state. This way, he questions the West's universalising assumptions about culture, identity, language and power and the institutional privileging of theoretical knowledge together with the very ontology of 'theory' as a discrete and knowable category of critical engagement.

Ake (1981, 68–87) presents the colonial impact as central for understanding the continent's history. Drawing on Walter Rodney (1972), he defines colonialism as an effective instance of intervention and take over in which local conceptions of space and time as well as pre-colonial modes of self-governance were dismantled; in which a new tradition was invented and presented to colonised populations as sacrosanct, so that in their very act of imagining and understanding themselves, colonial and postcolonial societies could acquiesce in the epistemic and moral legitimacy of European sovereignty and superiority. This way, he rehearses the familiar thesis of the postcolonial predicament by arguing (i) that heterogeneity and hybridity are written into the fabric of the postcolonial experience, and (ii) that there is a relationship of historical continuity however oblique and problematic between colonialism and nationalism. This aspect of Ake's argument is closely linked with Edward W. Said's (1978) position that there is practically no discursive basis for interrogating or writing about nationalism and subjectivity in colonial and postcolonial societies without colonialism. He says in spite of formal independence, the domineering impulse of the West on Africa are still apparent through the operations of the Western social sciences – the ideological apparatuses – which ensure the dependence and underdevelopment of the continent under changing historical conditions. These aspects of Ake's argument also reinforce the debate on postcoloniality. Hence his advocacy for decolonising the social sciences in the South through endogenising the very strategies of knowledge production on the continent.

Ake foregrounds the understanding of his position with an advocacy of the need for endogeneity in knowledge production on Africa. He presents this as the alternative to the continent's dependence on the West in the sphere of knowledge. He observes that Africa is not winning the battle to control its development agenda. To him, this is mainly because the struggle has been misconstrued as a battle over economic and political power. While not underestimating its economic and political dimensions, he argues that the struggle is mainly paradigmatic and that social scientists have a central role to play in this regard. His advocacy of the need for endogeneity in knowledge production on Africa is hinged on the need to transcend the erasures and extroversions that constitute the hallmark of imperial pedagogy. He cautions that failing to achieve this we risk reimporting the very hegemonies we claim to be working hard to overthrow – a failure – which he says must be resisted as a matter of nationalism and professional commitment.

The way out of this epistemic failure, he says, is to develop a form of scholarship which takes its local existential, intellectual and political contexts seriously while also seeking to be globally reputable. He advances this position through his pragmatic belief that all models of social action, modes of thought, paradigms and theories should be contextualised in a manner that enables us transcend the temptation of wrongly generalising from one context to the other without critically considering the specificities of individual case histories and cultures. He argues that far from being universal, the European invention of historical consciousness is only the result of its own perspectival imaginings, just as 'other perspectives' are also implicated in the polemics of their own constructions and positionalities. His aim is to assert the autonomy of South-driven intellectual thought generally through opposing perennially dominant historiographies which resist change and ethico-political persuasions.

He advocates the building of an alternative system of knowledge production based on an appreciation of the different histories which produce the diverse knowledge bases across the world. To him, this is a criterion for transcending the restrictive contexts of knowledge production in the modern world. It was precisely in the struggle to achieve this objective that Ake became a central figure in the movement that gained momentum in the 1970s and 1980s among the progressive forces within the social sciences community in Africa – a movement – which exposed the epistemic shortfalls of Western liberal scholarship and Marxist social sciences in their application to Africa. For Ake, the universality of empirical and theoretical knowledge is only a ruse which should be carefully broken down into distinctive cultural and historical components to be explored and pursued within the frameworks defined by one's cultural milieu and social experiences. In other words, searching for the universals vaguely defined as 'knowledge' or 'the truth' must proceed from an appreciation of one's context, experience and history. An understanding of Ake's aversion to dogma and orthodoxy thus helps us to appreciate his principled rejection of the pluralist, national integration and his modification of the neo-Marxist theories of underdevelopment and dependency in their application to Africa.

His considered solution is hinged on the development of a social science scholarship which in epistemic terms is rooted in its culture and locale to create canons in its own right, especially ones that take the

African policy-making nexus seriously. From this he criticises a major paradox and practice in the continent's universities namely, the idea of deploying and teaching, especially in African policy-making contexts, as 'nomothetic' what is rather 'idiographic' in other contexts. He argues that engaging a social science scholarship that derives the source-codes for its epistemologies from the 'life forms' and 'practices' of its context and people is a requirement for taking the practice of scholarship in Africa beyond its conception as translation or data gathering for 'others' in the global division of intellectual labour. Ake (1979) exposes the inclination of the Western social sciences towards teleological and vivisectomical analyses. He demonstrates and encourages further acknowledgement of the idiographic nature and particularities of the Western social sciences and thought rather than blindly treating them as either 'nomothetic' or 'universal'. He recommends an informed recourse to 'endogeneity' articulated through critical distancing and selective borrowing from other epistemic contexts.

Pitching endogeneity and ontology against the contradictions of Eurocentric extroversion and idiography, Ake challenges us to replace the practice of scholarship in Africa as extroversion and translation with its engagement as an objective reflection of Africanity through a careful reformulation of 'the African condition' and 'self'. While the practice of scholarship as 'translation' involves the articulation of knowledge according to Western academic standards, its 'rearticulation', 'redefinition' and 'reformulation', which Ake advocates, are based on the 'reconstitution' and 'reconstruction' of existing disciplinary fields and vocations following uniquely African critiques and interpretations; through an appreciation of endogeny and ontology as the objective bases of epistemology and philosophy rooted in an understanding of the disciplinary and institutional histories of existing knowledge producing frontiers; inspired by a corrective commitment to reclaim history and rewrite the careless deployment of the ideas of neocolonialism in constructing the African historical imaginaire. Ake is not alone in this advocacy. Rather, being an influential voice, he is complemented on the continent by others whose works have been noted earlier in this work. Taken together, such efforts challenge methodological and theoretical universalisms in expatriate social sciences scholarship on the continent.

Other areas also exist within the African contexts of knowledge production which have been positively affected by Ake's intellectual involvement. To foreground our claim on the relevance of Ake's works espoused here above, the next sections discuss the significance of his thesis on endogenous knowledge production for nation building and autochthonous reconstruction of the state in Africa.

On nation building in Africa

This section discusses the relevance of Claude Ake's political thought for nation building and state formation in Africa. It draws on two notable periods in African history as a basis for instantiating its position on the significance of Ake's political thought for state formation in Africa. The periods under reference are the immediate postindependence as well as the postconflict experiences in post-Cold War Africa. While nation building was an important theme in the historical and theoretical literature on Africa in the immediate postindependence period, Ake offers a seminal treatment of the disintegrative impact of the colonial presence on the emergent states in the continent. As an original contribution for understanding centrifugal pulls and movements of the excluded in postcolonial societies generally, his corpus is an important reading for all historians of Africa, whatever their regional specialisations. Focusing on the experiences of the 'new states' – as they were fondly called at that time – Ake engaged brilliantly with the emergent fissiparous challenges of the period. These had to do with rising conflicts based on postindependence political alliances; the emergence of separatist tendencies; the effects of modernisation on political stability in new and transitional societies; and the impacts of cultural heterogeneity, low regime legitimacy, economic backwardness and the ethnic factor on the continuity of these societies across the newly independent states. With respect to the post-Cold War context, this work highlights the background to the complex web of violent conflicts and wars that ravaged Africa in the 1990s and the challenges posed by the newly won peace to the reconstruction of postconflict states across the regions. The aim is to underline the relevance of Ake's thesis on the need for an autochthonous perspective as a basis for reinventing the state in Africa for the purpose of promoting democracy, development and reintegration.

On political integration in Africa

The historical context of Ake's work on this subject matter is the immediate postindependence period in African history. One of the crucial problems at this time was the integration of the 'new state', which was threatened by strong centrifugal forces. Instability, political conflict and state building thus emerged as important themes in constructing the postcolonial imaginary in Africa at that time. In addition to Claude Ake, other authorities also worked extensively on these themes.[6]

During the 1950s and 1960s – the decade of African independence – many efforts were sunk into attempts at strengthening relevant institutions as a way out of the legacy of conflict, instability and underdevelopment. Several initiatives were also undertaken to unify African countries on a continental and regional scale. The Casablanca and Monrovia groups; the Organisation of African Unity and later the Lagos Plan of Action were all conceived in this light. It was also in this context that Claude Ake carried out his first major study on this subject matter, produced first as a doctoral dissertation in Political Science at Columbia University. New York, at the United States, and later as a number of published academic articles and a book.

Although his concrete discussion is mainly on Africa (see Ake 1966; 1967a; 1967b; 1973 and 1974), however, its potential relevance is broader, particularly for the postcolonial world. And while the historical context of his study was the experiences of the newly independent states in Africa, in laying the groundwork for a general theory, his concern was extended beyond the immediate African experience.

Although Ake offers rigorous analyses on nation building, political integration and state building in Africa, such perspectives have not been sufficiently deployed or reflected in the literature. This is surprising given the heightened concern with these issues in the post-Cold War period in African history. Since the 1990s, fundamental changes have taken place within the state in Africa. Powerful external forces in the industrialised world have exerted considerable influence on events in the continent (Ellis 1996). Africa has also been affected by globalisation and the revolution in communication and information technology, which are rapidly changing the world as a whole. Globalisation has brought about fundamental changes in the conditions of human life. However, the academic literature on globalisation tends to focus more on the specific trends that appear to have pushed the implications and sources of social action beyond state borders.

The end of the Cold War marked the close of an era for Africa in an instructive manner. Although the continent recorded some achievements in democratisation and economic reform, the 1990s overall became the decade of endemic state crisis of an unprecedented magnitude for the continent (Young 2002, 532–57). Epitomised by the erosion of the 'stateness' of many African polities; the renewed salience of informal politics; and an adaptation to diminished state presence and service provision; the post-

Cold War conflict situations in Africa were significantly different from the Cold War experiences in the continent (Hale and Kienle 1997, 1–12; Cooper 2006, 184).

Africa has thus become a conflict zone, with state failure and violence affecting Angola, Burundi, Liberia, Mozambique, Namibia, Nigeria, Rwanda, Sierra Leone and the Congo. The consequences of these conflicts have also been deleterious to the development and security of the continent. In 1996, armed conflicts in Africa accounted for half of all war-related deaths worldwide and resulted in more than 8 million displaced persons, refugees and returnees. Economic growth has continued to elude Africa, with most of the world's heavily indebted and least developed countries also located in the continent. This is not surprising. Countries engaged in conflicts and wars generally have dismal records of socioeconomic growth compared with those at peace (Adejumobi 2001). In Nigeria, violent conflict has crippled oil production; accelerated governance failure and fundamentally inhibited state capacity in the Niger Delta region. The corrupt and rent-seeking orientation of the elite has also driven various ethnic, regional and religious communities into developing subnational conceptions of ethnic citizenship (Joseph 2003, 165). In Sierra Leone, notwithstanding the return to democratic rule, huge problems remain in terms of illicit mining and the smuggling of diamonds, governance weaknesses and regional instability (Grant 2005). These examples underline the continued relevance of the problem of political integration in the post-Cold War period and into the 21st century.

Generalisations about African politics and political systems across the continent have been made difficult by the extent to which African societies both differ from one another and have changed since independence (Allen 1995). Nevertheless, given the context of predatory rule and other familiar stigmas of African politics, anti-state mobilisations have been widespread and have undermined development and state capacity. The unique historical configuration of the postcolony – inherent in the bifurcation of society into two contradictory publics – still underlies many of the political problems in Africa today.[7] The institutions and trajectories of change and power that simultaneously generate the structural dynamics of conflict, political disorder and disruption through a segregated citizenship – laid down in the colonial era – have also not been fundamentally altered (Berman 1998, 307; 318). These realities emphasise the continued relevance of Ake's thesis on the problem of political integration as a template for understanding the impediments to unity in contemporary Africa. Ake describes the emergent political complex in post-Cold War Africa as 'humanitarian emergencies'

(Ake 1996). He says these have been mostly (i) state-centred and hinged on the deployment of state power, (ii) associated with identity claims and identity solidarities if only as ideological representations, and (iii) have been prevalent in those countries which face – in an acute form – the contradictions of capitalist modernity such as dislocations in the economy, power and status hierarchies.

A recapitulation of Ake's thesis on political integration is now in order. Ake's (1967a, 1) study was developed from an analysis of the problem of political integration in the new states to the more general question of their capacity for undertaking social change on a large scale and for withstanding the disruptive impact of such change. His aim was to formulate a theory of the conditions of political integration; engineered large-scale social change; political stability and the relation between the three phenomena.

Drawing on Hans Kohn (1955), Elie Kedourie (1961) and Sidney Verba (1965, 513–23), Ake locates political culture as central to political integration. He adopts Sidney Verba's (1965, 513) definition of political culture as comprising the system of empirical beliefs; expressive symbols and values which defines the situation in which political action takes place; and frames the problem of political integration as one of developing a political culture and of inducing commitment to it. He argues that this problem is a shorthand expression for two other related problems namely a) How to elicit from subjects deference and devotion to the claims of the state; b) How to increase normative consensus governing political behaviour among members of the political system (Ake 1967a, 1).

Some points from Ake's (1967a, 3–4) illustrations on political integration are worth underlining:

A political system is integrated to the extent that the minimal units (individual political actors) develop in the course of political interaction a pool of commonly accepted norms regarding political behavior and a commitment to the political behavior patterns legitimised by these norms. ...

A political system is malintegrated to the extent that political exchanges are not regulated by a normative culture. In malintegrated political systems the emphasis is on effective rather than on legitimate means for pursuing goals; in highly integrated political systems the emphasis is on legitimate rather than on effective means. ...

In a minimally integrated political system – and such a political system can only be an ideal type – the 'subjects' ... obey the rulers not out of a sense of obligation but only because they are obliged to.

Populations in a minimally integrated political system are referred to as 'subjects' and not citizens mainly because such a system of relations is, strictly speaking, 'pre-civil'. Ake's view of political integration leans towards the consensus theory of social integration which sees value consensus as the pervasive character of society and for which the role of coercion in social integration is the subordinate one of controlling deviance. However, a political system held together purely by normative consensus – what one might call optimal integration – is only an ideal type. We know of no political system in the world that does not deploy legitimate coercion in some form or other. Ake refrains from using the term 'national integration' not only because 'nation' suggests a highly integrated human grouping but also because the concept of 'nation' is both controversial and problematic – especially as different writers explain the bond of nationality using different categories, such as a common ancestry, a common culture, history, language, social communication and will.

For Africa, Ake (1967a, 96) defines the problem of political integration as entailing the transformation of a multiplicity of traditional societies into coherent political societies; increasing cultural homogeneity and value consensus; together with eliciting deference and devotion from the individual to the claims of the state.

He identifies 'cleavages in the nationalist movement', 'elite competition', 'cleavages in the social structure' and 'the problems of policy' as major centrifugal forces which impeded integration in these states in the immediate postcolonial period (Ake 1967a, 17–35). The nationalist movement was thrown into colossal disarray by 'the confrontation of special interests' within the nationalist movement; 'the impact of an expanded franchise'; 'conflict based on the weight of imperial diplomacy' and 'the inability of the new government to cope with rising demands by the masses for rapid economic and social development'. At least in the short run, independence brought about popular disenchantment with the nationalist party, partly because of the state's failure to quickly meet the expectations of those who had fought under its banner and partly due to the sacrifices and unpopular measures needed for rapid economic expansion and social development.

Comprising trade unions pressing for higher wages and the ending of racial discrimination; intellectuals angered by their subordination to semiliterate colonial officials; syncretistic movements reacting against the inroads of Christianity into the native culture; traditional authorities smarting from their diminishing influence as well as those who held the colonial government responsible for all social ills, the nationalist movement in Africa was not a united body of people with a common approach to social problems but a coalition of special interests. The manoeuverings by these groups not only undermined the solidarity of the nationalist movement but also stimulated previously politically inarticulate interest groups to seek political influence. At independence there were no common coins of national unity – ethnic, psychological or socioeconomic. There were also no leaders of stature to serve as national symbols, but rather individuals who personified sectarianism. In Sudan the anti-colonialist agitation eventually led to the factionalisation of politics along old ethnic and religious lines. In Ghana ethnic particularism, politically manifested in the National Liberation Movement; the Muslim Association Party and the Northern Peoples Party threatened the supremacy of Nkrumah's Convention Peoples Party. Uganda's National Congress was frightened by the breakaway Uganda Congress Party, which expressed Ganda tribalism. In Kenya, the Kenya African National Union dominated by the Luo, the Kikuyu and other bigger tribes was opposed by the Kenya African Democratic Union, which insisted on the protection of minority rights through a loose federal constitution. In Nigeria, the contentious relations between the majority and minority ethnic groups led to the appointment of a special commission in 1957, to look into ways of allaying minority fears in the country.

Economically, in spite of self-rule, multinational corporations still control the commanding heights of the national economies, while the new bourgeoisie have been more statist than bourgeois. Elite competition was manifested in 'the differences in the ideological orientations of the leaders'; 'the suspicion between professional politicians and alienated intellectuals whose oppositionalism spilled over to the postcolonial regime'; 'the competition for office that came with independence' and 'ethnic competition'. (Ake 1967a, 27–9). These were complicated by the rifts between older leaders and their successors. The older leaders, who had spearheaded the nationalist struggles, considered themselves deserving of unquestioned obedience, while the younger generation, more ambitious and impatient, argued that those who had liberated the nation no longer had the right to misgovern it. In Burma, the older generation of leaders condemned their successors as half-educated upstarts who had failed to prove their competence in the competitive examination of colonialism, while the new politicians described their forerunners and the intellectuals as pitiful victims of colonial indoctrination who must be resocialised to better appreciate their national culture and history (Ake 1967a, 19).

Cleavages in the social structures of these states were manifested in the uneasy relationship between the leaders and their masses; the disenchantment with the revolution and its leaders who could not immediately translate 'the development slogan' and other abstract notions of democratic rights into concrete economic benefits and immediate material improvements as well as bitterness at the politicians who enriched themselves at the expense of the people (Ake 1967a, 30–1). The termination of colonial rule therefore diminished the atmosphere of crisis which had made it easier for leaders to enlist popular enthusiasm and cheaply dramatise their heroism. Their charismatic appeal was thus weakened, especially as grand politics was toned down to administration and the efficiency of political parties came under serious scrutiny. There was also a communication gap between the largely Westernised leaders and the masses, who were still in the grip of traditional modes of action and thought. While the latter were confused by the language of rationality and secularism which their leaders deployed, the leaders were frustrated by the masses' attachment to tradition, which was supposedly detrimental to modernity. The masses that had supported the liberation struggles saw the overthrowing of alien rule as a means to other ends. Unfortunately, only a few saw their lot improving. The living conditions of most people remained largely unchanged. Educational and medical facilities could not be transformed overnight, yet taxes must be paid. The emergent reality thus meant fulfillment for a few and disillusionment for the majority of the populations.

These cleavages later played out in the problems linked with 'integral decolonisation' and other initiatives with which the leaders sought to resocialise their masses from colonial indoctrination to the real conditions of their milieu; and also from their traditional ties to the rational-bureaucratic culture required for a successful industrial revolution. The problems of policy were noted in such areas as 'the attempt to adopt one of the indigenous languages as lingua franca'; 'the controversies that surrounded their educational reform' and 'the difficulty of finding acceptable cultural symbols around which the new nations could be united'. Transforming these states into symbols that inspired popular loyalty was therefore an enormous challenge. Ake (1967a, 31–4) observed that in spite of some potentially unifying elements – 'the unifying capacity of Christianity and Islam'; 'the language and political philosophy of the imperial powers' and 'the bonds of wider economic interaction' – on balance, the disintegrative pressures on the nationalist movements far outweighed the centripetal factors. These tensions notwithstanding, Ake recognised the Convention Peoples Party in Ghana, the India National Congress and the Parti Democratique de Guinee as major nationalist parties which displayed considerable solidarity.

Ake postulates the conditions under which political integration and stability are attainable by these states.[8] The primary prerequisite for a high degree of integration, according to Ake, is the acquisition of a mature political culture and the essential preliminary for this is the broadening and intensification of social communication. Following Karl Deutsch (1961), Ake argues that to improve their communicative efficiency, these states must undertake social mobilisation, namely, the process through which major clusters of old economic, psychological and social commitments are broken down or eroded and people become available for new patterns of behavior and socialisation.

It needs to be underlined that the problem of political integration is not confined to Africa, but is shared by the postcolonial world as one of the regressive features differentiating the state in the East from its counterparts in the advanced capitalist societies.[9] Ake's reflections on the problem of political integration therefore, continue to resonate in the post-Cold War period and even the 21st century.[10] However, the failure to accord such works the seriousness that they deserve, has undermined several intellectual attempts at grasping the trajectory of both development and state reconstruction across postconflict settings on the continent. Thus, while his longstanding engagement with political integration across the South has guaranteed a place for Ake in the literature on nation building and state transformation, the failure to deploy such South–South interventions in policy and theoretical thinking on these issues and themes highlights the weaknesses in nation building projects across the periphery. How are we to understand this neglect of the intellectual contributions on the global South by one of its best and clearest thinkers? The next section examines the relevance of Claude Ake's political thought for state reconstruction on the continent.

On state reconstruction in Africa

Since the end of the Cold War, the state in Africa has passed through several destructive civil wars and internecine conflicts. The imperative of reconstructing damaged economies and devastated societies; overcoming entrenched divisions and healing old wounds as well as reintegrating displaced populations and shattered communities thus loomed large across these settings. Countries that have undergone civil conflicts in post-Cold War Africa – especially as the situations in Liberia and Sierra Leone illustrate – have been subjected to a combination of ecological stresses, widespread socioeconomic problems, identity politics, episodes of unrest and pressures for democratisation. This is the curious context for deploying Claude Ake's political thought as a basis for an autochthonous reconstruction of the state in postconflict Africa.

Ake (1985a) defines the state as a set of interactions and relationships among social classes and groups organised and sustained by political power. He describes it as the fundamental instrument of political power in a class-based society. Although he acknowledges the existence of other, non-capitalist forms of the state's domination; he presents the state as essentially a capitalist phenomenon and locates the particularities of the capitalist mode of production as the ideal-typical setting for the development of the state's domination. According to him, the thoroughgoing generalisation of commodity production and exchange relations which characterises this mode of production allows for a high degree of autonomisation of class domination. He demonstrates this by illustrating the relationship between the pervasive autonomisation of commodity exchange and the autonomisation of class domination. Under the capitalist mode of production, particularly under the conditions of pervasive commoditisation, including that of labour power, society becomes highly atomised, so that people are first and foremost commodity bearers, even when their sole commodity is their labour power. In the process, society is reduced increasingly and perpetually to a market economy, governed and operated by the logic of the market and the dictates of capital, and social life revolves around the norms of competition and individualism, so that, as they pursue their particular interests, members of this market economy become collectively dependent and individually interdependent on the forces of the market. Such forces are reproduced through their daily interactive decisions which function as an independent force that dominates and subordinates them. Ake calls this 'the autonomising matrix of domination for solidarity' (Ake 1985a, 106) which coerces all into interdependence and subordination, and behind which is the domination of man by man as well as the domination of labour by capital. These forms of domination, according to him, are constituted in such a manner that economic domination seems to operate independently of the social groups that dominate and is therefore perceived as a natural force within society or, at any rate, as an impersonal market force.

Ake captures 'autonomisation' as the very essence of the state and identifies the autonomisation of the mechanisms of domination as the central feature of the state, both in political theory and also in the advanced capitalist societies. According to him, this does not mean that the state is entirely neutral, but that it is significantly autonomous and independent of the existing hegemonic social classes within it. He argues that the state's autonomisation is concretely expressed in two ways. One, in the fact that economic domination operates independently of the social groups that dominate and is perceived as a natural force – or at any rate – as an impersonal force. He calls this 'market forces'. Two, in the political sphere. Ake argues that the autonomisation of domination is generated and reproduced through the mediation of commodity production and exchange in the manner in which the state is constituted. According to Ake (1985a, 106–7), 'autonomisation … institutionalises the equal treatment of unequals that underlies the capital relation'. Thus epitomised as the rule of law, autonomisation reproduces the rule of capital over labor by the very rights it guarantees.

Applied to Africa, Ake (1985b, 1–32) argues that an understanding of the character, history and nature of the state is very important for capturing the dynamics of Africa's socioeconomic formations, because the state is the central locus of politics and therefore the major determinant of the directions of most societal processes. He traces the history of the state in Africa first through an examination of colonialism and the capitalist penetration of the region; and second through the eventual political legacy of colonialism for the continent (Ake 1993; 1996, 1–6). Having characterised the capitalist mode of production as 'the ideal-typical setting' for the development of the state's form of domination, he refrains from referring to the social formations in Africa as 'independent states', because, he says, the specific form of capitalist development which occurred in Africa is both 'enclave' and 'peripheral'. Furthermore, he says, 'the process of state formation in the continent is bogged down by knotty contradictions which stubbornly resist transcendence' (Ake 1981, 3). Speaking of these contradictions, he refers to the wholesale importation of the mentalities, practices and routines of the colonial state into its postcolonial successor and the limited nature of the state's independence that results from that historical process (Ake 1996, 3). According to him, 'in Africa, there are few social formations that are capitalist or socialist enough as to be identifiable as clearly boasting the state's form of domination' (Ake 1985a, 108). The unique feature of the state in Africa is limited autonomisation. This means that it is institutionally constituted in such a manner that it enjoys limited or no independence from the existing social classes, particularly the hegemonic social classes, and so, it is not just immersed in the ensuing struggles, but is also overwhelmed and taken over, usually by the hegemonic social classes.

Ake stresses that the limited autonomy of the state in Africa engenders conflict in a number of ways. In so fraught a context, the stakes in the struggles for state power are very high and often assume a zero-sum game approach. In the process, the state is immersed in the struggles between contending elements and is often hijacked by the hegemonic social classes within it. This leads to an exclusive politics articulated in a struggle for power based on efficiency norms rather than legitimacy norms; the triumph of the vicious circle over the virtuous; the centralisation of power; the imposition of domination and political control; the alienation of the leaders from the masses; and the deployment of extremism in the exercise of power. In effect, the people tend to retreat into their primary groups, which become the beneficiary of their residual loyalty; and to explore other extra-juridical and non-state means of reproducing their material and social existence, which often have very high conflict potential. In the process, society becomes deeply divided and alienation is endemic (Ake 1996, 3). Anxiety, bitterness and distrust among contending groups also become so pronounced that the state stumbles and totters on the brink of disaster, headed for disintegration in a circle of political recrimination, violence and war (see also Ake 1982, 1–3).

Under these circumstances, Ake argues, state building is subverted and becomes the political equivalent of primitive accumulation in a rather violent form. It entails conquest and subjugation since state building is projected as an arbitrary power. It revokes the autonomy of communities and subjects them to alien rule within an otherwise independent political system by laying claim to the resources of subordinated territories and through its exertion of force in resource wars and against pro-democratic resistance (Ake 1997, 2). As a result of the over-centralised nature of the state, access to state power in much of Africa is difficult. State building thus assumes a high conflict profile. These experiences feed into the explosion of conflicts and wars over natural resources and state power, leading to the collapse and subversion of the state in some parts of the continent. A classic case in point is offered by post-Cold War Sierra Leone.

The limitations of state reconstruction frameworks based on the neo-liberal peace paradigm have been covered in other works in the literature.

This work therefore, limits its enquiry to Ake's specific contribution in rebuilding the state in postconflict and postwar Africa.

Ake did not use the concepts of 'peacebuilding' and 'state reconstruction' that are central in this work. His publications also did not address the question of reinventing the state in postconflict Africa. While the context of his works on Africa's civil wars and conflicts was the post-Cold War period, Ake (1997, 3–9) deals with these challenges in terms of humanitarian emergencies. This section makes explicit the connection between peace building and state reconstruction in postconflict Africa.

Although the continent recorded remarkable achievements in multi-party democratisation and economic reform (Young 2002); the significance of the 1990s for sub-Saharan Africa lies in the coincidence of the transformation in the international system with a profound internal crisis of the state in the continent (Clapham 1997). Ake (1996; 1997) analyses the implications of Africa's exploitation and poverty – driven by both global and local forces – for the conflicts and wars in the region. Although his works provide only limited coverage of peacebuilding and state reconstruction in postconflict Africa, which only took centre stage a few years before his sudden death in 1996, nevertheless, some of his contributions and insights can be linked to ongoing debates and reflections on peacebuilding and state reconstruction in postconflict Africa.

As one of Africa's foremost political theorists, Ake acutely diagnosed the major failings inherent in the state in Africa. He also sketched out what is required to put them right. His insights therefore provide a valid starting point for looking anew at the problems crippling postconflict reconstruction as well as the pitfalls of the externally-driven conceptions underlying various agendas on how to rebuild the state in such contexts.

Ake argues that 'the rudimentary development' of the state form in Africa underlines the Hobbesian character of political struggles – usually based on the relations of raw power among contending groups and social classes – in which right is coextensive with power and security depends solely on the control of state power. The rudimentary development of the state form in Africa engenders the problem of conflicts and contradictions of the socioeconomic formation in which the possibility of resolving contradictions is severely limited as the differences between various groups in struggles are misrepresented as entirely absolute. This, he says, undermines the legitimation of power – a problem underlying the crises of authority and nation building on the continent – given the personalised use of the state's coercive resources (Ake 1985b, 4).

His major contribution in this regard is his critique of the state in Africa – recapitulated here above – focusing especially on its unique features and their implications for the continent. Having traced the history of the state in Africa first to colonialism and the capitalist penetration of the region and second, to the eventual political legacy of colonialism for the continent, and following his limited autonomy thesis on the state in peripheral capitalist societies as well as the characterisation of the social formations in Africa as colonial creations, Ake asserts that the states in Africa are best understood as states in formation. He exposes the major contradictions in the composition of the state in Africa and concludes that, unless it is fundamentally transformed, it cannot meet the expectations of modern statehood. These contradictions and weaknesses, he says, inhibit competitive politics, equality and formal freedom. They also exacerbate the problem of political instability for which Africa has become deservedly notorious (Ake 1985b, 5–10).

Ake's contribution here lies in his advocacy of the autochthonous transformation of the state in Africa using endogenous knowledge production on the continent. As is widely known, the disposition and legacy of Western scholarship on the state is basically to universalise a particular cultural construction of state–society relations in which specific notions of civil society and statehood are conjoined and epistemologically asserted on the rest of the world through the projection of the Western gaze as the exclusive perspective on power. Rather than building on such notions, Ake draws on Africa's cultural and historical contexts and experiences – which sharply differ from the known trajectory of the state in the West – as a basis for provincialising such imperial notions of power and statehood. His task in this engagement is to recreate received knowledge generally as a basis for speaking to social realities on the continent. His intervention suggests that in seeking to transform the state, we must go beyond idealised conceptions of civil society and state–society relations borrowed and imagined from the western experience. He suggests that we must look inwards and focus more closely on the actual roots and sociocultural categories of state–society relations which, although are uniquely African, are not accommodated within the Western conception of the Gemeinschaft–Gesellschaft. I have in mind here the political society.[11]

He admonishes us to rethink existing understandings of colonialism and its legacies for the continent; the role of multinational capital, dependent capitalism, the centralisation of power as well as the impact of authoritarian and corrupt elites in Africa. He presents democratisation as the most salient option for addressing the normless struggles over ethnic conflict, resource wars, state power and Africa's humanitarian emergencies.

In the context of Ake's reflections, one understands the historic fault lines in Africa's experience with state formation. In this connection, the failure to transform the character of the state on the continent – in spite of formal political independence – engenders conflict over state power and the resources that access to state power offers. Far from being transcended; this failure is very much still with us. Twentieth century anticolonial demands for self-rule in Africa achieved the vision of a quasi-independent state but failed to transform the structures of the colonial state or imagine alternative conceptions of nationhood and statehood independent of the European model. The modern state has everywhere in Africa been patterned on the European model, with all its contradictions for postcolonial societies. Put differently, the historical patterns and global conditions which gave rise to the state in Africa have not been fundamentally altered. This is a major limitation of the nationalist response to the colonial intervention. It explains the continent's vulnerability to ideological and policy tinkering by neo-imperial brains trusts, with all their hardnosed arguments on the lack of development in Africa. It also explains why the postcolonial state in its present form has been embattled, ineffectual and subjected to several reform programmes by the external donor community and international financial institutions. With neoliberalism, the wheel has only come full circle.

State building in Africa therefore operates within the framework of a borrowed knowledge system whose representational structure corresponds to the very structure of power, which intellectual and nationalist leaders on the continent seek to repudiate (Chatterjee 1986). The anticolonial vision has been influential throughout the postcolonial world, instituting the foundations of modern critiques of socially unjust practices of caste, oppression of women, lack of rights for labouring and subaltern classes, and of colonialism itself (Chakrabarty 2000, 4). However, it has been ineffectual in erecting the foundations of an independent state free from neo-imperial dominance and capable of delivering the expectations of a truly developmental state.

Thus, nationalism may have succeeded in liberating the nation from colonialism but not from the knowledge system of the West, which continues to dominate the continent. Through their opposition to colonialism, nationalist elites in Africa checked a specific political form of metropolitan capitalist dominance. Although they rejected the dominant rhetoric such as the civilising mission of the West – the white man's burden – they ignored the need for an epistemological revolution in the Western knowledge system on which the operations of the state are premised. While the lessons of decolonisation and what it means for world history are irreversible, this failure explains the continued dominance of the continent by the knowledge system of the West in the postcolonial era.

Africa therefore inherited the European system of administration and government in its original form based on borrowed technologies of power; imitated administration and constitutional principles, merely replacing the personnel. The elites of the 'new states could not think'of an entirely new system (Pylee 1967, 15). Having replicated the Western model, the state in Africa thus remains 'an imposed institution inappropriate to the African condition'. This way, decolonisation foreclosed other significant alternatives that were once at the centre of attention, such as supranational federations and pan-Africanism; and put in place a kind of state headed by a ruling class conscious of its own fragility and interests. The failure by successive regimes on the continent to see to the reality of change in this regard is what Frantz Fanon (1968, 119–65) describes as 'the pitfalls of national consciousness'.

Ake (1979; 1996 and 1997) establishes a connection between development, knowledge production and state building on the continent; and bemoans 'the poverty of ideas' with which state building has been undertaken since decolonisation. Put together, his works indicate that democratisation cannot ignore the character of the state. After all, the colonial state was not just the agency that brought the modular forms of the modern state to the colonies; it was also the agency destined never to fulfill its normalising mission in the postcolony. And the postcolonial state throughout Africa and Asia has 'only expanded and not transformed the basic institutional arrangements of colonial law and administration, [of] the army, the bureaucracy, the courts, the police [and] the various technical services of government' (Chatterjee 1994, 15; Thompson and Garratt 1934; Dutt 1947; Habib 1995).

A major characteristic of the modern regime of power is a certain governmentalisation of the state, which secures legitimacy not necessarily through the direct involvement of citizens in matters of the state, but rather by claiming to provide for the well-being of the population. Marked by the triumphant advance of governmental technologies, all of which promise to deliver more well-being to the governed at very low costs, the twentieth century witnessed a steep increase in the welfarist functions and role of the state. In this type of state, the purpose of classifying and enumerating population groups is mainly to facilitate welfare administration; this purpose leads to the proliferation of censuses and demographic surveys, thus making the workings of government accountable in quantifiable terms and the idea of representation by numerical population a reality. However, while the history of citizenship in the modern West moves from the institution of civic rights in civil society to that of political rights in the fully developed nation-state, leading ultimately to the relatively recent phase where government from the social point of view develops the economy, looks after the citizens and actually takes over society, in Africa the chronological sequence is quite different, mainly because in these societies the career of the state has been foreshortened. In other words, in contrast to the experience of the state in the West, where governmental technologies developed after the political consummation of the nation in the state, in Africa, given the context and the enduring impact of colonial rule, the development of governmental technologies actually predated the nation-state.

Given the implications of the fraught manner in which the technologies of government developed under colonialism and the problematic context of elite control and popular legitimacy, two sets of conceptual connections emerged in terms of the relations between the state and the citizens/populations in Africa. One concerns the connection between the civil society and the nation-state, rooted in popular sovereignty and the granting of equal rights to citizens. The other concerns the connections between populations and government agencies pursuing multiple policies of security and welfare. While the first connection relates to a domain already described in democratic political theory in the last century, the second relates to a different domain of politics, yet to be fully explored and researched in Africa. This is the domain of the political society.

In terms of the formal structures of the postcolonial state, especially as set down in the constitution and the laws, each individual is a citizen with equal rights to all others; and is therefore to be regarded as a member of civil society. But this claim is far from being borne out in practice. Most Africans are only ambiguously, contextually and tenuously rights-bearing citizens in the sense imagined by the constitution. In the real world, they are far from being equal, free and proper members of civil society; nor are they regarded or treated as such by the organs of the state. Although they are not entirely outside the democratic and demographic reach of the state, since they are controlled and looked after by the various governmental agencies, the political relationship existing between these left out populations and the state does not conform to what is envisaged in the constitutional depiction of state–society relations. Thus, while the idea of civil society continues to drive an interventionist political project as an ideal, it is demographically limited as an actually existing form in Africa. This demographic limitation of civil society, deepening the split in the domain of politics between an organised elite domain and a marginalised, unorganised subaltern domain, is what we call the political society. The history of the state in postcolonial Africa confirms the exclusion of this group from the developmental policies of government, most of which have been targeted at specific segments of the state's populations, above all the elite. Due to their lack of representation in civil society, members of the political society are therefore organised in informal associations, often transgressing the strict bounds of legality in their struggles to earn a living. This problem characterises the relationship between democracy and modernity in most parts of Africa. Until it is resolved, state building remains an uncompleted project in the continent.[12]

The state's inadequacy in representing large population groups in society creates a context in which opposing claims are negotiated on a political terrain where, on the one hand, governmental agencies have an obligation to look after the poor and underprivileged; and on the other hand, particular population segments receive attention from government agencies according to the varying calculations of political expediency, and according to the varying degrees of threat they are able to pose to the existence of the state and its institutions. It is precisely in seeking to accommodate the alienated groups of political society that this work explores the autochthonous transformation of the state in Africa using endogenous knowledge production, as described in Ake's works. After all, the civil wars and conflicts in the continent are deeply connected to the disruptive activities of marginalised population groups across the regions. Hence the need to imagine alternative conceptions of nation building and state formation capable of delivering a more inclusive form of state–society relations beyond the received conceptions inherited from the colonial past.[13]

There is the need to expand the existing demographic representational reach of the civil society in Africa as a basis for incorporating into the state several indigenous institutions that, although are hitherto neglected, are nevertheless crucial components of both the political society and of state–society relations. Examples of such indigenous formations include the administrative-political institutions of power centred on the Emir, Oba and Obi in Nigeria; Shaka Zulu in South Africa; the Kabaka of Buganda in Uganda; and the leopard skin chiefs among the Nuer in

Sudan; or the newly created chiefs; age-group, kindred and peer-group associations; community development associations; credit and thrift unions; occupational, professional and trade guilds; religious and spiritual associations linking the people with their ancestral roots; town and village unions; women's groups; and other social networks. Existing in various forms and sometimes overlapping, these are either entirely traditional – that is, created and nurtured by the people as well as rooted in the indigenous cultures, histories and traditions of the people, and carried over from Africa's pre-colonial past – or relatively recent, representing indigenous responses to the limitations of the inherited institutions of the colonial and postcolonial state in Africa.

Since the 1990s, the failure of governmental institutions inherited from the colonial state has informed the development of as well as search for alternative institutions – largely indigenous institutions – for providing essential security and social services for African populations. This failure has also awakened an interest in the relevance of traditional African institutions and knowledge systems.[14] Such neglected institutions have played active roles in governance and socioeconomic development, especially at the grassroots level in pre-colonial and colonial Africa. They have been active in building local bridges, health centres, police stations, roads and schools; in defence and the administration of justice, law and order; in erecting and maintaining community banks and court houses; and in labour mobilisation for community projects, conflict resolution, mutual aid, peacekeeping, revenue generation, security and welfare.[15] They also furthered the articulation of the nationalist vision during the decolonisation process. As Titilope M. Oladejo (2013) recounted in her work on Ibadan, market women were organised to enhance political campaigns in the colonial and postcolonial periods. They were involved in the activities of the Action Group (AG) and the National Council for Nigeria and Cameroons (NCNC) as well as various traditional power struggles at the local levels. Before the advent of party politics in Southwestern Nigeria, the Iyalode of Ibadan was central to the establishment and planning of the Dugbe market in 1915. Between the 1930s and 1940s, market women collaborated with educated women to form Ibadan Women's Party in 1947. Between 1951 and 1960, Iyalode Abimbola represented market women at the Butcher Commission of Inquiry to justify the suspension of Salami Agbaje as the Otun Balogun. Following this development, a major political figure within Southwestern Nigeria, Adegoke Adelabu took up the grievances of Ibadan market women on the enforcement of bans on street trading as an opportunity to mobilise women generally into the

NCNC-led Mabolaje Grand Alliance as a basis for gaining victory in the Ibadan District Council election of 1954. The marginalisation and neglect of such population groups in postcolonial Africa – on a momentous scale have however – been linked with the operations of various neoliberal establishments.

Demanding that these institutions modernise and transform themselves is hardly feasible; nor would discarding them as anachronistic relics of the African past help matters. It has already been made clear that the attempt to transplant Western institutions and structures of civil society and state–society relations into Africa has not worked well so far; nor is a nativist resort to traditionalism or traditional fundamentalism to be recommended.

Thus, drawing on Claude Ake's intellectual works, one of the most effective options for the autochthonous transformation of the state in Africa lies in a convergence between the articulation of international inter-ventionism and the operations of indigenous institutions – a convergence that offers a promising way of addressing the disjuncture between the global and the local in the continent. There are several ways of actualising this. One way is by training those officers and personnel attached to various indigenous institutions for the purpose of adapting them to the normative standards of the modern state. Most importantly, rather than basing their judgments on blind assumptions about these institutions, international actors should endeavour to properly understand the operations of governance structures in Africa and other non-Western societies. This should be pursued as the normative premise for fighting corruption, advancing devolution in local government administration, education, good governance, human rights and institution-building. This is critical for sustainable state construction and reconstruction processes in the continent. The trajectory of state and power in Africa, Asia and the postcolonial world does not always conform to the known experience of the state in the West. The task of critical theory is not to dismiss or characterise these societies in terms of any lack, but to study them – on their own terms – as an interesting contrast and establish the implications of such differences in the manner in which societies are constituted in the East.

Conclusion

This chapter has tried to articulate Claude Ake's contributions to knowl-edge production and state reconstruction in Africa. As we have tried to show, Ake's aim was not to reshape 'the modern African left' through transcending the classical university-based African Marxism of the 1960s and 1970s; although this was achieved to some extent. Rather, his task was to contribute towards recreating the social sciences in Africa as a unified body of knowledge relevant for speaking to social realities on the continent. This was his conception of the role of the social scientists in advancing social progress through decolonising knowledge production on the continent. It should also be cleared that Ake does not criticise all branches and methods of the Western social sciences. Nor does he fault all shades of European thought. What he questions are the ideological orientations; imperialist character and value-assumptions underlining them in their application to Africa, especially given their role in the continent's dependence and subordination in the sphere of knowledge.

With respect to state reconstruction, beyond the critique of externally driven state reconstruction projects in postconflict and postwar Africa, the chapter highlighted the limitations of the nationalist response to the colonial intervention as well as the ruinous impact of status quo elite politics for development and state transformation in Africa. In doing this, it drew attention to the relevance of Ake's works for advancing an autochthonous intervention on the conditions for reinventing the state in postconflict Africa.

In pointing out the limitations of the neoliberal peacebuilding approach, this chapter is not breaking any new ground. The limitations of state reconstruction frameworks based on the neoliberal peace paradigm have been covered in the literature on this subject matter.[16] While several studies have focused on the post-Cold War conflicts in Africa, few of these efforts have historicised the state in relation to such wars or linked them to the character of the state on the continent. Consequently, such works gloss over the need for state transformation as a prerequisite for sustainable peacebuilding in postconflict societies. Drawing on Ake's seminal thinking, this chapter fills this gap and establishes the need to focus attention on the autochthonous transformation of the state as a central component of peacebuilding programmes in postconflict contexts.

How else does one account for the transformations taking place within the continent without engaging the state? Ake's focus on the state in Africa is by no means the only approach towards understanding the conflicts and wars across the regions. His argument regarding the limited autonomy of the state in Africa is also neither his only thesis nor his strongest position on the state in Africa. Rather, by drawing on his position on the limited autonomy of the state in Africa, we have drawn attention to an instructive approach that we consider relevant to comprehending ongoing transformations on the continent. Far from limiting our analytical options, the aim has been to enrich and expand such options by highlighting the salient features and other attributes of the state hitherto glossed over in extant literature on the state in Africa.

One interesting outcome of recent debates on Orientalism and post-coloniality has been a renewal of interest in the intellectual history of colonial Africa. Theoretically, a major contribution by Ake to the understanding of African political thought is his redirection of attention to the state, its character and unique features and their implications for conflicts and socioeconomic transformation on the continent. While Georg W. F. Hegel, Karl Marx, Friedrich Engels, Vladimir I. Lenin and more recently Nicos Poulantzas and Ralph Miliband have contributed significantly to our understanding of the state in the advanced capitalist societies in the West, Claude Ake, Hamza Alavi and Samir Amin are instructive voices in understanding its trajectory in Africa and other peripheral-postcolonial societies. According to Ake (1985a; 1996), the European model of the nation-state is the major institution engrafted by the core on to the peripheries in the form of the state in Africa.

However, unlike the European model, which developed within Europe, the state in Africa is a force imposed on society from without. This logical inversion of state formation in Africa underlines the alienness of the state in Africa – its lack of conformity with the expectations and practices of the people. This is what makes the state inadequate on the continent. In effect, while most of the state forms in pre-colonial Africa arguably approximated statehood – at least to the extent that they were developed within the indigenous societies in which they operated – the same is not the case with the colonial and postcolonial state in Africa.

Put differently, while the 'stateness' of the socioeconomic formations in Africa as systems of authority monopolising the deployment of force over given territories is not in doubt, their 'Africanness', 'autonomy' and 'autochthoneity' are matters of continuing debate. For that reason, the descriptive referent 'the state in Africa' rather than 'the African state' is generally adopted in this work. The state's alienness is evident in its existence as a suspended power standing aloof and in abstraction from the society, mainly for the purpose of maintaining law and order and as a basis for maximising the political conditions of exploitation. This situation also explains the overdeveloped status of the state's apparatuses of violence relative to its education, health and welfare systems. Regrettably, local elites under successive regimes on the continent have demonstrated neither the discipline nor the willingness to transform these inherited structures of the state.

Following Ake, one understands the contradictory effects of global capitalism and its connections with new forms of empire, governmentality and violence. He insists that we recognise the insufficiency of dominant categories of analysis that all too often are anodyne and aseptic. Old models of citizenship, empire and the state have thus become anachronisms. In Ake's works, new models – especially those of the autochthonous transformation of the state based on endogenous knowledge production – now fire our analytical and political imagination of the state. The trajectory of state formation in Africa, as elsewhere in the global South, does not always conform to the known experiences in the West. The task of empirical research and indeed political theory is not to dismiss this interesting contrast, but to explain it and establish its implications for how society is constituted in the region. Although the rise of mass politics in 20th century Africa has led to the development of new techniques of governing population groups, the proliferation of security and welfare technologies has created modern governmental bodies that administer populations but do not provide citizens with an arena for democratic deliberation.

Under these conditions, multiparty democracy is no longer 'government of the people, by the people and for the people'. It has rather become a world of power whose startling dimensions and unwritten rules deny the expectations of the voiceless mass of the dominated populations. Such politics – especially as operated outside the traditionally defined arena of civil society and the formal legal institutions of the modern state – engenders the tensions that underlie conflicts and wars.[17] Ake considers the global conditions within which such local forms of popular politics – based on conflict and war – have not only appeared but transformed community violence and global society.

In reinventing the state in Africa, Ake charges us to engage the epistemological bases of state building and state formation from the perspective of knowledge production. This, according to him, is mainly because the ideological control and exploitation of the continent have been achieved, for the most part, through the continent's dependence on the West in the sphere of knowledge. The hegemonic status of European historiography has contributed to a longstanding neglect of knowledge produced from the global South. Hence the series of interventions across the different disciplines; bound and localised by their own historically produced rules of formation but also thematically connected by their convergence on the state, the most contested concept in postcolonial societies. While several efforts have been made to transcend the knowledge systems of Europe, a persistent contradiction has been the assertion of an inseparable complicity between this borrowed knowledge and its epistemic privileging over other local and often incommensurable knowledge.

Africa's dependence in the sphere of knowledge has serious implications for the untransformed character of the state; the spread of conflict and the continent's lack of development. It is the failure to imagine alternative forms of the modern state independent of the European model that underpins Africa's continued dependence on the West for inspiration and solutions to its problems. This also underlies the interventionist basis of neoliberalism and other foreign recipes, which have hardly been helpful to the continent. Far from being autochthonous, state building and knowledge production in Africa operate within a borrowed context (Kaviraj and Khilnani 2001). 'The knowledge of backwardness is never very comforting. It is even more disturbing when its removal requires coming to terms with a culture that is alien' (Chatterjee 1986, 11). State transformation is an urgent task on Africa's agenda, and the question of 'Africanising the state' in Africa through endogenous knowledge production is critical. Other crucial considerations for Africa in this regard include (i) what kind of state should be constructed (ii) what kinds of relationships should be forged across state lines and (iii) what kinds of recognition within states should be given to the affinities to which the citizens subscribe (Cooper 2006, 186).

Although the restoration of their states' capacities is a critical component of the democratic order, postconflict societies must work towards the progressive transformation of their governance and public administrations with a view to rekindling socioeconomic development. The political processes in these states should also be reconstituted in a manner that genuinely engages and incorporates their citizens in the state relegitimation process. While their overall frameworks remain largely based on imitations developed in the West, efforts should be made to endogenise these states by evoking innovative practices at the local level. It is important to think of means of transcending the legacies of the colonial past. The one-sided reference to the colonial past in the unmaking of Africa's present and future histories is flawed. By focusing exclusively on the role of external actors, Africans wrongly absolve themselves of their failings and are thus reduced to the typical colonial role of helpless victims and chronically dependent actors, lacking the capacity for agency both to redress and transform the historic structures underlying the reproduction of crisis on the continent.

Notes

1. For an account of Ake's biographical and theoretical orientations, including further details on his paradigm shifts, see Jeremiah O. Arowosegbe (2012).

2. Claude Ake's works are not without their limitations. For example, Ake (1979) spoke of 'Western social science' – in the singular. There are however, several other strands within Western social sciences – from the social democratic to the radical Marxist. In this sense, the foundation of Ake's counter narratives developed and foregrounded within Marxism, is a strand of this broader Western intellectual archive – albeit the dominant aspects of the emancipatory counter narratives. Even here, it should be understood as heterogeneous. However, an engagement with such weaknesses is not the focus of this study.

3. For a list of important works that have examined aspects of Claude Ake's works, see Jeremiah O. Arowosegbe (2008a; 2008b; 2011a; 2011b).

4. Although from the above quotation, Ake makes an exception of the Marxist intellectual tradition, he does not explain his basis for such an exception. This hiatus has however been treated in another work. For an elaborate account of this treatment, see Kelly Harris (2005, 73–88).

5. For operational and politically suggestive discussions of the North–South dichotomy especially in the context of postcoloniality, see Dipesh Chakrabarty (1992), Dwaipayan Bhattacharyya (2004), Partha Chatterjee (2004) and SEPHIS Electronic Magazine (2004, 58–60).

6. See James S. Coleman (1955); Karl Deutsch (1961; 1963); Howard Wriggins (1961); Richard Sklar (1967); Aristide Zolberg (1967; 1968); Arend Lijphart (1971); Aidan Southall (1974); William Tordoff (1977; 1984).

7. For a detailed articulation of this position, see Peter P. Ekeh (1975).

8. For a detailed treatment of these conditions and Ake's illustrations on the experiences of some historical political systems, see Ake (1967a, 96–150).

9. For illustrations from the experiences of other societies across the postcolonial world, see Mahmood Mamdani (2003).

10. For an account of how this problem undermines the prospects for South–South solidarity, see Chakrabarty (2005).

11. Partha Chatterjee (2004, 27–51). I am grateful to Partha Chatterjee for first bringing this thoughtful insight to my attention. See his (2004) argument in which he tackles this question head on.

12. Societies like Sierra Leone's have been profoundly damaged by a combination of forces – the experience of colonial rule, appallingly corrupt postcolonial regimes, armed conflicts, brutal civil wars, endemic disease, healthcare exclusion and social violence as well as several missing links in the standard answers proposed by the international community. The combination of these factors has left hardly any foundations on which to build the autochthonous state forms advocated by Ake.

13. For other accounts of such an approach relating to governmentality, see James Ferguson (1990); Arturo Escobar (1995); Christopher Bayly (1996); Akhil Gupta (1998) and Michael Watts (2003).

14. For a list of relevant works within the literature on this subject matter, see Claude Ake (1990, 7–21); James Wunsch and Dele Olowu (1990); George Ayittey (1991); Basil Davidson (1992) and Vincent Ostrom, David Feeny and Hartmut Picht (1988).

15. For further illustrations on the relevance and weaknesses of indigenous African institutions, see Dele Olowu and John Erero (n. d., 1–19).

16. For a few examples, see Samir Amin (1989); C. Colclough and James Manor (1991); Christopher Allen (1999); Said Adejumobi (2001); J. Milliken and K. Krause (2002); Keith Krause and Oliver Jutersonke (2005) and Thandika Mkandawire (2005).

17. For a foregrounding of this analysis, see Partha Chatterjee (2004). See especially the back and inner pages of the text. For an understanding of his argument on the operations of members of the political society, see 27–51.

Conclusion

When the chips are down, politics is the chessboard of power.

— Jeremiah O. Arowosegbe, 2014

This book has been concerned with an examination of Claude E. Ake's intellectual works. It has offered a genealogical account of his biographical and theoretical orientations. It presented him as one of the most fertile and influential voices within the social sciences community in Africa. As was earlier noted, while the ideas of intellectuals and nationalist leaders in Africa provide a popular entrée to African politics (Clapham 1970, 1), the exploration of their contributions and profiles still remains a largely underdeveloped genre. This is especially the case with academics, intellectuals and scholar-activists across the continent. Yet, by challenging existing hierarchies and oppressive institutions as well as truth regimes and the structures of power that produce and support them, engaged scholars occupy a uniquely critical position in the society. The world therefore has a lot to learn from their contributions and failings as progressive social forces. Claude Ake's works have been examined as a basis for filling this crevasse.

A measure of a philosopher's greatness is evaluated in terms of the appeal and continuing relevance of their work, especially after their death. Others may disagree violently in their assessment and interpretations of their major ideas and positions. Yet such disagreements in part serve to testify to their greatness. Although it may be too early to measure Ake's greatness as a political philosopher, nevertheless, one can safely suggest that other considerations notwithstanding, Ake was a great political philosopher.

Beyond a resurgence of the appeal of ideology, the 1960s and 1970s witnessed the radicalisation of politics in most parts of the world. Although Ake died relatively young, he belongs to a revolutionary pantheon that has exerted and continues to impact on contemporary political developments. The various works published in assessment of his corpus, also testify to his contribution to African political thought. Ake provides a compelling account of the material and political costs of the European colonisation of the continent – in short a record of the dynamics of rapid social change – as well as an outline for a different future for colonial and postcolonial Africa.

This book has tried to trace the development and genesis of Ake's political thought.[1] In doing this, we focused on his contribution to the social sciences in Africa and the global enterprise on knowledge production. We located him within the tricontinental intellectual project of postcolonial studies, which we defined as a South-driven critique of historicism. In the process, historicism was described as a revisionist Western (mis)conception of history, which obfuscates, rather than furthering the understanding of Africa. We also defined postcolonial studies as a South–South critique of political modernity and the very idea of the political – a practice – which involves by implication, an engagement with the practice of history writing from the South. Furthermore, we argued that the impact of the imperial presence and other legacies of the European Enlightenment are central for understanding the continent's present and future histories. The aim is to further research on aspects of the issues raised in Ake's works. This was done by suggesting vital reasons why Ake's works are considered worth reading – at least in the understanding of this researcher.

Stemming from the premise that the contributions and profiles of intellectuals and nationalist figures in Africa and the diaspora are still a largely underdeveloped genre, this book critically assesses Claude Ake's intellectual works and draws attention to vital aspects of those works that are relevant not just for accounting for, but also for transcending Africa's intellectual lag in the area of history writing and knowledge production. It argues out the connections between Ake's works and the subject field of postcolonial studies. In doing this, the aim has been to establish the relevance of such works for mapping the genealogies of the colonial and postcolonial in African history. This is a major area of omission with respect to the interventions made on Ake's works. Having underlined the centrality of endogenous knowledge production as the essential material precondition for development in Africa, the book has explored Ake's corpus as a basis for pondering on the impact and place of colonialism in the making of world history. Our approach has been to discuss his contribution to the social sciences community in Africa.

To recapitulate, Ake's position on the impact and place of colonialism in world history sees colonialism as epochal and fundamental in the making of African history. Following Walter Rodney (1972), Ake (1985a; 1985b) argues that under colonialism, Africans actually lost power. Their collective capacity for independent initiatives was also lost. The enormous impact of the colonial presence reduced them to mere spectators not only in the making of world history but also in determining their future interests. On the ruins of the colonial project emerged the caricature of a state system that is neither modern nor traditional. The decision by the emergent postcolonial elites to appropriate and consolidate rather than transforming the inherited structures of colonialism – especially the economies and state – not only constitutes the dilemma of the present juncture but also explains the perpetuation of the logic of the colonial condition (Cooper 2005).

Drawing on Ake's works as a basis for understanding the African crises, this volume has discussed the general question of knowledge production in Africa; its constituents and pitfalls; its enabling precepts and the prospects, which these open up, focusing specifically on the contributions of the late Claude Ake to this question. The aim has been to establish Ake's contribution to the humanities and social sciences in Africa as well as the global industry of knowledge production from the perspective of postcolonialism. The book is not concerned with examining Ake's contribution to the subject matter of knowledge production in Africa per se. It is also not concerned with the question of knowledge production on the continent alone as its central focus. Rather, knowledge production on Africa is examined as the major context for interrogating Ake's writings and also for assessing the problematic situations surrounding the state, within which democracy and development take place in the continent.

As we have tried to show, Ake's engagement with the extroversions of the Western social sciences in its application to Africa and other non-metropolitan histories is only a case in point on the ambiguity of the Enlightenment and more broadly European thought in its reference to non-metropolitan societies at large. Similar efforts are found in the works of other scholars within this mode across Africa and in Asia and Latin America. Put together, such efforts represent bold initiatives in asserting the identities of African and other non-Western cultures – inter alia – through carefully rewriting the intellectual and nationalist histories of these societies on their own terms. Importantly, (i) through re-appropriating their vantage location in the home ground – the African soil – as the ultimate 'firma terra' (Mafeje 2000); (ii) by establishing the centrality of race in the making of the Enlightenment and all shades of imperial thought (Ghosh and Chakrabarty 2002) and (iii) by exposing the ambiguity and dualism that lie at the heart of liberalism and other European philosophical traditions (Chatterjee 1994), postcoloniality decentres Europe and more broadly the West from being the source of all legitimate signification and makes room for other ways of being (see Argyrou 2001) through carefully asserting the abstract possibility of other universes of theoretical reflections (Kaviraj 1992). It challenges Europe's tendency to absolutise theoretical insights and fights to redress the entrenched inequality of ignorance characterising the global system of knowledge production. Through its intellectual project of narrative history writing, postcoloniality counters the misrepresentation of the continent in terms of a lack; an absence and an incompleteness, which translates into perpetual inadequacy and inferiority – through the imperial project of transition narrative. This way, postcoloniality simultaneously advocates and asserts the originality of the African voice as the most authentic expression of the African condition and an end to African studies not just in Europe and North America but also in South Africa.

While the nationalist past provides the background for understanding anticolonial nationalism and decolonisation in Africa, the antecedents of intellectual and political struggles in colonial and postcolonial Africa, together with the African experiences of struggles in the pre-colonial era shaped Ake's scholarship and writings. These experiences – together with the intellectual renditions, which accompanied the struggles for independence and local ownership of the social sciences in Africa – constitute the actual intellectual roots and sources of Ake's radical inspiration; paradigms shift and revolutionary inclinations. As a public intellectual, Ake had a long history of political activism which preceded his career as a scholar and continued throughout his life. That experience enriched his scholarship greatly in speaking to an audience much larger than the academy and also in transforming the terms of engagement with knowledge production in Africa (Isaacman, 14–20). In his mode are Basil Davidson, Francis Deng, Joseph Harris, Susan Geiger and Walter Rodney.

Aspects of the intellectual traditions into which Claude Ake's works are inserted are not only rooted in Marxist thought, but also feed into the more contemporary debates on postcolonial studies and subaltern studies – the connections of which are yet to be explicitly established and foregrounded in the literature. While Ake's publications are marked by an original brand of Marxism, some of his contributions and insights can be linked to the discussions on postcolonial studies and subaltern studies scholarship. This book attempted to make this link explicit. At the moment, the interventions made to Ake's works can be grouped into three. First are those which directly focus on the celebration of his intellectual pedigree and stature through the biographical accounts and tributes that they provided. These include J. 'Bayo Adekanye (1996); L. Adele Jinadu (1996); Guy Martins (1996); the *Yale Bulletin and Calendar* (1996); CASS (1997) and James H. Mittleman (1997). The second comprises his interlocutors who engaged with some of the issues raised in his corpus. Julius O. Ihonvbere (1989); Okechukwu O. Ibeanu (1993); Archie Mafeje (1997); Andrew O. Efemini (2000) and Kelly Harris (2005) are known examples in this respect. Although indirectly, the third category draws on the works of leading authorities within the fields of African studies, postcolonial studies and subaltern studies, which help to deepen historical reflections as well as theoretical understandings of the questions bearing on autochthoneity and endogeneity in knowledge production; the state and other postcolonial concerns examined in Ake's works. Of particular relevance are those texts, which help to animate the debate on the relationship between 'the colonial' and 'the postcolonial' in the making of African history. In doing this, the intention has been to keep alive and potent a long cherished tradition of critique and resistance with respect to the production of knowledge on the continent (see also West 1990, 33).

Given the endemic nature of the African crises, it will not do to end matters by merely advocating a more proactive engagement by African scholars with the methodological implications of their liberatory intellectual ethics (Mama 2007). In addition to such efforts, there is the need for more focused and incisive analyses of the origins and impacts of the continent's crises – as a basis for proffering lasting solutions to them. This is therefore, a call on African scholars to rededicate themselves towards improving the material conditions of their people – inter alia – through a fearless articulation of the ideational and ontological connotations of Africanity and Afrocentrism.

To actualise such an expectation, efforts must be made not only to revive Africa's rich heritages and traditions in the bid to make sense of modernity, but also to invoke and retrieve aspects of its imaginary golden past, which are useful for thinking through its present and future histories.

As Amitav Ghosh (2002, 147) puts it, history is never more compelling than when it gives us insights into oneself and the ways in which one's own experience is constituted. History writing in Africa must therefore create those conditions that would enable us redeem ourselves by ourselves. In other words, while good history writing on the continent may well involve acknowledging the efforts of non-African contributors, it also centrally involves making choices and judgments of our own – as Africans. Africans and other non-Western cultures cannot afford to renounce their traditions in their quest for modernity, for it is these traditions, which enable them not only in accounting for their pasts, but also in imagining a liberated future.

Notes

1. It is best taken as the author's assessment of Ake's intellectual corpus as well as a modest invitation for others to come up with such works.

Bibliography A:
Works by Claude E. Ake

Books

1967a.   *A theory of political integration.* Homewood. Illinois: Dorsey Press.

1978.   *Revolutionary pressures in Africa.* London: Zed Books.

1979b.   *Social science as imperialism: the theory of political development.* Ibadan: Ibadan University Press.

1981.   *A political economy of Africa.* England: Longman.

1985b.   *Political economy of Nigeria.* Lagos and London: Longman.

1996a.   *Democracy and development in Africa.* Washington. DC: The Brookings Institution.

2000.   *The feasibility of democracy in Africa.* Dakar: CODESRIA.

Monographs

n.d.   *Social sciences and development.* Dakar: CODESRIA.

1992c.   *The feasibility of democracy in Africa.* Ibadan: Ibadan University Press.

1992g.   *The new world order: a view from the South.* Lagos: CASS and Malthouse Press.

1994h.   *The democratization of disempowerment in Africa.* Lagos: CASS and Malthouse Press.

1996b.   *Development strategy for Nigeria after the structural adjustment programme.* Ibadan: Development Policy Centre.

1996d.   *Is Africa democratizing?* Lagos: CASS and Malthouse Press.

1996f.   *The marginalization of Africa: Notes on a productive confusion.* Lagos: CASS and Malthouse Press.

1997e.   *Why humanitarian emergencies occur: Insights from the interface of state, democracy and civil society.* Helsinki: UNU-WIDER.

Chapters in books

1976b.   The congruence of political economies and ideologies in Africa. In Gutkind, Peter C. W. and Immanuel Wallerstein. eds. *The political economy of contemporary Africa.* Beverly Hills: Sage Publications.

1985a.   Indigenization: problems of transformation in a neo-colonial economy. In Ake, Claude. ed. *The political economy of Nigeria.* Lagos and London: Longman.

1985d.   The Nigerian state: antimonies of a periphery formation. In Ake, Claude. ed. *The political economy of Nigeria.* Lagos and London: Longman.

1988a.   Building on the indigenous. In Ministry of Foreign Affairs. ed. *Recovery in Africa.* Stockholm: Ministry of Foreign Affairs.

1989.   Peculiarities of the socio-political structures of the developing countries. In Volkor, M. ed. *The general course of economic theory.* Moscow: Progress Press.

1990a.   Sustaining development on the indigenous. In The World Bank. ed. *The long term perspective study of sub-Saharan Africa.* Washington: The World Bank.

1990b.   The role of students in the social and political development of Africa: the West African Students' Union. In UNESCO. ed. *UNESCO General History of Africa.* Paris: UNESCO.

1991b.   How politics underdevelops Africa. In Adedeji, Adebayo, O. Teriba and P. Bugembe. eds. *The challenge of African recovery and development.* London: Frank CASS.

1992b.   Points of departure: a keynote address. In Onoge, Omafume F. ed. *Nigeria: The way forward.* Lagos: Spectrum Books Limited.

1992f.   The legitimacy crisis of the state. In Kennett, D. and Tukumbi Lumumba-Kasongo. eds. *Structural adjustment and the crisis in Africa: Economic and political perspectives.* Lewiston. New York: Edwin Mellen Press.

1993b.   Deeper into original sins: the context of the ethical crisis in African public services. In Rasheed, A. and D. Olowu. eds. *Ethics and accountability in African public services.* Nairobi: AAPAM.

1993c.   Development and underdevelopment. In Krieger, J. ed. *Oxford companion to the politics of the world.* Oxford: Oxford University Press.

1993f. Nigeria. In Krieger, J. ed. *Oxford companion to the politics of the world.* Oxford: Oxford University Press.

1993i. Rethinking African democracy. In Diamond, Larry and Mark F. Plattner. eds. *The global resurgence of democracy.* Baltimore: The Johns Hopkins University Press.

1994b. A world of political ethnicity. In Berg, V. D. and Ulbe Bosma. eds. *Poverty and development: Analysis and policy, the historical dimensions of development, change and conflict in the South.* The Hague: Ministry of Foreign Affairs.

1994c. Academic freedom and the material base. In Diouf, Mamadou and Mahmood Mamdani. eds. *Academic freedom in Africa.* Dakar: CODESRIA.

1995l. The democratization of disempowerment in Africa. In Hipler, J. ed. *The democratization of disempowerment in the Third World.* The Transnational Institute: Pluto Press.

1995m. The new world order: a view from Africa. In Hans-Henrik, H. and G. Sørensen, eds. *Whose world order: Uneven globalization and the end of the Cold War.* Boulder. Colorado: Westview Press.

1996g. The political question. In Oyeleye O. Oyediran. ed. *Governance and development in Nigeria.* Ibadan: Oyediran Consult International.

1997a. Dangerous liaisons: the interface of globalization and democracy. In Hadenius, A. ed. *Democracy's victory and crisis.* Cambridge: Cambridge University Press.

1997b. Democracy and development in Africa: the residual option. In Adetula, Victor A. O. ed. *Claude Ake and democracy in Africa: A tribute.* Jos: AFRIGOV.

1997c. Global processes, identity and social movements. In Hadenius, A. ed. *Democracy's victory and crisis.* Cambridge: Cambridge University Press.

1997d. Political ethnicity and state-building in Nigeria. In Van Horne, Winston A. ed. *Global convulsions: Race, ethnicity and nationalism at the end of the twentieth century.* New York: State University of New York Press.

Articles in scholarly journals

1991a. As Africa democratizes. *African Leadership Forum* 1 (2):239–44.

1965. Pan-Africanism and African governments. *The Review of Politics* 27 (4):532–42.

1966. Charismatic legitimation and political integration. *Comparative Studies in Society and History* 9 (1):1–13.

1967b. Foreign relations of nation building states. *The Review of Politics* 29 (1):121–23.

1967c. Political integration and political stability: a hypothesis. *World Politics* 19 (3):486–99.

1967d. Right, utility and Rousseau. *Western Political Quarterly* 20 (2):21–52.

1968. Africa: the politics of unity. *The Review of Politics* 30 (1):102.

1969. Political obligation and political dissent. *Canadian Journal of Political Science* 2 (2):245–55.

1970. The social contract theory and the problem of politicization: the case of Hobbes. *Western Political Quarterly* 23 (3):463–70.

1972a. Tanzania: the progress of a decade. *African Review* 2 (1):112.

1972b. The scientific status of political science. *British Journal of Political Science* 2 (1):109–15.

1972c. The scientific status of political science: rejoinder. *British Journal of Political Science* 2 (2):131–32.

1973. Explaining political instability in new states. *Journal of Modern African Studies* 11 (3):347–59.

1974. Modernization and political instability: a theoretical exploration. *World Politics* 26 (4):576–91.

1976a. Explanatory notes on the political economy of Africa. *Journal of Modern African Studies* 14 (1):201–61.

1979a. Comments on the survival of communities. *Current Anthropology* 20 (2):249–74.

1980a. Comments on asymmetrical reciprocity. *Current Anthropology* 21 (1):299–314.

1980b. Sciences sociales et développement. *Africa Development/ Afrique et Développement* 5 (4):248–9.

1983. The political economy approach: historical and explanatory notes on a Marxian legacy in Africa. *Africa Development* 8 (2):22–35.

1984a. Introduction. *Africa Development/ Afrique et Développement* (special issue on Nigeria). 9 (3):6–8.

1984b. Presidential address to the Nigerian Political Science Association. 1982. *Africa Development/ Afrique et Développement* (special issue on Nigeria). 9 (3):9–13.

1984c. The commodification of the social sciences. *International Social Science Journal* 36 (4):615–25.

1984d. The state of the nation: intimation of disaster. *Africa Development* 9 (3).

1985c. The future of the state in Africa. *International Political Science Review* 6 (1):105–14.

1987a. History as the future of the social science. *Tarikh: Journal of the Historical Society of Nigeria* 9 (1).

1987b. Notes on the political economy of unemployment in Africa. *African Journal of Political Economy* 2 (2):67.

1987c. The African context of human rights. *Africa Today* 34 (1,2):152–76.

1987d. The problem of implementation of the two-party system. *Nigerian Journal of Policy and Strategy* 2 (1).

1988b. The future in perspectives. *Annals of the Social Science Council of Nigeria* 3 (1):124–41.

1988c. The limits of pluralism in Nigeria. *Nigerian Journal of Critical Social Science* 1 (1).

1988d. The political economy of development: does it have a future? *International Social Science Journal* 40 (4):485–97.

1991c. L'Afrique vers la democratie. *Africa Forum* 1 (2).

1991d. Rethinking democracy in Africa. *Journal of Democracy* 2 (1):32–44.

1992a. Devaluing democracy. *Journal of Democracy* 3 (3):101–2.

1992h. Wo ist die Substanz? Über die Dürftigkeit von Modellen der Demokratisierung für den Süden. *Der Überblick* 28 (3):14–15.

1993j. The unique case of African democracy. *International Affairs* 69 (2):239–44.

1993k. What is the problem of ethnicity in Africa? *Transformation* 22 (1):176–94.

1995d. Approches et orientations socio-politiques pour le développement durable en Afrique. *Afrique 2000* 22 (1):13–29.

1998. L'économie politique du développement a-t-elle un avenir? *Revue Internationale des Sciences Sociale* 118 (1):34–43.

Articles in newsmagazines and newspapers

1985e. Why is Africa not developing? *West Africa*. June 17.

1992d. The feasibility of democracy in Africa. (1). *Weekly Sunray*. June 28.

1992e. The feasibility of democracy in Africa. (2). *Weekly Sunray*. July 5.

1993a. Against the removal of oil subsidy. *Daily Sunray*. February 5.

1993d. Irrelevant remedies and false hopes. *The Guardian*. February 12.

1993e. Is Africa democratizing? *The Guardian*. December 15.

1993g. Of subsidies, remedies and false hopes. *National Concord*. February 12.

1993h. Our interim future. *The African Guardian*. September 20.

1994a. 12 June and beyond. *Tempo*. August 18.

1994d. Endangered species. *The Nigerian Economist*. August 22.

1994e. Lifting the haze. *Tell*. October 24.

1994f. Present realities. *Daily Sunray*. October 18.

1994g. Present realities. *The News*. October 24.

1994i. The marginalization 1). *The Nigerian Economist*. May 9.

1994j. The marginalization of Africa (2). *The Nigerian Economist*. May 16.

1994k. The marginalization of Africa (3). *The Nigerian Economist*. May 23.

1994l. The marginalization of Africa (4). *The Nigerian Economist*. May 30.

1994m. The marginalization of Africa (5). *The Nigerian Economist*. June 6.

1994n. Time for a democratic agenda. *Tell*. August 22.

1995a. A plausible transition. *AM News*. September 17.

1995b. A plausible transition. *Tell*. September 25.

1995c. A plausible transition. *The News*. September 25.

1995e. Democracy, governance and development in Africa. *AM News*. June 12, 13 and 14.

1995f. Is democratization conducive or ...? *Independent Monitor*. October 22.

1995g. June 12 and beyond. (1). *The Guardian*. October 2.

1995h. June 12 and beyond. (2). *The Guardian*. October 3.

1995i. Ogoni lessons. *AM News*. September 17.

1995j. Ogoni lessons. *Daily Sunray*. September 25.

1995k. Ogoni lessons. *Independent Monitor*. October 22.

1995n. Why I am resigning. *AM News*. December 7.

1995o. Why we organized the seminars. *Daily Sunray*. January 31.

1996c. For Africa, the way forward. *The Guardian*. November 13.

1996e. Shelling Nigeria. *AM News*. January 18.

Bibliography B:
Works on Claude E. Ake

Primary sources

Abiodun, J. O. 1998. Remembering Claude Ake: the social scientist. In CASS. ed. *The challenge of African development: tributes and essays in honour of professor Claude Ake*. Port Harcourt: CASS.

Adekanye, Bayo. J. 1996. Obituary: Claude Ake. *Review of African Political Economy* 23 (70):563–4.

Adetula, Victor A. O. ed. 1997. *Claude Ake and democracy in Africa: A tribute*. Jos: African Centre for Democratic Governance.

Africa–America Institute. 2004. Claude Ake memorial awards programme. USA.

African Studies Association and the Africa–America Institute (ASA/AAI). 2003. *Claude Ake memorial awards programmes*. Philadelphia: African Studies Centre. University of Pennsylvania.

Arowosegbe, Jeremiah O. 2008. The social sciences and knowledge production on Africa: the contribution of Claude Ake. *Africa Spectrum* 43 (3):333–51.

Arowosegbe, Jeremiah O. 2008. Decolonizing the social sciences in the global South: Claude Ake and the praxis of knowledge production in Africa. *Working Paper 79*. Leiden: African Studies Centre.

Arowosegbe, Jeremiah O. 2011. Claude E. Ake: political integration and the challenges of nationhood in Africa. *Development and Change*. 42 (1):349–65.

Arowosegbe, Jeremiah O. 2011. State reconstruction in Africa: the relevance of Claude Ake's political thought. *International Affairs* 87 (3):651–70.

Arowosegbe, Jeremiah O. 2011. Reflections on the challenge of reconstructing postconflict states in West Africa: insights from Claude Ake's political writings. *Discussion Paper 54*. Uppsala: Nordic Africa Institute.

Arowosegbe, Jeremiah O. 2012. The making of an organic intellectual: Claude Ake. biographical and theoretical orientations. *African and Asian Studies* 11 (1):123–43.

Arowosegbe, Jeremiah O. 2013. Claude E. Ake and the praxis of knowledge production in Africa. *Africa Development* 38 (3 and 4):1–19.

Arowosegbe, Jeremiah O. 2016. Endogenous knowledge and the development question in Africa. *Cambridge Review of International Affairs* 29 (2):611–635.

Awa, Eme O. 1998. Professor Claude Ake: a tribute. In CASS. ed. *The challenge of African development: tributes and essays in honour of professor Claude Ake*. Port Harcourt: CASS.

Awolowo (Obafemi) Foundation. 1998. Tribute to professor Claude Ake. In CASS. ed. *The challenge of African development: tributes and essays in honour of professor Claude Ake*. Port Harcourt: CASS.

Bangura, Yusuf. 1997a. Claude Ake: a tribute. In Adetula. Victor A. O. ed.*Claude Ake and democracy in Africa: a tribute*. Jos: African Centre for Democratic Governance.

Bangura, Yusuf. 1997b. Claude Ake: A tribute. African Association of Political Science. *AAPS Newsletter*.

Balogun, Hairat A. 1998. Tribute to professor Claude Ake. In CASS. ed. *The challenge of African development: tributes and essays in honour of professor Claude Ake*. Port Harcourt: CASS.

CASS. 1997. Professor Claude Ake. 1939–1996: a ceremony in honour of professor Claude Ake. Port Harcourt: CASS.

CASS. ed. 1998.*The challenge of African development: tributes and essays in honour of professor Claude Ake*. Port Harcourt: CASS.

Drillbits and Tailings. 1997. In memoriam: Claude Ake. *Drillbits and Projects*. November 27.

Efana, L. 1996. In memoriam: Claude Ake (1939–1996). *Nordic Journal of African Studies*5 (2):98–100.

Efemini, Andrew O. 2000. *Claude Ake's philosophy of development: implications for Nigeria*. Port Harcourt: University of Port Harcourt Press.

Essien-Ibok, A. 1998. Substantiation on Claude Ake. In CASS. ed. *The challenge of African development: tributes and essays in honour of professor Claude Ake*. Port Harcourt: CASS.

Fafowora, Dapo. 1997. A tribute to Claude Ake. In Adetula. Victor A. O. ed. *Claude Ake and democracy in Africa: a tribute*. Jos: African Centre for Democratic Governance.

Founou-Tchigoua, B. 1996. Tribute to Claude Ake. *CODESRIA Bulletin* 4.

Guy, Martins. 1997. Claude Ake: a tribute. In Adetula. Victor A. O. ed. *Claude Ake and democracy in Africa: a tribute*. Jos: African Centre for Democratic Governance.

Harris, Kelly. 2005. Still relevant: Claude Ake's challenge to mainstream discourse on African politics and development. *Journal of Third World Studies* 22 (2):73–88.

Ibeanu, Okechukwu O. 1993. The state and the market: reflections on Ake's analysis of the state in the periphery. *Africa Development* 18 (3):117–31.

Ihonvbere, Julius. ed. 1989. *The political economy of crisis and underdevelopment in Africa: selected works of Claude Ake*. Lagos: JAD Publishers.

Iyam, O. O. 1998. Claude Ake: The passing of an exemplary academic and intellectual. In CASS. ed. *The challenge of African development: tributes and essays in honour of professor Claude Ake*. Port Harcourt: CASS.

Jega, Attahiru M. 2006. Democratization in Nigeria: problems and prospects. A paper presented at the 8th Claude Ake Memorial Lecture. Lagos: Nigerian Institute of International Affairs. February 28.

Jinadu, Liasu Adele. 1996. Claude Ake (1939–1996): an appreciation. *African Journal of Political Science* 1 (2).

Jinadu, Liasu Adele. 1997. Claude Ake: an appreciation. In Adetula. Victor A. O. ed. *Claude Ake and democracy in Africa: a tribute*. Jos: African Centre for Democratic Governance.

Jinadu, Liasu Adele. 1998. Claude Ake: the man and social scientist. In CASS. ed. *The challenge of African development: tributes and essays in honour of professor Claude Ake* 232–239. Port Harcourt: CASS.

Jinadu, Liasu Adele. 2004. Social science and the challenge of peace and development in Africa: the contribution of Claude Ake. Seminar paper presented as a Visiting Claude Ake Professor. Uppsala: Department of Peace and Conflict Research. Uppsala University.

Le Sueur, James D. ed. 2003. *The decolonisation reader*. London and New York: Routledge.

Ly, B. 1997. Tribute to Claude Ake. In Adetula. Victor A. O. ed. *Claude Ake and democracy in Africa: a tribute*. Jos: African Centre for Democratic Governance.

Mabogunje, Akinola. 1998. Ake: a celebration of dignity. In CASS. ed. *The challenge of African development: tributes and essays in honour of professor Claude Ake*. Port Harcourt: CASS.

Martins, Guy. 1996. Claude Ake: a tribute. *CODESRIA Bulletin* 2.

Martins, Guy. 1997. Claude Ake: a tribute. In Adetula. Victor A. O. ed. *Claude Ake and democracy in Africa: a tribute*. Jos: African Centre for Democratic Governance.

Mittleman, James. 1997. Tribute to Claude Ake. *CODESRIA Bulletin* 2.

Mwalilino, W. 2000. An interview with Claude Ake. *West Africa Review* 2 (1):1–17.

Ninsin, Kwame A. 2002. Book Review. Ake, C. 2000. The feasibility of democracy in Africa. Dakar: CODESRIA Books Series. *African Journal of Political Science* 7 (1).

Nzongola-Ntalaja, Georges. 2000. *Democracy and development in Africa: a tribute to Claude Ake*. A paper presented at the 4th Annual Lecture in Honour of Claude Ake. Ibadan: University of Ibadan.

Oculli, Okello. 1997. Ake, the critical theorist. In Adetula, Victor A. O. ed. *Claude Ake and democracy in Africa: a tribute*. Jos: African Centre for Democratic Governance.

Oyovbaire, Sam Egite. 1997. Remembering Claude Ake. In Adetula, Victor A. O. ed. *Claude Ake and democracy in Africa: a tribute*. Jos: African Centre for Democratic Governance.

Ozo-Eson, Peter I. and Ukoha Ukiwo. eds. 2001. *Ideology and African development*. Abuja and Port Harcourt: African Centre for Democratic Governance and CASS.

Sawyer, Akilagpa. 1997. Claude Ake: a committed scholar. institution-builder and pan-Africanist. In Adetula, Victor A. O. ed. *Claude Ake and democracy in Africa: a tribute*. Jos: African Centre for Democratic Governance.

Tamuno, Tekena. 1998. Claude Ake. his life and works: a tribute. In CASS. ed.*The challenge of African development: tributes and essays in honour of professor Claude Ake*. Port Harcourt: CASS.

Thoahlane, A. L. 1998. Tribute to professor Claude Ake. In CASS. ed. *The challenge of African development: tributes and essays in honour of professor Claude Ake*. Port Harcourt: CASS.

Tolofari, S. 2001. In remembrance of Claude Ake.

Ukiwo, Ukoha. 1997. The apotheosis of Ake. In Adetula. Victor A. O. ed. *Claude Ake and democracy in Africa: a tribute*. Jos: African Centre for Democratic Governance.

Uwujaren, W. 1996. The exit of a patriot: the passage of Ake closes the chapter for one of Nigeria's brightest minds. *The News*. 25 November.

Yale Bulletin and Calendar. 1996. Obituaries: Claude Ake.

Other publications

Acharya, A. and B. Buzan. 2010. *Non-Western international relations theory: perspectives on and beyond Asia*. London: Routledge.

Ade Ajayi, Jacob F. and Tekena N. Tamuno. eds. 1973. *The University of Ibadan. 1948–1973: a history of the first twenty-five years*. Ibadan: Ibadan University Press.

Adejumobi, Said. 2001. Citizenship, rights and the problem of conflicts and civil wars in Africa. *Human Rights Quarterly* 23 (1):148–70.

Adekanye, 'Bayo J. 1996. Obituary: Claude Ake. *Review of African Political Economy* 23 (70):563–64.

Adesina, Olujimi O. 2006. Sociology. endogeneity and the challenge of transformation. *An inaugural lecture*. Grahamstown: Rhodes University Press.

Africa Information Service. ed. 1973. *Return to the source: selected speeches of Amilcar Cabral*. London and New York: Monthly Review Press.

Ahmed, Aijaz. 1992. *In theory*. London: Verso.

Alagoa, E. J. 1986. Nigerian academic historians. In Bogumil Jewsiewicki and David Newbury. eds. *African historiographies: what history for which Africa?* Beverly Hills. London and New Delhi: Sage Publications. pp. 189–96.

Alatas, Sayed Farid. 2006. A Khadunian exemplar for a historical sociology for the South. *Current Sociology* 54 (3):397–411.

Allen, Chris. 1995. Understanding African politics. *Review of African Political Economy* 22 (65):301–20.

Allen, Christopher. 1999. Warfare, endemic violence and state collapse in Africa. *Review of African Political Economy* 81 (1):367–84.

Alpers, Edward and Pierre-Michelle Fontaine. eds. 1982. *Walter Rodney, revolutionary and scholar: a tribute*. Los Angeles: University of California.

Amin, Samir. 1989. *Eurocentricism*. London: Zed Books.

Amin, Samir. 1989. La question democratique dans le tiers monde contemporain. *Africa Development* 14 (2):5–25.

Amin, Samir. 1990a. *Delinking: towards a polycentric world*. London: Zed Books.

Amin, Samir. 2004. Modernité et interpretations religieuses. *Africa Development* 29 (1):7–53.

Anderson, Perry. 1976. The antinomies of Antonio Gramsci. *New Left Review* 1/100.

Argyrou, Vassos. 2001. Review article. Provincialising Europe: reflections on questions of method and strategy. *Social Anthropology* 9 (2):217–22.

Asad, Talal. ed. 1973. *Anthropology and the colonial encounter*. New York: Humanities Press.

Ashcroft, Bill. et al. eds. 1995. *The postcolonial studies reader*. London and New York: Routledge.

Ashcroft, Bill. et al. 1998. *Postcolonial studies: the key concepts*. London and New York: Routledge.

Awe, Bolanle. 2000. The institute of African studies in an African university. In B. A. Mojuetan. ed. *Ibadan at 50. 1948–1998: Nigeria's premier university in perspective*. Ibadan: Ibadan University Press. pp. 79–95.

Ayandele, E. A. 1966. *The missionary impact on modern Nigeria. 1842–1914.* London.

Ayittey, George. 1991. *Indigenous African institutions*. New York: Transnational.

Babu, Abdulrahman M. 1982. Introduction. In Yashpal Tandon. ed. 1982. *University of Dar es Salaam debate on class, the state and imperialism*. Dar es Salaam: Tanzania Publishing House. pp. 1–12.

Bates, et al. eds. 1993. *Africa and the disciplines*. Chicago: University of Chicago Press.

Bayart, Jean-Francois. 2010. Postcolonial studies: a political invention of tradition? *Public Culture* 23 (1):55–84.

Bayly, Christopher S. 1996. *Empire and information: intelligence gathering and social communication in India. 1780–1870*. Cambridge: Cambridge University Press.

Berman, Bruce. 1998. Ethnicity, patronage and the African state: the politics of uncivil nationalism. *African Affairs* 97 (388):305–41.

Beckman, Bjorn and Gbemisola Adeoti. eds. 2006. *Intellectuals and African development: pretensions and resistance in African politics*. Dakar: CODESRIA.

Bhabha, Homi K. 1994. *The location of culture*. London: Routledge.

Bhambra, G. 2007. *Rethinking modernity: postcolonialism and the sociological imagination*. New York: Palgrave Macmillan.

Bhattacharyya, Dwaipayan. 2004. Book review. Partha Chatterjee. *The politics of the governed: reflections on popular politics in most of the world*. Delhi: Permanent Black. pp. 58–60.

Biko, Steve. 1973. White racism and black consciousness. In H. van der Merwe and D. Welsh. eds. *Student perspectives on South Africa*. Cape Town: David Philip.

Boggs, C. 1976. *Gramsci's Marxism*. London: Pluto Press.

Bollen, Kenneth A. 1983. World systems position. dependency and democracy: the cross-national evidence. *American Sociological Review* 48 (4):468–79.

Booth, William C. et al. 2003. *The craft of research*. Chicago and London: University of Chicago Press.

Bradshaw, York W., Paul J. Kaiser and Stephen N. Ndegwa. 1995. Rethinking theoretical and methodological approaches to the study of African development. *African Studies Review* 38 (2):39–65.

Buchanan, Ian. 2010. *Oxford dictionary of critical theory*. Oxford: Oxford University Press.

Buck-Morss, Susan. 2009. *Hegel, Haiti and universal history*. Pittsburgh: University of Pittsburgh Press.

Burke, Edmund. 1788/1991. Opening of impeachment. 16 February 1788. In Marshall. P. J. ed. *Writings and speeches of Burke*.Volume 6. Oxford: Clarendon Press.

Burke, Peter. 2005. *History and social theory*. Ithaca. New York: Cornell University Press.

Campbell, Horace. 1983. Walter Rodney and the Marxist method in African history. *History teachers' conference*. Dar es Salaam: University of Dar es Salaam.

Campbell, Horace. 1991. The impact of Walter Rodney and progressive scholars on the Dar es Salaam school. *Social and Economic Research* 40 (2):99–135.

Campbell, Horace. 1986. The impact of Walter Rodney and other progressive scholars on the Dar es Salaam school. *African Association of Political Science Newsletter*. July–September. 14–30.

Campbell, Trevor A. 1981. The making of an organic intellectual: Walter Rodney (1942–1980). *Latin American Perspectives* 8 (1):49–63.

Caute, David. 1970. *Frantz Fanon*. New York: The Viking Press.

Chabal, Patrick. 2005. Area studies and comparative politics: Africa in context. *Africa Spectrum* 40 (3):471–84.

Chakrabarty, Dipesh. 1987. Towards a discourse on nationalism. *Economic and Political Weekly* 22 (28):1137–8.

Chakrabarty, Dipesh. 2000. *Provincialising Europe: postcolonial thought and historical difference*. Princeton. New Jersey: Princeton University Press.

Chakrabarty, Dipesh. 2005. Legacies of Bandung: decolonisation and the politics of culture. *Economic and Political Weekly* 40 (46):4812–818.

Chakrabarty, Dipesh. 1992. Postcoloniality and the artifice of history: who speaks for 'Indian' pasts? Representations 37:1–26.

Chatterjee, Partha. 1974. Modern American political theory with reference to underdeveloped nations. *Social Scientists* 2 (12):24–42.

Chatterjee, Partha. 1986. *Nationalist thought and the colonial world: a derivative discourse*. London: Zed Books.

Chatterjee, Partha. 1993. *The nation and its fragments: colonial and postcolonial histories*. Princeton. New Jersey: Princeton University Press.

Chatterjee, Partha. 2004. *The politics of the governed: reflections on popular politics in most of the world*. New York: Columbia University Press.

Chatterjee, Partha. 2011. *Lineages of political society: studies in postcolonial democracy*. New York: Columbia University Press.

Chaudhuri, K. N. 1978. *The trading world of Asia and the English East India Company. 1660–1760*. Cambridge: Cambridge University Press.

Clapham, Christopher. 1970. The context of African political thought. *Journal of Modern African Studies* 8 (1):1–13.

Clapham, Christopher. 1997. International relations in Africa after the Cold War. In William Hale and Eberhard Kienle. eds. *After the Cold War: security and democracy in Africa and Asia*. London and New York: Tauris Academic Studies.

CODESRIA. 1996. *The state of academic freedom in Africa*. Dakar: CODESRIA.

Cohn, Bernard S. 1996. *Colonialism and its forms of knowledge: the British in India*. Princeton. New Jersey: Princeton University Press.

Coleman, James S. 1955. The problem of political integration in emergent Africa. *Western Political Quarterly* 8 (1):44–57.

Colclough, C. and James Manor. 1991. eds. *States or markets? neoliberalism and the development policy debate*. New York: Oxford University Press.

Cooper, Frederick. 1994. Conflict and connection: rethinking colonial African history. *American Historical Review* 99 (5):1516–545.

Cooper, Frederick. 2005. *Colonialism in question: theory, knowledge and history*. Berkeley. London and Los Angeles: University of California Press.

Cooper, Frederick. 2006. *Africa since 1940: the past of the present*. Cambridge: Cambridge University Press.

Coquery-Vidrovitch, Catherine. 2006. French historiography on Africa: a historical and personal contextualisation. *Africa Spectrum* 41 (1):107–26.

Craig, Albert M. et al. 2008. *The heritage of world civilisations*. New Jersey: Pearson Education.

Crofton, Ian. 2011. *World history: 50 key milestones you really need to know*. London: Quercus Publishing.

Dabashi, Hamid. 2013. Can non-Europeans think? What happens with thinkers who operate outside the European philosophical 'pedigree'? http://www.aljazeera.com/indepth/opinion/2013/01/2013114142638797542.html (accessed 7 June 2016).

Davidson, Basil. 1992. *The black man's burden: Africa and the curse of the nation-state*. New York: Times Books.

Deng, Lual A. 1998. *Rethinking African development: toward a framework for social integration and ecological harmony*. Trenton. New Jersey and Asmara: Africa World Press.

Derrida, Jacques. 1967. *De la grammatologie*. Paris: Les Éditions de Minuit.

Derrida, Jacques. 1978. Structure. sign and play in the discourse of the human sciences. In Jacques Derrida. *Writing and difference*. Trans. Alan Bass. Chicago: University of Chicago Press.

Deutsch, Karl. 1961. Social mobilisation and political development. *American Political Science Review* 55 (3):493–514.

Deutsch, Karl. 1963. ed. *Nation building*. New York: Atherton Press.

Dhaouadi, Mahmoud. 1990. Ibn Khaldun: the founding father of Eastern sociology. *International Sociology* 5 (3):319–35.

Dieng, Amady Aly. 2007. Reflections: an interview with Samir Amir. *Development and Change* 38 (6):1149–159.

Dike, Kenneth O. 1956. *Trade and politics in the Niger Delta. 1830–1885*. London.

Diouf, Mamadou. 1994. L'echec du modeledemocratique du Senegal. 1981–1993. *Africa Spectrum* 29 (1):47–64.

Diouf, Mamadou. 1996. Urban youth and Senegalese politics: Dakar. 1988–1994. *Public Culture* 8 (2):225–49.

Diouf, Mamadou. 2003. Engaging postcolonial cultures: African youth and the public space. *African Studies Review* 46 (2):1–12.

Duchesne, R. 2011. *The uniqueness of Western civilisation*. Boston and Leiden: Brill.

Dutt, Rayani Palme. 1947. *India today*. Calcutta: Manisha.

Efemini, Andrew O. 2000. *Claude Ake's philosophy of development: implications for Nigeria*. Port Harcourt: University of Port Harcourt Press.

Ekeh, Peter P. 1975. Colonialism and the two publics in Africa: a theoretical statement. *Comparative Studies in Society and History* 17 (1):91–112.

Ellis, Stephen D. K. 1996. Africa after the Cold War: new patterns of government and politics. *Development and Change* 27 (1):1–28.

Entwistle, H. 1979. *Antonio Gramsci: conservative schooling for radical politics*. London: Routledge.

Escobar, Arturo. 1995. *Encountering development*. Princeton. NJ: Princeton University Press.

Essien-Udom, E. U. 1962. *Black nationalism: a search for an identity in America*. Chicago and London: University of Chicago Press.

Fafunwa, Babatunde A. 1974. *History of education in Nigeria*. London: George Allen and Unwin.

Fage, J. D. 1969. Slavery and the slave trade in the context of West African history. *Journal of African History* 10 (3):393–404.

Fajana, Adewunmi. 1978. *Education in Nigeria. 1842–1939: an historical analysis*. Ibadan: Longman.

Falola, Toyin. 2004. *Nationalism and African intellectuals*. Rochester. New York: University of Rochester Press.

Fanon, Frantz. 1967. *Towards the African revolution*. New York: Grove.

Fanon, Frantz. 1968. *Wretched of the earth*. New York: Grove.

Feierman, Steven. 1993. African histories and the dissolution of world history. In Bates. et al. eds. *Africa and the disciplines*. Chicago: University of Chicago Press.

Ferguson, James. 1990. *The anti-politics machine: 'development'. Depoliticisation and bureaucratic power in Lesotho*. Cambridge: Cambridge University Press.

Foucault, Michel. 1973. *The order of things: an archaeology of the human sciences*. New York: Random House.

Frank, Andre Gunder. 1969. *Latin America: underdevelopment or revolution*. New York: Monthly Review Press.

Frankfurt Research Centre for Postcolonial Studies. 2011. *Colonial legacies. postcolonial contestations: decolonising the social sciences and the humanities*. Frankfurt: Goethe University. Frankfurt Research Centre for Postcolonial Studies. Call for abstracts. 16–18 June 2011.

Furnivall, John Sydenham. 1939. *Netherlands India*. Cambridge: Cambridge University Press.

Gamble, Andrew. 1981. *An introduction to modern social and political thought*. Basingstoke and London: Macmillan.

Geuss, Raymond. 2008. *Philosophy and real politics*. Princeton: Princeton University Press.

Ghosh, Amitav and DipeshChakrabarty. 2002. Reflections: a correspondence on provincializing Europe. *Radical History Review* 83:146–72.

Gonsalves, Ralph. 1978. The Rodney affair and its aftermath. *Caribbean Quarterly*.

Gordon, R. 1990. Early social anthropology in South Africa. *African Studies* 49 (1):15–48.

Gramsci, Antonio. 2001. The formation of intellectuals. In Leitch, Vincent. ed. *Norton anthology of theory and criticism*. New York: Norton. 1135–1143.

Gramsci, Antonio. 1971. The intellectuals. In *Selections from prison notebooks*. New York: International Publishers. Translated and edited by Quintin Hoare and Geoffrey Nowell Smith. 3–23.

Grant, Andrew. 2005. Diamonds, foreign aid and the uncertain prospects for postconflict reconstruction in Sierra Leone. *The Round Table* 94 (381):443–57.

Gupta, Akhil. 1998. *Postcolonial developments*. Durham. NC: Duke University Press.

Gutkind, Peter C. W. and Immanuel Wallerstein (eds). 1976. *The political economy of contemporary Africa*. Beverly Hills. California: Sage.

Habib, Irvan. 1995. *Essays in Indian history: towards a Marxist perception*. New Delhi: Tulika.

Hale, William and Eberhard Kienle. eds. 1997. *After the Cold War: security and democracy in Africa and Asia*. London and New York: Tauris Academic Studies.

Hall, Martin. 1998. "Bantu education"? a reply to Mahmood Mamdani. *Social Dynamics: A Journal of African Studies* 24 (2):86–92.

Harris, Kelly. 2005. Still relevant: Claude Ake's challenge to mainstream discourse on African politics and development. *Journal of Third World Studies* 22 (2):73–88.

Hart-Davis, Adam. ed. 2007.*History: the definitive visual guide from the dawn of civilisation to the present day*. London: Dorling Kindersley.

Harvey, David. 1989. *The condition of postmodernity: an inquiry into the origins of cultural change*. Oxford: Blackwell Publishers.

Hegel, Georg W. F. 1975. *Lectures on the philosophy of world history.* Cambridge: Cambridge University Press.

Hobson, John M. 2004. *The Eastern origins of Western civilisation.* Cambridge: Cambridge University Press.

Hobson, John M. and S. Hobden. eds. 2002. *Historical sociology for international relations.* Cambridge: Cambridge University Press.

Holsinger, Bruce W. 2002. Medieval studies, postcolonial studies and the genealogies of critique. *Speculum* 77 (4):1195–227.

Horrocks, Chris and Zoran Jevtic. 2009. Introducing Foucault: a graphic guide. London: Icon Books.

Hountondji, Pauline. 1977. *Sur la 'philosophie africaine'.* Paris: Maspero.

Hountondji, Pauline. 1983. *African philosophy: myth and reality.* Bloomington and Indianapolis: Indiana University Press.

Hountondji, Pauline. 1997. *Endogenous knowledge: research trails.* Dakar: CODESRIA.

Ibeanu, Okechukwu O. 1993. The state and the market: reflections on Ake's analysis of the state in the periphery. *Africa Development* 18 (3):117–31.

Ihonvbere, Julius O. ed. 1989. *The political economy of crisis and underdevelopment in Africa: selected works of Claude Ake.* Lagos: JAD Publishers.

Isaacman, Allen. 2003. Legacies of engagement: scholarship informed by political commitment. *African Studies Review* 46:1–41.

Jameson, Fredric. 2002. *Singular modernity: essay on the ontology of the present.* London: Verso.

Jewsiewicki, Bogumil. 1986. Introduction: one historiography or several? A requiem for Africanism. In Jewsiewicki, Bogumil and David Newbury. eds. *African historiographies: what history for which Africa?* Beverly Hills. London and New Delhi: Sage Publications.

Jewsiewicki, Bogumil and David Newbury. eds. 1986. *African historiographies: what history for which Africa?* Beverly Hills. London and New Delhi: Sage Publications.

Jewsiewicki, Bogumil. 1987. The African prism of Immanuel Wallerstein. *Radical History Review* 39:50–68.

Jewsiewicki, Bogumil. 1989. African historical studies: academic knowledge as usable past and radical scholarship. *African Studies Review* 32 (3):1–76.

Joseph, Richard. 2003. Africa: states in crisis. *Journal of Democracy* 14 (3):159–70.

Kant, Immanuel. 1991. *An answer to the question: What is enlightenment?* Cambridge: Cambridge University Press.

Kaviraj, Sudipta. 1992. The imaginary institution of India. In Chatterjee, Partha and Gyanendra Pandey. eds. *Subaltern studies VII: Writings on South Asian history and society.* Delhi. New York and Oxford: Oxford University Press.

Kaviraj, Sudipta. 2000. Modernity and politics in India. *Daedalus* 129 (1):137–62.

Kaviraj, Sudipta and Sunil Khilnani. 2001. eds. *Civil society: history and possibilities.* Cambridge: Cambridge University Press.

Kaniki, M, ed. 1980.*Tanzania under colonial rule.* London: Longman.

Kedourie, Elie. 1961. *Nationalism.* London: Hutchinson and Company.

Kennedy, Dane. 2003. Imperial history and postcolonial theory. In James D. Le Sueur. ed.*The decolonisation reader.* London and New York: Routledge. pp. 16–7.

Kohn, Hans. 1955. *Nationalism: Its meaning in history.* Princeton. NJ: D. Van Nostrand.

Krause, Keith and Oliver Jutersonke. 2005. Peace, security and development in postconflict environments. *Security Dialogue* 36 (4):447–62.

Lalu, Premesh J. 2009. *The deaths of Hintsa: Postapartheid South Africa and the shape of recurring pasts.* Cape Town: Human Sciences Research Council Press.

Landau, Cecile, Andrew Szudek and Sarah Tomley. 2011. *The philosophy book.* London: Dorling Kindersley Limited.

Laski, Harold J. 1948. *A grammar of politics.* London: George Allen and Unwin Limited.

Latin American Weekly Report. London. 20 June 1980.

Legassick, Martin J. 1974. Capital accumulation and violence in South Africa. *Economy and Society* 3 (3):253–91.

Lijphart, Arend. 1971. Cultural diversity and theories of political integration. *Canadian Journal of Political Science* 4 (1):1–14.

Lugard, Frederick. 1911. Dual mandate. Oxford: Clarendon Press.

Lyotard, Jean-Francois. 1983. *The differend: phrases in dispute.*

Lyotard, Jean-Francois. 1979. *The postmodern condition: a report on knowledge.*

Macamo, Elisio S. 2012. In defense of 'useless' research in African studies. A paper presented at the African Studies Centre. Leiden. the Netherlands. 21 June.

Macey, David. 2000. *Dictionary of critical theory*. Johannesburg and London: Penguin Books.

Mafeje, Archie. 1976. The problem of anthropology in historical perspective: an inquiry into the growth of the social sciences. *Canadian Journal of African Studies* 10 (2):307–33.

Mafeje, Archie. 1997. Democracy and development in Africa: a tribute to Claude Ake. *African Journal of International Affairs* 1 (1):1–17.

Mafeje, Archie. 2000. Africanity: a combative ontology. *CODESRIA Bulletin* 1 (1):66–71.

MacGaffey, Wyatt. 1986. Epistemological ethnocentrism in African studies. In Jewsiewicki, Bogumil and David Newbury. eds. *African historiographies: what history for which Africa?* Beverly Hills. London and New Delhi: Sage Publications.

Makgoba, William Malegapuru. ed. 1999. *African renaissance: the new struggle*. Cape Town: Mafube Publishing.

Mama, Amina. 2007. Is it ethical to study Africa? preliminary thoughts on scholarship and freedom. *African Studies Review* 50 (1):1–26.

Mamdani, Mahmood. 1976. *Politics and class formation in Uganda*. London and New York: Monthly Review Press.

Mamdani, Mahmood. et al. 1988. Social movements, social transformation and the struggles for democracy in Africa. *Economic and Political Weekly* 23:973–81.

Mamdani, Mahmood. 1990. *The intelligentsia, the state and social movements: some reflections on the experiences in Africa*. Dakar: CODESRIA.

Mamdani, Mahmood. 1992. Africa: democratic theory and democratic struggles. *Economic and Political Weekly* 27:2228–32.

Mamdani, Mahmood. 1993. *The intelligentsia, the state and social movements in Africa*. Dakar: CODESRIA.

Mamdani, Mahmood and Ernest Wamba-dia-Wamba. 1995. *African studies in social movements and democracy*. Dakar: CODESRIA.

Mamdani, Mahmood. 1996a. *Citizen and subject: contemporary Africa and the legacy of late colonialism*. Princeton: Princeton University Press.

Mahmood Mamdani. 1996b. Centre for African Studies: some preliminary thoughts. *Social Dynamics: A Journal of African Studies* 22 (2):1–14.

Mamdani, Mahmood. 1998. Teaching Africa at the post-apartheid University of Cape Town: a critical view of the 'Introduction to Africa' core course in the social science and humanities faculty's foundation semester. 1998. *Social Dynamics: A Journal of African Studies* 24 (2):1–32.

Mamdani, Mahmood. 2003. From conquest to consent as the basis of state formation: reflections on Rwanda. In Pandey, Gyanendra and Peter Geschiere. eds. *The forging of nationhood*. Amsterdam: SEPHIS and New Delhi: Manohar.

Mamdani, Mahmood. 2011. The importance of research in a university. A paper presented as a keynote speech at Makerere University Research and Innovations Dissemination Conference. Hotel Africana. 11 April.

Mantena, Karuna. 2010. *Alibis of empire: Henry Maine and the ends of liberal imperialism*. Princeton: Princeton University Press.

Martins, Guy. 1996. Claude Ake: a tribute. *CODESRIA Bulletin* 2:12–5.

Martin, William and Michael West. 1995. The decline of the Africanists: Africa and the rise of new Africas. *Issue: A Journal of Opinion* 23 (1):24–6.

Marx, Karl. 1852/1869. *The Eighteenth Brumaire of Louis Bonaparte*. Hamburg: Die Revolution.

Massad, Joseph. 2004. The intellectual life of Edward W. Said. *Journal of Palestine Studies* 33 (3):7–22.

Mazrui, Ali A. 2005. Pan-Africanism and the intellectuals: rise, decline and revival. In Mkandawire, Thandika. ed. *African intellectuals: rethinking politics, language. gender and development*. Dakar: CODESRIA.

Mathews, Joseph Brown and R. E. Smalleross. 1976. Partners in plunder. *The Current*. Bombay. 17 January.

Mbembe, Achille. 2001. *On the postcolony*. Berkeley: University of California Press.

Mbembe, Achille. 2002. African modes of self-writing. *Public Culture* 14 (1):239–73.

Mehta, Uday Singh. 1999. *Liberalism and empire: a study in nineteenth century British liberal thought*. Chicago and London: University of Chicago Press.

Mill, John Stuart. 1861/1991. *Considerations of representative government*. Buffalo. New York: Prometheus Books.

Mill, John Stuart. 2003. *Autobiography*. Project Gutenberg e-Book, produced by Marc D'Hooghe. http://www.gutenberg.org/cache/epub/10378/pg10378-images.html (Accessed 03/11/2017).

Milliken, J. and K. Krause. 2002. State failure. state collapse and state reconstruction: concepts. lessons and strategies. *Development and Change* 33 (5):753–74.

Mittleman, James H. 1997a. A tribute to Claude Ake. *CODESRIA Bulletin* 2.

Mittleman, James H. 1997b. A tribute to Claude Ake. *Issue: A Journal of Opinion* 25 (1):3–4.

Mkandawire, Thandika. ed. 2005a. *African intellectuals: rethinking politics. language. gender and development.* Dakar: CODESRIA.

Mkandawire, Thandika. 2005b. Maladjusted African economies and globalization. *Africa Development* 30 (1 and 2):1–33.

Momoh, Abubakar. 1999. Kwame Nkrumah and the African liberation: the limits of praxis. *Unpublished PhD Dissertation.* Lagos: University of Lagos.

Momoh, Abubakar. 2002. The philosophy and theory of the national question. In Momoh, Abubakar and Said Adejumobi. eds. *The national question in Nigeria: comparative perspectives.* Aldershot. United Kingdom: Ashgate Publishing.

Momoh, Abubakar. 2003. Does pan-Africanism have a future in Africa? In search of the ideational basis of Afro-pessimism. *African Journal of Political Science* 8(1):31–57.

Moore, Brooke Noel and Richard Parker. 2007. *Critical thinking.* London and New Delhi: Mc Graw Hill.

Mudimbe, Valentine Y. 1988. *The invention of Africa: gnosis, philosophy and the order of knowledge.* Bloomington and Indianapolis: Indiana University Press.

Mudimbe, Valentine Y. 1994. *The idea of Africa.* Bloomington and Indianapolis: Indiana University Press.

Nabudere, Dani Wadada. 1977. *The political economy of imperialism.* London and New York: Zed Books.

Nabudere, Dani Wadada. 1978. Cited in Jinadu. Liasu A. 2004. *Social science and the challenge of peace and development in Africa: the contribution of Claude Ake.* Uppsala: Uppsala University. p. VI.

Nabudere, Dani Wadada. 1982. Is imperialism progressive? In Yashpal Tandon. ed. 1982. *University of Dar es Salaam debate on class. the state and imperialism.* Dar es Salaam: Tanzania Publishing House. pp. 252–82.

Nandy, Ashis. 1983. *The intimate enemy: loss and recovery of the self under colonialism.* Calcutta. Delhi and Madras: Oxford University Press.

Nandy, Ashis. 1995. History's forgotten doubles. *History and Theory* 34 (2):44–66.

Nietzsche, Friedrich. 1957. *The use and abuse of history.* New York: Liberal Arts Press.

Nkiwane, Tandeka C. 2001. Africa and international relations: regional lessons for a global discourse. *International Political Science Review* 22 (3):279–90.

Nnoli, Okwudiba. 1978. *Ethnic politics in Nigeria*. Enugu: Fourth Dimension Publishers.

Norton, W. A. 1916. Quoted in H. Phillips. 1993. *The University of Cape Town 1919–1948: the formative years*. Cape Town: University of Cape Town Press.

Ntsebeza, Lungisile. 2008. The Mafeje and UCT saga: an unfinished business. *CODESRIA Bulletin* 3 and 4:36–43.

Ntsebeza, Lungisile. 2012. African studies at UCT: an overview. In Nhlapo, Thandabantu and Harry Garuba. eds. *African studies in the postcolonial university*. Cape Town: University of Cape Town in association with the Centre for African Studies. 1–20.

Nuttall, Sarah and Carli Coetzee. eds. 1998. *Negotiating the past: the making of memory in South Africa*. Cape Town: Oxford University Press.

Nyong'o, Peter Anyang'. 2004. Political scientists and the democratic experiment in Africa. Billy Dudley Memorial Lectures Series Number 1. Organised by the Nigerian Political Science Association. Held at the University of Ibadan. Ibadan. Nigeria. 25 June.

Offiong, Daniel A. 1980. *Imperialism and dependency*. Lagos and London: Fourth Dimensions Publishers.

Ojo, Olatunde. 1985b. Self-reliance as a development strategy. In Claude Ake. ed. *The political economy of Nigeria*. Lagos and London: Longman. pp. 141–72.

Oladejo, Titilope Mutiat. 2013. Ibadan market women and politics. 1900–1995. *Unpublished PhD Dissertation*. Ibadan: University of Ibadan.

Olowu, Dele and John Erero. n.d. Governance of Nigeria's villages and cities through indigenous institutions. *Unpublished paper*. Ile-Ife: Obafemi Awolowo University. 1–19.

Olukoshi, Adebayo O. 2006. African scholars and African studies. *Development in Practice* 16 (6):533–44.

Ostrom, Vincent. David Feeny and Hartmut Picht. 1988. eds. *Rethinking institutional analysis and development*. San Francisco: ICS Press.

Pandey, Gyanendra and Peter Geschiere. eds. 2003. *The forging of nationhood*. Amsterdam: SEPHIS and New Delhi: Manohar.

Parrott, David. ed. 2011. *History: the ultimate visual guide to the events that shaped the world year by year*. London: Dorling Kindersley. pp. 255–61.

Petras in *Los Angeles Times*. 23 June 1980.

Phillips, H. 1993. *The University of Cape Town 1919–1948: the formative years*. Cape Town: University of Cape Town Press.

Prakash, Gyan. 1994. Subaltern studies as postcolonial criticism. *American Historical Review* 99 (5):1475–90.

Pylee, Moolamatton Varkey. 1967. *Constitutional history of India: 1600–1950.* Bombay: Apt Books.

Radhakrishnan, Rajagopalan. 1993. Postcoloniality and the boundaries of identity. *Callaloo* 16 (4):750–71.

Rassool, Ciral Shahid. 2004. The individual. auto/biography and history in South Africa. *Unpublished PhD Dissertation.* Cape Town: University of the Western Cape.

Reid, Richard. 2007. *War in pre-colonial eastern Africa.* Athens. Ohio: Ohio University Press.

Rodney, Walter. 1969. *The grounding with my brothers.* London: Bogle L'Ouverture.

Rodney, Walter. 1972. *How Europe underdeveloped Africa.* London: Bogle-L'Ouverture.

Rogers, J. A. 1945. A comment submitted to the editorial director of the University of North Carolina Press on Eric E. Williams' book manuscript. *Crisis.* 10 July. 203–4.

Rostow, Walt W. 1960. *The stages of economic growth.* Cambridge: Cambridge University Press.

Said, Edward W. 1978. *Orientalism: western conceptions of the orient.* London: Routledge and Kegan Paul.

Sanjek, Roger. 1993. Anthropology and its hidden colonialism: assistants and their ethnographers. *Anthropology Today* 9 (2):13–8.

SEPHIS. 2004. *Global South SEPHIS e-Magazine* 1 (1): 1–68.

Shilliam, B. 2009.*German thought and international relations.* New York: Palgrave Macmillan.

Singh, Shyam. 2011. World social science report: whither India and South Asia. *Economic and Political Weekly* 46 (1):10–2.

Shivji, Issa. 1970. *Tanzania: the silent class struggle.* Cheche: University of Dar es Salaam.

Shivji, Issa. 1973. *The silent class struggle continued.* Dar es Salaam: Tanzania Publishing House.

Sklar, Richard. 1967. Political science and national integration: a radical approach. *Journal of Modern African Studies* 5 (1):1–11.

Slater, Henry. 1986. Dar es Salaam and the post-nationalist historiography of Africa. In Jewsiewicki, Bogumil and David Newbury. eds. *African historiographies: what history for which Africa?* Beverly Hills. London and New Delhi: Sage Publications.

Somjee, Abdulkarim Husseinbhoy. 1984. *Political society in developing countries.* Basingstoke and London: Macmillan Press.

Spivak, Gayatri Chakravorty. 1988. 'Can the subaltern speak?'In Gary Nelson and Lawrence Grossberg. eds. *Marxism and the interpretation of culture.* Chicago and Urbana: University of Illinois Press. pp. 271–313.

Spivak, Gayatri Chakravorty. 1985. Subaltern studies: deconstructing historiography. In Ranajit Guha. ed. *Subaltern studies IV.* Delhi.

Southall, Aidan. 1974. State formation in Africa. *Annual Review of Anthropology* 3 (1):153–65.

Stuart, Sim and Borin van Loon. 2009. *Introducing critical theory.* London: Icon Books Limited.

Swai, Bonaventure. 1981. Rodney on scholarship and activism: part one. *Journal of African Marxists* 1 (1):31–43.

Swai, Bonaventure. 1982. Rodney on scholarship and activism: part two. *Journal of African Marxists* 2 (1):38–52.

Swingewood, Allan. 2000. *A short history of sociological thought.* Basingstoke and London: Macmillan Press Limited.

Tandon, Yashpal. ed. 1982. *University of Dar es Salaam debate on class. the state and imperialism.*Dar es Salaam: Tanzania Publishing House. pp. 252–82.

Tanzania Zamani. 1974. Tanzania Zamani 14 (1):1.

The Current. Bombay. 17 January 1976.

Editorial. 1984. *Journal of African Marxists* 5:2–6.

The Guardian. 25 June 1980.

The News magazine. 1996.

Thompson, Edward and Garret T. Garratt. 1934. *Rise and fulfilment of British rule in India.* Allahabad: Central Book Depot.

Tordoff, William. 1977. Zambia: the politics of disengagement. *African Affairs* 76 (302):60–9.

Tordoff, William. 1984. *Government and politics in Africa.* Basingstoke and London: Macmillan Press.

Trouillot, Michel-Rolph. 1995. *Silencing the past: power and the production of history.* Boston: Beacon Press.

Uwujaren, W. 1996. The exit of a patriot: the passage of Ake closes the chapter for one of Nigeria's brightest minds. *The News.* November 25.

Van den Berghe, Pierre L. 1973. *Power and privilege at an African university*. London: Routledge and Kegan Paul.

Van der Merwe, N. J. 1979. African studies. In A. Lennox-Short and D. Welsh. eds. *UCT at 150: reflections*. Cape Town: David Philips. pp. 62–7.

Vansina, Jan. 1986. "Knowledge and Perceptions of the African Past." In Jewsiewicki, Bogumil and David Newbury. eds. *African historiographies: what history for which Africa?* Beverly Hills. London and New Delhi: Sage Publications. pp. 28–41.

Verba, Sidney. 1965. Comparative political culture. In Pye, Lucian and Sidney Verba. eds. *Political culture and political development*. Princeton. NJ: Princeton University Press. pp. 513–23.

Wa Thiong'o, Ngugi. 1985. The commitment of the intellectual. *Review of African Political Economy* 32 (?):18–24.

Wa Thiong'o, Ngugi. 1986. *Decolonising the mind: the politics of language in African literature*. London: James Currey.

Warren, D. M. 1990. *Strengthening indigenous Nigerian associations and organisations for rural development: the case of Ara community*. Ibadan: Nigerian Institute of Social and Economic Research.

Watts, Michael. 2003. Development and governmentality. *Singapore Journal of Tropical Geography* 24 (1):6–34.

Weinberger-Thomas, C. 1999. *Ashes of Immortality*. Chicago: University of Chicago Press.

West, Cornel. 1990. The new cultural politics of difference. In Russell Ferguson. et al. eds. *Out there: marginalisation and contemporary cultures*. New York: Cambridge and London: The New Museum of Contemporary Art and MIT Press.

White, Luise. et al. eds. 2001. *African words. African voices: critical practices in oral history*. Bloomington. Indiana: Indiana University Press.

Williams, Eric Eustace. 1944/1994. *Capitalism and slavery*. Chapel Hill and London: University of North Carolina Press.

Witz, Leslie and Ciral S. Rassool. 2008. Making histories. *Kronos: Southern African Histories* 34:6–15.

Wriggins, Howard. 1961. Impediments to unity in the new states: the case of Ceylon. *American Political Science Review* 55 (1):313–20.

Wunsch, James and Dele Olowu. 1990. eds. *The failure of the centralised state*. Boulder. CO: Westview.

Yale Bulletin and Calendar. 1996. Obituaries.

Young, Robert T. C. 1990. *White mythologies: writing history and the West.* London and New York: Routledge.

Young, Crawford. 2002. Deciphering disorder in Africa: is identity the key? *World Politics* 54 (4):532–57.

Young, Crawford. 2004. The end of the postcolonial state in Africa? reflections on changing African political dynamics. *African Affairs* 103 (410):23–49.

Zeleza, Paul Tiyambe 2003. *Rethinking Africa's globalization. Volume I: the intellectual challenges.* Trenton. New Jersey: Africa World Press.

Zolberg, Aristide. 1967. Patterns of national integration. *Journal of Modern African Studies* 5 (4):449–67.

Zolberg, Aristide. 1968. The structure of political conflict in the new states of tropical Africa. *American Political Science Review* 62 (1):70–87.

Index

political thought 144, 151, 152, 170
professional associations, role in
47–49
relevance of his work 30
teaching experience 47
Amin, Samir 9, 19, 42, 66, 164
anthropology 61, 79, 87, 99–100, 112,
114
anthropologists 7, 115, 122
anti-colonial 4, 12, 14, 41, 53, 104,
117, 126, 137, 149, 157
nationalism 44, 72, 117, 125, 172
apartheid 15, 114, 115, 116
archaeology 61, 79
area studies 85, 112, 117, 119, 123,
124, 125
aristocracy 36, 93
Arouet, François-Marie *see* Voltaire
astronomers 89
autochthonous, autochthoneity 110,
166
reconstruction 144, 152
transformation 135, 156, 160, 162,
163, 165
autonomisation 152, 153, 154
autonomy 15, 134, 136, 142, 154, 156,
163, 164

B

Babu, Abdulrahman M. 57, 58
Bhabha, Homi K. 14, 15–16, 18, 106
blackness 100, 127
bourgeois 35, 39, 41, 42, 56, 57, 99,
140, 149
British 54, 69, 103, 104, 106, 108, 109,
111, 114
imperialism 37, 96

C

Campbell, Horace 54, 55, 56, 57, 58,
61
capitalism 1, 6, 11, 34, 35, 37, 38, 39,
41, 57, 61, 62, 93, 109, 111, 137
global 96, 165
international 8, 140

capitalist powers 7, 51
capitalist societies 5, 9, 117, 151, 153,
156, 164
Caribbean 13, 55, 60, 63, 64
centuries 5, 38, 54, 89, 91, 104, 159
17th 86, 89, 105
18th 51, 94, 95, 96, 103
19th 60, 91, 95, 97, 103, 105, 108,
11
20th 4, 16, 54, 90, 91, 107, 112,
128, 157, 158, 165
21st 54, 91, 146, 151
Chakrabarty, Dipesh 19, 127, 128, 157
Chatterjee, Partha 7, 24, 40, 99, 105,
106, 107, 108, 110, 128, 157, 166
China 10, 21, 91, 124
citizens 124, 148, 158, 165, 166
citizenship 95, 109, 140, 146, 159, 165
civil society 30, 39, 81, 140, 156, 159,
160, 162, 165
class relations 72
civilisation 6, 9, 10, 87, 88, 91, 96,
102, 104, 124, 137, 138
CODESRIA (Council for the
Development of Social Science
Research in Africa) 43, 66, 137
coercion 38, 54, 148, 152
coercive 39, 105, 155
Cold War *see* wars
colonial 5, 38, 89, 91, 104, 159; *see
also* anticolonial
archive 15, 119, 120
discourse 4, 17, 103, 107
domination 6, 45, 82, 96
foundations 4, 81
legacies 24, 55
neo- 9, 51, 55
powers 7, 54, 106, 107
pre- 53, 72, 141, 161, 164, 172
rule 6, 15, 24, 51, 60, 106, 128,
150, 159
societies 6, 105, 107; *see also*
postcolonial societies
state 7, 51, 106, 117, 153, 157, 158,
161, 164; *see also* postcolonial
state

post-independence 107
religions 7, 90, 93, 94, 113
 Christianity 91, 92, 94, 149, 150
 Islam 91, 96, 150
 Buddhism 91
 Hinduism 91
Renaissance 48, 90, 91
research funding 53, 66, 82, 118, 123
Revolutionary pressures in Africa
 (Claude e. Ake) : 137
revolutions 36, 91, 95, 109
Rodney, Walter 45, 58–64
Rousseau, Jean-Jacques 92, 94, 129
ruling class 38, 39, 40, 54, 158; *see also* working class

S

Said, Edward W. 17, 141
 Orientalism: Western conceptions of the orient 13, 18
Saro-Wiwa, Kenule 68, 70
scholar-activists 29, 43, 71, 169
Scientific Revolution 88, 89, 90
Second World War *see* Wars
self-rule 24, 149, 157
slave trade 58, 64, 109
slaves 80, 95
 black 109
 Negro 109
slavery 58, 61, 95, 109
Smith, Adam 92, 93
social formations 108, 153, 156
social groups 36, 37, 59, 152, 153
social movements 30, 42, 72
Social reality 22, 34, 83, 85
social sciences community in Africa 21, 71, 134, 136, 142, 169, 171; *see also* Western social sciences
Social science as imperialism: The theory of political development 64, 135, 139
social scientists 7, 19, 66, 134, 136, 141, 163
social structure 34, 72, 148, 150
social transformation 55, 61

social change 11, 61, 88, 103, 147, 170
socialism 39, 53, 61, 63, 65, 103
socialisation 32, 33, 38, 151
South Africa; *see also* African Studies
 history 15; *see also* African history
 post apartheid 113, 114, 115, 116
South-South Exchange Programme for Research on the History of Development 21
Spivak, Gayatri C. 15
state; *see also* colonial states, new states, postcolonial states
 building 94, 96, 144, 145, 154, 157, 158, 160, 165, 166
 formation 60, 144, 153, 157, 160, 164, 165
 modern 30, 103, 106, 109, 156, 157, 158, 162, 165, 166
 power 52, 68, 147, 154, 155, 157
state reconstruction 134, 135, 151
 in Africa 151–162, 163
stateness 145, 164
structures of power 3, 29, 71, 127, 169
struggles 34, 47, 51, 61, 105, 108, 123, 125, 154
 African experience 33, 72, 172
 class 39, 41
 decolonisation 72, 117
 democratic 44
 ideological 39
 liberation 150
 nationalist 41, 43, 117, 149
 pan-African 125
 political 44, 65, 72, 78, 155, 172
 power 161
subaltern studies 2, 3, 4, 13, 16, 173
sub-Saharan Africa 9, 48, 155

T

Tandon, Yashpal 57
Tarikh: Journal of the Historical Society of Nigeria 121
theorists 13, 14, 16, 18, 24, 34, 43, 44, 50, 86, 108, 155; *see also* poststructuralist